KNACK®
MAKE IT EASY

SLOW
COOKING

KNACK®

SLOW COOKING

Hearty and delicious meals you can prepare ahead

Linda Johnson Larsen

Photographs by Christopher Brown

Guilford, Connecticut
An imprint of Globe Pequot Press

Editor in Chief: Maureen Graney
Editor: Imee Curiel
Text Design: Paul Beatrice
Layout: Joanna Beyer
Cover photos by Christopher Brown
All interior photos by Christopher Brown with the exception of p. 9 (right) and p. 17 courtesy Crock-Pot; p. 13 © Monkey Business Images/Shutterstock; p. 16 (adjustable roasting rack) courtesy NorPro; p. 22 (left) by Alexey Avdeev/shutterstock; p. 22 (right) by Jack Schiffer/shutterstock; p. 23 (right) courtesy Brookstone; p. 121 (left) © Dobri/Dreamstime.com

CIP DATA: A catalogue record for this book is available from the British Library
Larsen, Linda Johnson.
Knack slow cooking : hearty & delicious meals you can prepare ahead /

Linda Johnson Larsen ; photographs by Christopher Brown.
  p. cm.
 Includes index.
 ISBN 978-0-7627-5926-2
1. Electric cookery, Slow. I. Title. II. Title: Slow cooking.
TX827.L37 2009
641.5'884—dc22

Globe Pequot Press International
Footprint Handbooks
6 Riverside Court
Lower Bristol Road
Bath
BA2 3DZ
UK
T+44(0)1225 469141
F+44(0)1225 469461

The following manufacturers/names appearing in *Knack Slow Cooking* are trademarks: Callebaut®, Godiva®, Lindt®, Pyrex®.

Printed in India by Replika Press Pvt Ltd

About the author

Linda Johnson Larsen is the author of many cookbooks, including *Knack Grilling Basics*, and is the Guide for Busy Cooks at About.com. She has created and tested recipes for major food companies since 1987. Linda has written articles for *Woman's Day*, and her recipes appeared regularly in America's *Quick & Simple* magazine. She lives in Minneapolis, Minnesota, USA. Visit the author at www.busycooks.about.com.

CONTENTS

INTRODUCTION

Many people own a slow cooker, even if it's just languishing in a kitchen cupboard or it's been consigned to the attic. But there are many reasons to pull out that neglected piece of equipment and put it to work – including better tasting, healthier food; time, energy and money savings; and less washing up.

This book, featuring easy, delicious recipes, straightforward instruction and commonsense safety information, will help you become a slow cooker pro and feed your family excellent food for less money. When the slow cooker is used correctly, with staggered cooking times for different foods and judicious seasoning, you can produce excellent quality meals with very little work.

As a cooking appliance, the slow cooker enjoyed a period in vogue in the 1970s, but its popularity faded during the last few years of the 20th century. It is now making a comeback, however. The ease of use, the excellent results, and the time and money it can save make it a valued appliance in the kitchen.

This book will focus on familiar slow-cooked foods and introduce you to more exotic, delicious recipes. A simple, clear layout, with photos of not only the completed dish but also steps along the way, makes learning easy. Once you have discovered the many ways to use the slow cooker, you will be able to adapt recipes to your taste and create your own meals to satisfy your family.

Each spread is self-contained, with tips and instructions on how to prepare and cook each recipe perfectly and safely. Simple variations that transform the recipe into something completely new are highlighted, showing you that mastering a few basic techniques will exponentially increase your repertoire. Alongside classic dishes such as pork carnitas, salt beef, baked beans, poached salmon and rice pudding, inventive new tastes and food combinations are introduced via the variations.

Topics covered include how to cook multiple foods at the same time, how to use the slow cooker to make unexpected recipes like cheesecakes and salads, why slow-cooked food is healthier for your family, and how to make entire meals using the slow cooker. Slow cooker safety is stressed, with safe cooking ranges and the final temperatures dishes should reach. You'll learn how to test the accuracy of your slow cooker.

It's good to own more than one slow cooker. Not only do the different sizes cook different types of food more successfully, but you can make an entire meal in a collection of slow cookers. The main dish will cook in the largest appliance, while potatoes stay warm in another. A chocolate bread pudding cooks without any attention while you're eating.

There is more to slow cooking than just filling up the pot and turning it on. Once you learn the special preparation methods some slow cooker recipes demand, all your attempts will turn out better.

There have been many advances in slow cooker technology over just the last five to six years. Electronic controls let you programme a cooking sequence into the appliance. For instance, you can set it to cook for an hour on high to get the temperature up quickly, then set it to low for the rest of the cooking time.

The delayed-start and keep-warm features are also great advances. They let you safely stretch the cooking time by a couple of hours on each side, so that you can be away from the house longer and still return to perfectly cooked food.

Food Safety

Food safety is one of the most important facets of cooking: the last thing you want is for someone to get ill from eating food you cooked, and the consequences can be serious.

Some people have questioned the safety of the slow cooker because it cooks at low temperatures. But there's no need to be concerned. The low setting cooks at 100°C and

enough to bring them quickly through the danger zone.

- Don't cool food in the slow cooker. The thick ceramic insert is designed to hold heat for a long time. If food is kept in the insert and placed in the refrigerator, it will take too long to cool below 5°C. Instead, just transfer the food to a food storage container and refrigerate promptly.

- Finally, watch the time that the food is not cooking. Perishable foods, which include meat, dairy products, eggs and cheese, cannot be safely left out at room temperature for longer than 2 hours, cooked or uncooked. If the ambient temperature is above 25°C, that safe time shrinks to 1 hour. Promptly refrigerate foods after cooking.

the high setting cooks at 150°C, both well above the 'danger zone' of 5–60°C. However, there are some food safety rules you need to follow:

- Don't cook meats from frozen in the slow cooker. The cold temperature of the meats can keep the entire temperature of the dish in the danger zone too long.

- Don't cook a whole chicken or whole turkey in this appliance; the slow cooker just can't heat these birds fast enough to prevent bacterial growth. And the slow cooker's heat doesn't reach the interior of whole birds fast

It's important to understand the preparation techniques and steps that will improve the quality of the finished dishes that come from your slow cooker. Browning meats adds colour and remarkable flavour to the food, while precooking some foods like beans and grains makes the end result very delicious and appealing.

Some vegetables should be cooked before they are added to the slow cooker. Onions and garlic are the most common ingredients that need precooking. These foods add great flavour and texture to recipes, but they can be harsh and overpowering when uncooked. Sauté them in oil or butter before adding to the recipe so they become sweet and mellow in the slow cooker.

Slow cooking a whole meal is easy. Pick a main dish, a vegetable dish and a dessert from this book. Choose the time when you want to serve dinner, and then write down a timetable.

Start the longest-cooking recipe first, then stagger the cooking times of the remaining dishes so everything will be done at the same time. You may want to time dessert to finish cooking an hour after the other foods, so you can enjoy a leisurely meal.

Dessert can sometimes be made ahead of time, so if that's the case, make it in the morning or the night before. Main dishes usually need to cook for longer than side dishes, so plan those in advance as well. Work backwards from your chosen serving time to figure out when to start the various slow cookers.

Care and Use

Caring for your slow cooker is easy. The inserts are usually dishwasher safe (but read the instructions!). However, it's a good idea, after you remove the food, to fill the insert with hot, soapy water and leave it to soak until you're ready to do the washing up.

If you use a plastic slow cooker liner, cleaning up is a breeze; just throw away the liner after you've removed the food. *Note:* Only use commercial slow cooker liners that are specifically made for use in the slow cooker. Ordinary plastic bags, even roasting bags, may melt and ruin your food and the slow cooker.

Never add cold water to a hot insert; the ceramic could crack. And speaking of cracks, if your insert develops cracks, even tiny hairline cracks, you shouldn't use it. Those cracks can harbour bacteria that may contaminate your food. And tiny cracks can develop into larger cracks, or the insert could break apart while it is holding hot food. The manufacturer should be able to supply a new insert: ask your retailer to order a replacement.

When you've learned how to make a basic recipe, start incorporating your own favourite flavours and ingredients. Almost all food can be cooked in a slow cooker, and the appliance blends and accents flavours beautifully.

Enjoy these recipes. As you get more experienced in slow cooking, you'll be able to branch out and invent your own recipes. Be sure to write them down: it's hard to recreate a masterpiece from memory.

HOW IT WORKS

A slow cooker is a simple appliance that works wonders with inexpensive food

Your slow cooker is ready to go straight out of the box. This versatile appliance stands alone, ready to transform tough cuts of meat and vegetables into flavourful feasts.

The true slow cooker consists of a round or oval metal housing that holds the heating element. It literally surrounds the food with heat as it cooks. This part of the slow cooker should never be immersed in water: wipe it clean with a damp cloth or sponge.

Most slow cookers have inserts that actually hold the food. Stoneware inserts are very thick and heavy, and are meant to retain heat. Handle them carefully, because they can chip or break easily. A crack in the insert means it must be discarded.

Slow Cooker Components

- Metal exterior
- Digital or manual controls
- Stoneware or metal insert
- Power lead
- Lid
- Instruction book

Slow Cooker Housing

- Slow cookers cook at two temperatures. Low setting reaches 100°C, while the high setting reaches 150°C. These settings are safe for food.

- Meats are the focus for food safety in a slow cooker. Meats need to be cooked to 70–80°C, depending on the type, so these temperatures are sufficient.

- Try to keep the housing unit clean. Wipe up spills straight away so they don't cook on to the housing.

The lid is an integral part of the slow cooker. It traps heat and moisture and helps heat circulate around the food. You must use the lid designed for your slow cooker so the food cooks properly.

The power lead is deliberately short to avoid accidents. Place the slow cooker on a heatproof surface, such as a large tile, to protect your worktop. And never use an extension lead with the slow cooker; a long lead invites accidents, especially if it hangs over the edge of a worktop.

Inserts

- Most new slow cookers now come with a removable stoneware or metal insert.

- This insert makes it easy to clean the slow cooker and to serve food. If your older slow cooker is in one piece, use cooking bags to make cleaning easier.

- Be careful with the stoneware inserts. If they crack or chip, you'll have to discard them. These blemishes can harbour bacteria.

- Most inserts are dishwasher-safe. Be sure to read the instruction booklet and follow information about cleaning and storage.

Sealed Lid

- Even though it's a loose fit, the lid on a slow cooker actually forms a seal with the insert.

- This seal is created by moisture and a little bit of pressure from the heat of the food.

- The low heat and the moisture circulate in the slow cooker. Condensation from evaporated liquid is kept in the appliance.

- There is little or no loss of moisture with this appliance; the food stays juicy and tender. Don't lift the lid more than you have to.

HOW TO FILL IT
Filling the slow cooker properly is crucial for the best results

Because all the food cooks at the same time, variable cooking times come into play when filling the appliance. Follow these rules to the letter for best results.

The foods that cook most slowly in the slow cooker aren't meats, as you'd expect, but hard root vegetables like potatoes, carrots and parsnips. These foods must be placed in the hottest part of the cooker, as close to the heat source as possible.

Always place root vegetables in the bottom of the slow cooker. They will become tender and sweet, and all the juices from meats and stocks, and the flavours from herbs and spices, will infuse them.

Also place rice and grains in the bottom of the slow cooker. They have to be completely covered with liquid as they cook or they will never become tender.

Place Root Vegetables

- Make sure that root vegetables are prepared as directed in the recipe. Most need to be peeled and cubed or diced.

- These vegetables should all be cut to about the same size, as they take the same amount of time to cook.

- Place vegetables evenly in the bottom of the slow cooker, and either layer them if the recipe suggests it, or mix together.

- Even if you're making roasted vegetables, you need to add a small amount of liquid so the vegetables don't burn.

Faster Cooking Foods

- Meats and more tender vegetables, along with dried fruits, are placed on top of root vegetables, beans or grains.

- You can cook very tender vegetables in the slow cooker. Add peas, spring onions and fresh herbs at the very end of cooking time.

- Dairy products, such as milk, cream and cheese, are also added at the very end of the cooking time.

- Stabilizers, such as flour, cornflour or arrowroot, are often stirred in with dairy products to help prevent curdling and keep the sauce smooth.

2

Fill a slow cooker between one-half and three-quarters full. If you use less food, you run the risk of burning. And if you use more, the food may not cook through or the slow cooker could overflow as foods release juices.

As you get more accustomed to the slow cooker, filling it will become second nature and you'll learn how to gauge quantities by eye instead of precisely measuring foods.

Correctly Filled

- Regardless of the recipe, slow cookers should be filled between $1/2$ and $3/4$ full.

- To gauge which size slow cooker you need, add up all the non-liquid ingredients by volume.

- If you have only one slow cooker you may have to scale the recipe up or down to cook the dish.

- Refrigerate or freeze extra portions for another meal.

Stirring the Food

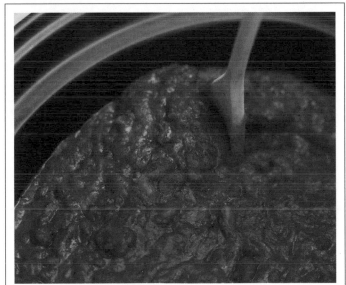

- Whenever you lift the slow cooker lid (even for stirring), it releases heat and extends the cooking time. Add another 20 minutes for each time the lid is lifted.

- When recipes specifically call for stirring, additional cooking time has already been factored in. Follow directions carefully and stir only as required.

- If you need to see the food, just spin the lid in place to remove condensation rather than lifting the lid.

SLOW COOKER SIZES
Large or small: these are the slow cookers you need

Since filling slow cookers correctly is so crucial to recipe success, owning a variety of sizes and shapes is important.

Slow cookers are among the most inexpensive kitchen appliances on the market. They can, especially with liners made of metal, literally substitute for a hob and an oven. You can bake, roast, boil and simmer in a slow cooker; all for less than £50. The models available range in size from diminutive 500-ml babies made for serving appetizers or sauces, to large 6.5-litre oval monsters that can serve a crowd.

The standard 3.5-litre slow cooker will handle most of your cooking needs. In it you can prepare a meal of, say, chicken and vegetables to feed a family of four.

The next addition to your slow cooker family should be a small model of 1.5–2 litres. With this, you can make a hot dip

Basic 3.5-Litre Round

- The basic 3.5-litre slow cooker should be in every kitchen. It's the perfect size for making pasta sauce or soup.

- This size is also ideal for keeping food such as mashed potatoes or other side dishes warm during festive meals.

- Most of these slow cookers come with a stoneware insert that fits snugly into the housing. Grease the insert before use to make washing up easier.

- As with all appliances, follow directions for care given in the instruction booklet.

1-Litre Slow Cooker

- Small slow cookers range from 500 ml to 2 litres. The very small sizes are used for melting chocolate or making appetizers.

- 1.5- and 2-litre models are ideal for small families, whether you're making soup or spicy chicken.

- Hot dips, snack mixes and tiny sauces cook perfectly in the small slow cooker, and you can use it for serving.

- If you're cooking for one or two people, a smaller slow cooker can prepare two chicken breasts or pork chops.

for a party and keep the dip hot and fresh while serving. After that, a 5–6.5-litre oval slow cooker is another great addition. These slow cookers hold larger cuts of meat, such as hams, roasts and large pieces of chicken, with ease. With a slow cooker this size, you can produce a complete meal for eight to ten people.

Keep your slow cooker family in good condition and it will serve you well for years.

···········GREEN●LIGHT············

When choosing the slow cooker to use for a recipe, especially if you're creating your own, just add up the volume of the ingredients and choose a slow cooker based on filling it half to three-quarters full. Think about appearance as well. An attractive slow cooker can be used to serve food as well as cooking it.

5.5-Litre Slow Cooker

- The 5.5-litre slow cooker is the one to purchase if you have a family larger than four people.

- It will cook 4 litres of soup or pasta sauce – enough to feed a family and have leftovers to freeze.

- A slow cooker of this size is also good for baking desserts and cooking porridge for breakfast.

- An 18 or 20-cm cake tin or springform tin will fit into this slow cooker with room for heat to circulate.

6.5-Litre Oval

- These large slow cookers make preparing a festive meal for a crowd a breeze.

- You should be able to fit a large joint or half a ham in this appliance, with room to spare.

- You can make whole meals for six to eight people by adding vegetables or fruits to the large cuts of meat.

- If you routinely cook for more than six people, you may want to purchase multiple large slow cookers.

SAUCES AND THICKENERS
Many slow cooker recipes need these additions for stabilizing

One of the critical parts of slow cooker success is creating sauces. Since foods release liquid when they are cooked in the slow cooker, and that liquid doesn't evaporate, it's essential that the sauces have a little extra help so they don't split or separate.

This is why many slow cooker recipes call for canned condensed creamed soups. The soups contain stabilizers, emulsifiers and other additives that keep the liquid stable over the long, slow, wet cooking time. But since condensed soups aren't very healthy, you can substitute a white sauce.

White sauces aren't difficult to make; they just take a little practice. Once you've learned how to make a white sauce, you can whip one up in about 10 minutes. And you control the sodium and other ingredients that your family eat.

White Sauce

Ingredients

Makes 250 ml

2 tablespoons butter

2 tablespoons plain flour

250 ml milk or single cream

1 teaspoon cornflour

Salt and white pepper

- In small saucepan, melt butter over medium heat. You can add chopped garlic, shallots or onion at this point.

- Add the flour and season with salt and pepper. Cook and stir with a wire whisk to incorporate the flour into the butter.

- Leave to cook gently for 2–3 minutes.

- Slowly add the milk or cream, whisking constantly.

- Cook and stir over low heat until the sauce thickens. Stir in cornflour and remove from heat; use as directed in recipe.

You can vary the basic white sauce recipe with the type of liquid you use. You can add herbs, spices, condiments such as mustard or flavoured vinegars and almost any kind of grated cheese.

If someone in your family is allergic to wheat or milk, you can still make a white sauce using a thickener other than wheat flour or a liquid other than milk or cream: variations are given below.

Sauces for Allergies

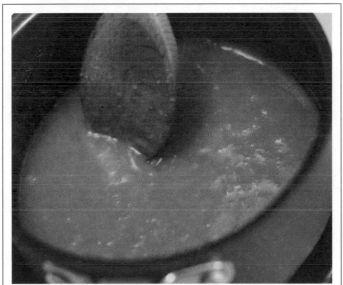

- For a milk allergy, simply substitute soy milk or rice milk for cow's milk. You can use dairy-free margarine in place of the butter.

- Or use chicken stock, beef stock or vegetable stock in place of the milk. The result is called a 'velouté' sauce.

- For wheat allergies, combine 1 tablespoon cornflour or arrowroot with 250 ml milk. Add this to the melted butter and cook for 3–4 minutes.

Oil-Based White Sauce

- An oil-based white sauce is based on the classic Cajun roux.

- Combine 2 tablespoons vegetable oil with 2 tablespoons flour in a small saucepan.

- Cook and stir over low heat just until the mixture takes on a tiny bit of gold. Then add 250 ml milk; cook and stir until thickened.

- Grated cheese can be added to any of these sauces; use 40 g cheese for 250 ml sauce.

ENTERTAIN WITH SLOW COOKERS
Slow cookers function as your own personal chef, making entertaining a breeze

Slow cookers are ideal for entertaining because the food cooks without any attention from you, it frees up your hob and oven and you can serve directly from the appliance.

You can remove the insert and place it on a trivet or hot pad on the table, or keep the slow cooker fully assembled and plug it in for a buffet.

It's possible to make an entire meal in a series of slow cookers. Serve a flavourful mulled drink along with a hot dip before dinner. Then offer a main dish like beef stroganoff or chicken verde; serve it over rice pilaf made in a small slow cooker, with some glazed carrots on the side. And for dessert, a chocolate cheesecake cooks to perfection in the slow cooker.

Multiple Slow Cookers

- The main problem if you are going to use multiple slow cookers is finding a heatproof surface.

- Slow cookers can damage laminate work-tops, so look out for large ceramic tiles in DIY stores to place under them.

- It's also helpful to place a note near (not on) each slow cooker with cooking times and any stirring instructions.

- Then relax, because everything is covered. All you need is a crisp salad, and dinner is served.

Make a Complete Meal

- For cooking an entire meal in slow cookers, you'll need different sizes and shapes.

- A joint requires a large, oval slow cooker, especially if you put vegetables around it, while mashed potatoes cook best in a 3.5-litre cooker.

- The smallest slow cookers are perfect for dips, while side dishes cook in the small to medium sizes.

- With several show cookers you can also easily stagger starting times if the foods cook for different times.

You have to keep an eye on the time, however. A keep-warm feature will keep the food at a safe serving temperature for 2 hours. If you only have low and high settings, place the slow cooker on low and stir it occasionally. After 2 hours, remove and refrigerate the food.

Even making one or two dishes in the slow cooker is like having your own personal kitchen assistant. And with the delayed-start and keep-warm features, entertaining has never been easier.

GREEN ● LIGHT

The slow cooker is the perfect choice when entertaining during the hot summer months. It doesn't heat up your kitchen, and you can prepare the food ahead of time and just add the ingredients to the slow cooker, stir and turn it on. Bean and vegetable dishes are a great complement to barbecued meats.

Drinks

- Any hot drink can be made or kept warm in a slow cooker during a party.

- The keep-warm or low setting is perfect. But when the amount of liquid in the slow cooker drops to less than a third, turn it off.

- If you're serving a large party or are holding a long open house, have more than one drink warming.

- Just stagger times so you can remove the old pot and put out the new one when it's ready.

Buffet Sets

- For a buffet, there's nothing better than a slow cooker set. You still have the flexibility of three separate slow cookers.

- Each has its own timer and heat regulation, so you can cook more than one dish.

- Start with the cooker on the table you'll use during the party; it will be too heavy to lift or move when full.

- Again, be sure to keep track of the time the food is sitting out – after 2 hours, remove it.

HOW TO ADAPT RECIPES
Adapt oven and stovetop recipes to the slow cooker

Many recipes that you cook in the oven and on the hob can be adapted to prepare in the slow cooker. There are just a few rules to follow.

First, choose a recipe. If it's a soup or stew, reduce the liquid by about half. Add a browning step if the recipe calls for beef or pork, and minced meats must be cooked and skimmed of fat before adding to the slow cooker.

Any recipes that call for long cooking times, such as braised or roasted meat dishes, are adaptable. Just remember to place root vegetables in the bottom of the slow cooker and top with meats and tender vegetables.

When cooking meat, first trim off any visible fat, since that will affect the taste and texture of the dish. Reduce liquids by two-thirds because of the slow cooker's moist environment.

Reducing Liquid

- For a soup, the liquid should just barely cover the solid ingredients when cooking starts.

- If there is excess liquid in the slow cooker when the soup is done, there are a few ways to reduce it.

- Spoon out some of the liquid, or turn the heat to high and cook with the lid off for 20–30 minutes.

- Or transfer the liquid to a pan and simmer on the hob until reduced, then return to the slow cooker.

Large Cuts of Meat

- Large cuts of meat cook well in the slow cooker; in fact, the cheaper the cut, the better the result.

- Coat the meat with seasoned flour and brown it first; this adds flavour and thickening for the gravy.

- Season the food well: dried herbs will stand up to the long cooking time, but their potency may be reduced.

- You can add some fresh herbs of the same type at the end of cooking time to add punch to the flavour.

For timing, multiply the cooking time required by your recipe by 6 for low-heat cooking, or by 3.5 for cooking on high. In general, to cook a 1.3-kg joint of meat will take 4 hours on high or 7 hours on low, while for chicken, breasts take 5 hours and thigh or leg meat 6–7 hours on low.

Then always check the food at the end of the shortest cooking time to make sure it doesn't overcook or burn.

ZOOM

The slow cooker is a very healthy way to cook foods. The long, slow cooking time reduces unhealthy compounds that form in high heat, called advanced glycation end products, or AGEs. So using your slow cooker can help lower the risk of developing diabetes, heart disease and cancer.

Adjust Ingredients

- When adapting recipes, add milk, cream, sour cream or cheese at the end of the cooking time, just to heat through.

- Some recipes are exceptions: cheesy dips cook for only a short period and you can add cheeses at the beginning.

- Add tender vegetables like peas at the end of cooking time.

- Dried beans should be soaked before adding to a slow cooker recipe; avoid adding salt or acid ingredients until the beans soften.

Layer Foods Properly

- Layering foods is crucial to success; hard vegetables go in the bottom, while tender vegetables go on top.

- Rice and pasta can be difficult to cook in the slow cooker. They should be placed on the bottom so they are covered with liquid.

- Usually, brown and wild rice work well. And smaller pasta like orzo or shells can be added during the last 15–20 minutes.

- Larger pastas should be cooked separately and added to the finished dish.

LADLES, SPOONS AND SIEVES
These tools will help you rearrange and remove food with ease

You don't need a lot of extra equipment to cook in your slow cooker. Ordinary utensils, such as knives, a swivel-bladed vegetable peeler and a frying pan to brown meats and cook off onions and minced meat, are standard in any kitchen.

Ladles and spoons are important tools for the slow cooker. You'll also need a strainer, especially if you make broths and stocks in your slow cooker. Have a selection of ladles on hand.

Ladles have a more rounded bowl, usually set at a right angle to the handle so it's easy to lift liquids. You should have a couple made of heat-resistant plastic, some made of steel or other metal and some pretty serving ladles. Ladles are perfect for serving and for adding more liquid to the slow cooker.

Regular and slotted spoons should be on hand too. Slotted spoons are great for removing meats to shred or chop, and

Silicone Ladle

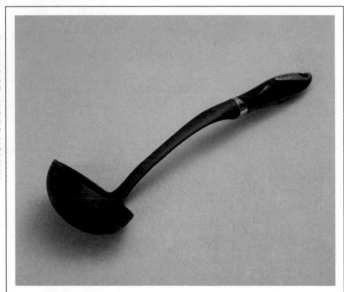

- You may want to have several ladles in different sizes. They are also available in different colours.

- Silicone ladles easily release food, and are good for serving sticky items like sauce for chicken or cheesy appetizers.

- For serving, you may want to use ladles of different materials, such as silver or china, to match your dinner service or cutlery.

Slotted Spoon

- Slotted spoons have holes, slots or decorative openings punched into the bowl. They are the same size as large serving spoons.

- They are ideal for scooping larger items out of liquid, while letting small pieces like chopped onions or garlic pass through.

- Spoons should be sturdy, with long handles so your fingers stay away from the heat and steam.

- These spoons can be made from metal, silicone, heat-proof rubber, china or ceramic.

for removing food from excess liquid. Stainless steel and wooden spoons are both good choices.

And skimmers will help you strain stocks as well as skim foam from the surface of simmering broths and stocks.

Buy the best quality, sturdiest items you can afford. Keep them in good working condition and on hand to help with your slow cooking chores.

········· GREEN●LIGHT ·············

When you find a ladle or spoon that you really like and that feels good in your hand, buy more than one. Utensils come and go on the market, and your favourite spoon may become unavailable. These tools are inexpensive and store easily.

Ladles and Spoons

- 1 metal ladle
- 1 silicone ladle
- 1 stainless spoon
- 2 wooden spoons
- 1 heatproof rubber scraper
- 1 colander
- Large and small sieves
- 1 large shallow skimmer
- 1 pair spring-loaded tongs

Spider Skimmer

- This type of skimmer or sieve usually has a bamboo handle and a mesh spoon.

- The handle stays cool when the spoon is immersed in boiling or simmering liquids.

- Strainers come in two forms: stand-alone colanders and sieves with a long single handle.

- A sieve with a handle usually has a hook on the opposite end so it can sit on top of a saucepan or bowl to strain broth or stock.

13

COOKING BAGS AND FOIL
Cooking bags and foil assist in preparation and cooking

A removable insert took the slow cooker to the next generation back in the 1980s. This advance made the appliance much easier to clean.

But making sure your slow cooker insert is sparkling clean is still a challenge. You can grease the insert before adding the food, but there is an even easier way. Heat resistant cooking bags, also called plastic liners, let you use your slow cooker with absolutely no washing up at all. Just place the liner in the slow cooker, fill it with food, turn it on, and cook.

Then all you have to do is remove and serve (or store) the food, lift out the liner and throw it away.

Foil is another essential slow cooker tool. Foil balls, made by crumpling the material in your fist, will help hold meat out of the liquid for roasting. And crossed foil strips fit neatly

Heat Resistant Bags and Liners

- Be sure that the cooking bags you use are specifically made for use in the slow cooker.

- As the name suggests, heat-resistant bags are specially designed to stand up to the heat of the slow cooker.

- Regular plastic bags should not be used in the slow cooker. They can melt and ruin your food.

- Products not designed for the slow cooker can emit chemicals into your food that may be harmful. So read labels.

Foil Balls

- Heavy-duty or regular foil can be used to make these balls. Make all the balls the same size so the meat sits solidly on them.

- This allows the meat to steam rather than braise sitting in liquid.

- The fat drains off the meat as it cooks, so the finished dish has much less fat.

- If you're concerned about aluminium, don't use the juices that accumulate around the foil balls. It won't affect the meat.

under a dish such as meatloaf so you can easily lift it out of the appliance when it's done.

Finally, paper towels also have a place in your slow cooking collection. When you're baking, place paper towels under the lid to catch condensing moisture, so it doesn't drip on to the top of the food.

With these inexpensive materials, using the slow cooker is even easier and less work for you.

Paper Towel under Lid

- Again, read labels to find out if the paper towel is approved for use with food.

- Microwave-safe paper towels are a good bet; they're approved for use with food, moisture and heat.

- Place 3–4 layers of paper towel on top of the slow cooker; make sure the paper towel is large enough to sit on top.

- Then cover with the lid of the slow cooker. Because you're placing paper next to heat, don't leave the house when cooking by this method.

Foil Strips

- To make foil strips, tear off two 60-cm pieces of 30-cm-wide aluminium foil.

- Fold the foil in half lengthwise, then fold in half again to make two strips 60 cm long and 7.5 cm wide.

- Cross the strips over each other in the bottom of the slow cooker. Allow the ends to extend beyond the lid.

- Add the food, cover and cook as directed. Use the foil to help remove the food from the slow cooker.

RACKS AND HOLDERS

Some recipes call for racks; and transporting a slow cooker is easy with a carrying case

When you think of the slow cooker as an oven, the only thing that is different is the amount of liquid the recipe creates. For some recipes, the food needs to be lifted out of that liquid. That's where racks and holders come into play.

Some manufacturers sell racks that are made to fit perfectly into the slow cooker. But you can find inexpensive metal racks

in any supermarket or kitchen shop. Just make sure they fit in your slow cooker without tilting or tipping. And always use heatproof racks, never plastic.

Meat racks are another great gadget for your slow cooker. There are V-shaped racks, which hold the meat out of the liquid, and racks to hold chicken or ham. Some of these racks

V-shaped Meat Rack

- Check that the rack fits into your slow cooker, and that it is short enough for the lid to fit snugly. There are even adjustable options.

- You can find racks made of aluminium, of metal coated with porcelain, and of stainless steel.

- The rack will hold the meat out of the liquid, while juices and fat drip down into the slow cooker.

- After skimming off the fat, the juices can be transferred to a saucepan to make delicious gravy.

Rack with Lifting Handles

- When you're cooking a large roast or ham in the slow cooker, removing it becomes a challenge.

- Foil strips aren't sturdy enough to lift the food; and if the food drops, it can splash hot liquid over you.

- There are racks with handles and even lifter baskets that you can put in the slow cooker before you add the meat.

- Just place the meat in the rack and make sure you can get to the handles. Use pan holders when lifting.

have handles built in, which makes removing the food from the slow cooker very easy.

And since slow-cooked recipes are the perfect choice for social events, you need a way to safely transport the food. Some slow cookers are made for transporting, with special locks; others have carrying cases that hold in the heat.

Take some time to browse through a kitchenware shop or even the baking supplies aisle of your supermarket to see what's new in gadgets and accessories. You may find something to make your life easier.

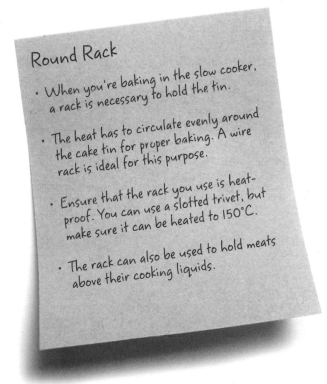

Round Rack

- When you're baking in the slow cooker, a rack is necessary to hold the tin.

- The heat has to circulate evenly around the cake tin for proper baking. A wire rack is ideal for this purpose.

- Ensure that the rack you use is heat-proof. You can use a slotted trivet, but make sure it can be heated to 150°C.

- The rack can also be used to hold meats above their cooking liquids.

···· YELLOW●LIGHT ····

Even if you have an insulated carrier that will keep the food in the slow cooker warm, you still have to follow food safety rules. Don't let the food sit in the slow cooker without cooking for more than 2 hours. Make sure you get to your destination within that time frame.

Carrying Cases

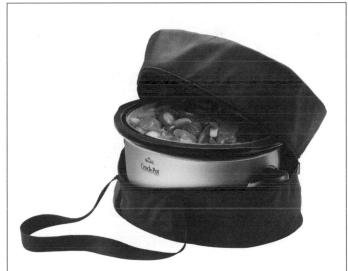

- When you want to take your slow cooker along to a party, it's a good idea to have some kind of case.

- There are cases specifically made for round and oval slow cookers that are insulated to conserve heat.

- These cases usually have sturdy handles, and they help keep you safe from spills while travelling.

- If you don't have a case, you can wrap the slow cooker in newspaper tied together, then in blankets.

TIMERS AND KEEPING WARM
Timing is everything with a slow cooker; and many models have keep-warm features

Because the slow cooker cooks slowly and safely, you can just assemble dinner, turn it on and leave the house. You can extend the cooking time to more than 10 hours, if you follow a few rules. Many newer models have built-in timers and keep-warm features, which can turn a 6-hour recipe into a 10-hour recipe, giving you more time away from the kitchen.

But you must follow the 2-hour rule. Never let perishable food (meat, eggs, dairy products) sit out at room temperature for longer than 2 hours. And that time shortens to 1 hour when the ambient air temperature is 26°C or higher. And, at the end of cooking, never let the food sit at room temperature for longer than 2 hours, or 1 hour in the summer.

Built-in Timer

- The newer slow cookers usually have built-in electronic timers for precise control of cooking times.

- Make sure that you read the manufacturer's instruction booklet completely so you understand how this feature works.

- Most of these slow cookers have three cooking temperatures: low, high and keep-warm.

- Others have up to five settings, including a buffet setting to keep food safe during parties.

Added Timer

- An added timer works by plugging into the slow cooker between the appliance and the power socket. Set the timer, turn on the slow cooker, and walk away.

- For best results, use an added timer that has been developed specifically for the slow cooker.

- While lamp timers may work, for safety's sake use a timer made for this purpose.

- When cooking poultry, you should reduce the delayed start time to 1 hour for food safety reasons.

Use these methods only if they are built into your slow cooker. Attaching a timing device to the slow cooker can be risky. Some people have used devices intended to turn on lights automatically to delay the starting time of their slow cookers, but it's not wise to gamble with your food.

Follow these rules strictly and precisely and you'll give yourself more freedom in the kitchen than ever before. And you'll eat well too.

Keep-Warm

- The keep-warm feature is built into many slow cookers. There really isn't a way to rig the appliance to create this feature.

- Timers made specifically for slow cookers often include this feature.

- Be sure that you count serving and eating time in that 2-hour window.

- If food stops cooking at 6.00 pm, you have until 8.00 pm to serve and eat the food. Don't think you can serve it at 8.00 pm and be safe.

Delayed Start

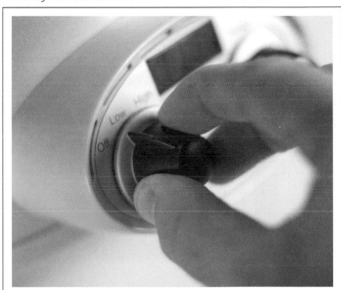

- All the ingredients must be cold when added to the slow cooker if you're going to use a timer for a delayed start.

- Never use room temperature food or warm sauces if you use delayed start; this will keep the food in the danger zone of 5–60°C for too long.

- Don't use the slow cooker to reheat food, especially with a timer.

- Reheat slow-cooked food in the oven or microwave or in a pan on the hob.

OPTIONS
The newest slow cookers come with some desirable extra features

These aren't your grandmother's slow cookers! The newest models come with all kinds of gadgets and options to make slow cooking even easier. Companies are constantly developing new products and updates to older products. In fact, it's worth taking time to browse the Internet for cooking equipment sites to find out what's new. Hinged lids, stainless steel liners, which are safe to use on the hob or in the oven,

and electronic controls are all huge recent advances in slow cooker technology.

When you lift off a hot lid covered with condensation and put it down on a worktop, a seal can form and the lid will stick tight to the worktop. (You need to slide it to the edge of the worktop to lift it off.) A hinged lid automatically prevents this and means you don't have to hold the lid while you stir.

Locking Lid

- A locking lid is a great feature that makes it easy to safely transport food in your slow cooker.

- Check that the locks really are fastened securely before you try to move the slow cooker.

- It's a good idea to place a hot slow cooker filled with food in an insulated case.

- These models often come with a spoon that attaches to the lid. Remember to wash off the spoon every time you stir, for food safety.

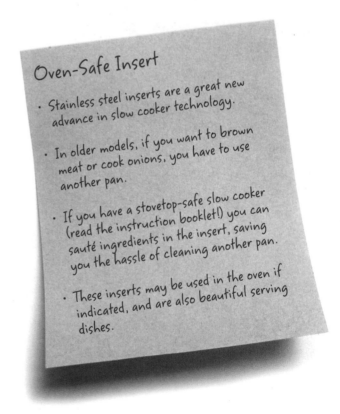

Oven-Safe Insert

- Stainless steel inserts are a great new advance in slow cooker technology.

- In older models, if you want to brown meat or cook onions, you have to use another pan.

- If you have a stovetop-safe slow cooker (read the instruction booklet!) you can sauté ingredients in the insert, saving you the hassle of cleaning another pan.

- These inserts may be used in the oven if indicated, and are also beautiful serving dishes.

Electronic controls make the slow cooker even more versatile. Delayed start, keep-warm and integrated meat probes all help to keep your food safe for hours.

These improvements do make the appliances more complicated. You may want to read reviews of slow cookers on sites such as Amazon.co.uk before buying one. And don't be afraid to add your voice to the reviews.

• • • • • • • • • • • • • • RED ● LIGHT • • • • • • • • • • • • • •

If the power goes off while your food is cooking, and you don't know exactly how long it was off, you have to throw away the food. A power cut of 2 hours or less is safe. Power cuts are a concern for manually controlled slow cookers. If you're at home while the power is off, monitor the time. It's better to be safe than sorry.

Hinged Lid

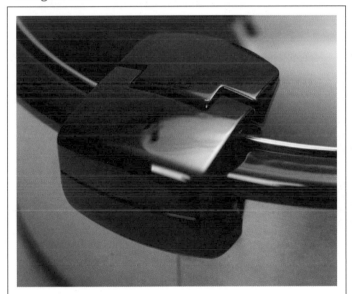

- Lids drip hot water when lifted, and steam will rush up from the food. You can be burnt by steam, and hot water can drip on your hands or arm.

- Hinged lids help prevent this from happening.

- If the lid is attached to the slow cooker and you have to unlock it before removal, it prevents sudden temperature changes.

- Glass lids can break or crack if they are put under cold water when they're hot.

Electronic vs. Manual Controls

- Some of the new, more sophisticated slow cookers have complicated controls; read the instruction booklet carefully.

- The newest even have built-in indicators that tell you if the power went off, and for how long.

- You can programme these slow cookers for many different combinations of cooking times and temperatures.

- A meat probe is another great feature; it will let you know when meat is safely cooked.

THERMOMETERS
Knowing the final temperature of food is the key to perfect results

If you don't have a food thermometer, get one now. They are very important to successful and safe cooking, not only with the slow cooker but with every other method.

There are several types of thermometer, ranging from a simple probe with a dial reading, to electronic digital thermometers that keep track of food as it cooks, and instant-read thermometers that give you almost instant results.

Correct placement of the thermometer in the food is crucial. For accurate results, when checking the temperature of meat, the probe has to be in lean meat, not in fat, and not touching bone.

The least complicated thermometer, a dial thermometer, should be pushed about 5 cm into the food for an accurate reading. Digital, instant-read and fork thermometers can take

Instant-Read Thermometer

- There are several types of instant-read thermometers. Permanent models come with a dial or electronic reading.

- Single-use instant-read thermometers can be used only once and are made of temperature-sensitive material.

- These thermometers can't remain in the food as it is cooking because the controls aren't heatproof.

- You can find these thermometers in kitchenware stores and in most large supermarkets or department stores.

Thermometer with Probe

- This sophisticated digital thermometer does more than just check the temperature of the food.

- You can programme it to alert you with a beep at certain times in the cooking process, as when the meat reaches a certain temperature.

- This type of thermometer is a little more expensive, but it's worth it if you cook a lot of meat.

- The probe stays in the meat while it's cooking; a lead attaches the probe to the base unit.

an accurate reading with just a 2.5-cm insertion, making them useful for thin foods.

Before you use a new thermometer to check foods, make sure it's properly calibrated. Bring some water to a boil, and place the tip in the water. It should read 100°C (or 212°F). If it doesn't, you can return the thermometer to the shop, or add or subtract the amount it's out to your readings in food.

Built-in Thermometer

- Some of the newest slow cookers have built-in thermometers.

- These thermometers are inserted into the food through a small hole in the lid. Follow manufacturer's instructions for use.

- The hole is designed to hold the probe and not release much heat as the food is cooking.

- The probe stays in the meat during the cooking process, and an alarm will alert you to a preset temperature.

Thermometer on Fork

- A thermometer on a fork is typically used for barbecuing meats, but can also be used for other cooking methods.

- There is a sensor near the tip of the fork that has to be fully inserted in the food for an accurate reading.

- Be sure that the probe isn't touching fat or bone, which will skew the reading.

- Most food thermometers are reliable to within about 2 degrees. Take this into account when determining whether your food is done.

MULLED DRINKS
Hot spiced drinks are a wonderful treat from your slow cooker

Mulling is the addition of spices to hot liquids to create flavourful drinks. Mulling spices include cinnamon, cloves, nutmeg, allspice and star anise, and dried citrus peel is another classic flavouring. You can use whole, broken or ground spices in your mulled drinks.

If you want to serve a clear liquid, tie up whole spices in a piece of muslin or use a tea infuser; remove the spices just before serving. You can also grind the spices and add to the liquid. Or whole spices, such as star anise and cloves, can be left in the drink as they give it an attractive appearance.

Serve the hot drinks directly from the slow cooker so they stay warm during your party.

Ingredients

Serves 8

1 cinnamon stick

4 whole cloves

2 tablespoons grated orange zest

150 g raisins

150 g dried cherries

2 litres cloudy apple juice

500 ml orange juice

50 ml lemon juice

Mulled Apple Juice

- Cut a 25-cm-square piece of muslin and spread it on the work surface.

- Place spices and orange zest in the centre of the muslin. Gather up the corners and, using kitchen string, tie into a bundle.

- Place bundle in 3.5-litre slow cooker. Top with dried fruit, then pour remaining ingredients into slow cooker.

- Cover and cook on low for 6–7 hours or on high for 3–4 hours, until juice is hot. Remove spice bundle before serving.

Mulled Wine

In 3.5-litre slow cooker, combine 2 bottles dry red wine with 120 ml honey and 120 ml water. Place 1 broken cinnamon stick, 1 cracked nutmeg, 2 teaspoons orange peel and 6 whole cloves in a tea infuser and add. Cover and cook on high for 2–3 hours until hot.

Glogg

Pour 2 bottles dry red wine into a 3-litre slow cooker. Add 2 cinnamon sticks, 150 g raisins, 1 split vanilla pod, $\frac{1}{2}$ teaspoon ground cardamom and 100 g sugar. Peel 1 orange in large pieces and add peel to slow cooker. Add 120 ml aquavit. Cover and cook on high for 2 hours.

Combine Spices

- Muslin is used because it is so permeable. The flavours of the spices can easily escape through the thin cloth to flavour the liquid.

- You can find single muslin in the food storage aisle of large supermarkets, or in your nearest kitchen shop.

- Use 100 per cent white cotton kitchen string to tie the muslin bundle closed.

- Remove the bundle before you serve the mulled apple juice. Fish it out with a spoon and squeeze the liquid out, then discard.

Add Liquids

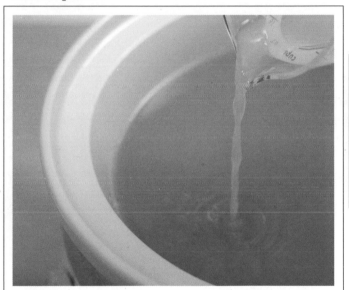

- Cloudy and clear apple juice will both work in this recipe. Cloudy juice is unfiltered and has more body and a fresher flavour.

- Other fruit juices will be delicious in this recipe; try pineapple or mango juice.

- Encourage your guests to scoop up some of the plumped fruits along with the drink as they enjoy this warming recipe.

- It's a good idea to offer small spoons so your guests can eat the flavoured fruit.

DRINKS & APPETIZERS

HOT PUNCH
Serve a crowd easily with these simple and flavourful punch recipes

Punch is traditionally served at large parties, but you can also serve it at a smaller gathering by cutting the quantities in half. The slow cooker is the perfect appliance for cooking and keeping the drink warm.

A hot punch can be made with or without alcoholic ingredients. Keep in mind that the low heat will not burn off all of the alcohol, even over long cooking times.

You can keep the punch warm for 2–4 hours after it finishes cooking. If you want to add more punch, it's better to make a new batch instead of just adding more ingredients to the original.

Serve your punch in handled mugs with cinnamon stick stirrers, a slice of orange or lemon, or grated spices.

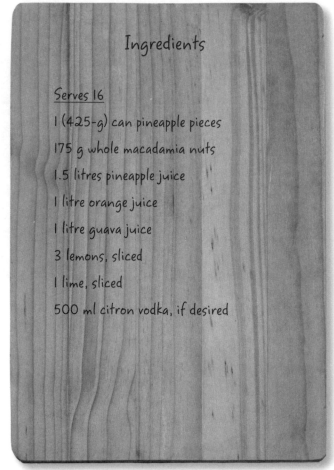

Ingredients

Serves 16

1 (425-g) can pineapple pieces

175 g whole macadamia nuts

1.5 litres pineapple juice

1 litre orange juice

1 litre guava juice

3 lemons, sliced

1 lime, sliced

500 ml citron vodka, if desired

Hot Tropical Punch

- Combine all ingredients except lemons, lime and vodka in a 5.5-litre slow cooker.

- Cover and cook on low for 6–7 hours, or on high for 3–4 hours, until punch is steaming and blended.

- Add lemon slices, lime slices and vodka to the slow cooker. Cover and cook on high for 30 minutes until punch is hot again.

- To serve, ladle punch, some of the pineapple pieces, a few nuts and a lemon or lime slice into each mug.

Cranberry Punch
Place 50 g dried sweetened cranberries in 3-litre slow cooker along with 75 g sugar. Add 2 litres cranberry juice, 1 cinnamon stick and 250 ml orange juice. Cover and cook on low for 2–3 hours until steaming and blended.

Wassail
In a 3.5-litre slow cooker, combine 100 g sugar, 120 ml honey, 500 ml water and 250 ml orange juice. Add 1.5 litres cloudy apple juice, 50 ml lemon juice, 2.5 cm piece peeled fresh ginger, 2 cinnamon sticks and 1 star anise. Cover and cook on low for 4–5 hours until steaming.

Prepare Fruit

Stir Punch

- Always wash fruits before slicing to avoid passing bacteria from the skin to the flesh and juice.

- Use a food-grade soap or washing solution and rinse thoroughly before you slice or chop.

- Slice the fruit 3–5 mm thick right through the rind. Carefully remove and discard any seeds.

- Other whole nuts you can use in hot punch are shelled cashews and walnuts; they keep their crispness even when cooked in liquid.

- Stir the punch gently so you don't break up the fruit. Use a wooden spoon or large ladle.

- Add the lemon and lime slices at the end of cooking time so the volatile oils in the skin don't become bitter.

- If you aren't going to use the citron vodka, add 75 ml lemon juice just before serving.

- As they help themselves to the punch, your guests automatically stir it, so it stays blended.

DRINKS & APPETIZERS

HOT CHOCOLATE
Warm and creamy hot chocolate is a treat on cold days

Everyday hot chocolate is often made from an instant mix. Real hot chocolate, made with cocoa powder and real chocolate, is another experience entirely.

The slow cooker melts the chocolate perfectly, with less chance of burning. The long cooking time also brings out the complex flavour of real chocolate. Use all plain or all milk chocolate, or a mixture for more depth of flavour.

For a nice frothy texture, whisk the hot chocolate with an eggbeater or immersion blender. The whipping cream will provide the foam.

Garnish your hot chocolate with anything from a candy cane to a cinnamon stick or tiny marshmallows. A sprinkle of freshly grated nutmeg or cardamom provides the perfect finishing touch.

Ingredients

Serves 8–10

1 (375-g) can evaporated milk

350 ml whipping cream

2 litres whole milk

2 tablespoons cocoa powder

350 g plain chocolate chips

175 g milk chocolate chips

175 g white chocolate chips

Pinch of salt

2 teaspoons vanilla extract

Classic Hot Chocolate

- In 4.5-litre slow cooker, combine all ingredients except vanilla. Mix well.

- Cover and cook on low for 2–3 hours, stirring every 30 minutes, until chocolate is melted and mixture is smooth.

- Beat mixture with eggbeater or immersion blender until frothy. Turn off slow cooker while using immersion blender.

- Stir in vanilla and serve hot from the slow cooker, topped with marshmallows or whipped cream.

Because chocolate burns easily, don't use high heat to cook your hot chocolate. White chocolate burns more easily than darker varieties. As you stir the chocolate, scrape the sides so the chocolate isn't directly exposed to heat for long periods.

Hot Chocolate Schnapps
In a 3.5-litre slow cooker, combine 1 (400-g) can sweetened condensed milk, 2 litres whole milk, 225 g chopped plain chocolate and 175 g milk chocolate chips. Cover and cook on low for 3–4 hours, stirring once, until steaming. Add 120 ml peppermint schnapps, stir and serve.

DRINKS & APPETIZERS

Mix Chocolate and Milk

Whipped Cream

- Combine all ingredients well, using a wire whisk or eggbeater.

- As the chocolate melts, incorporate it into the liquid. Use a heatproof spatula to scrape the bottom of the slow cooker.

- If the chocolate sits at the bottom of the slow cooker too long it can burn, so it's important to move it around.

- The little bit of salt may seem strange, but it brings out the flavour of the chocolate.

- A topping of whipped, sweetened cream melting slowly into the warm chocolate is decadent and delicious. And it's easy to make.

- Put 120 ml whipping cream in a small chilled bowl. Add 1 tablespoon icing sugar.

- Beat with an eggbeater or an electric mixer until the cream forms peaks. Don't overwhip. Beat in $1/2$ teaspoon vanilla extract.

DIPS

Dips cook to creamy perfection in your slow cooker

Most parties start with appetizers, and they very often include some kind of dip. Warm dips are less common but very welcome, especially during the cold autumn and winter months. But keeping them hot is tricky. You can place the serving bowl on a hotplate, but that can burn the bottom of the dip. A slow cooker is the perfect cooking and serving appliance for this type of food.

Hot dips are almost always creamy with cheese and dairy products. Those ingredients don't cook well in the slow cooker, so we need some buffering ingredients. A white sauce is a good choice for this job.

The dip will brown a little around the edges and on top as the cheese cooks; this is desirable. If you don't want this to happen, stir the dip twice during the cooking time.

Ingredients

Serves 8

2 tablespoons butter

1 leek, chopped

4 cloves garlic, finely chopped

450 g frozen spinach, thawed and
   drained

2 (400-g) cans artichoke hearts,
   drained and chopped

250 ml mayonnaise

250 ml white sauce

175 g grated Havarti cheese

75 g grated Parmesan cheese

Rich Artichoke Dip

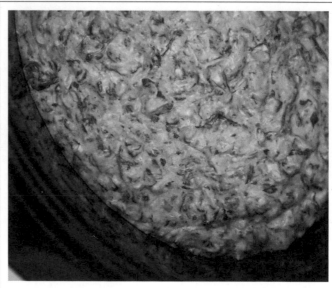

- Melt butter in medium pan or flameproof 3.5-litre slow cooker insert. Cook leek and garlic until tender.

- In slow cooker, combine leek mixture with all remaining ingredients except 25 g of the Parmesan cheese; mix well.

- Cover and cook on low for 6–7 hours, or on high for 3–4 hours, stirring once during cooking time, until mixture is bubbling.

- Sprinkle with remaining Parmesan cheese and serve with crudités and crackers.

Cheese Fondue

Cook 2 cloves crushed garlic in 1 tablespoon olive oil. Place in 3-litre slow cooker and add 350 ml dry white wine and 250 ml apple juice. Toss 225 g grated Emmental and 225 g grated Cheddar cheese with 2 tablespoons cornflour and add. Cover and cook on low 1–2 hours, stirring occasionally, until cheese melts.

Pizza Dip

Cook 1 chopped onion and 3 cloves crushed garlic in 2 tablespoons butter. Add to 3-litre slow cooker along with 225 g cream cheese, 1 (275-g) can tomato and herb pizza sauce, and 2 diced tomatoes. Add 115 g grated mozzarella cheese and 25 g grated Parmesan. Cover and cook on low 2–3 hours, stirring occasionally.

Prepare Vegetables

Mix Ingredients

- Frozen spinach holds an incredible amount of water. For this recipe's success, the spinach has to be well drained.

- Squeeze the thawed spinach in your hands, then place in paper towels and press to remove as much water as possible.

- The chokes, or prickly centres, of the artichokes should have been removed; inspect them before chopping.

- If the choke remains, just scrape it off gently with a spoon. Be sure to use non-marinated artichoke hearts.

- If your slow cooker has a metal insert, by all means use it to cook the leeks and garlic.

- Be careful with the insert; you may need to protect your hands if it gets hot as the food cooks on the hob.

- You can use low-fat mayonnaise in this recipe.

- Serve the dip with sturdy crackers and some crisp French bread, buttered and toasted.

SNACK MIXES

Snack mixes are well seasoned and crisp when cooked in the slow cooker

Crisp snack mixes don't have to be left to groups of men watching football games. They can be sophisticated and elegant, as well as flavourful and crunchy.

Once again, the slow cooker comes to the rescue with low, even heat that makes a crisp mix with no burned edges.

This is one of the few recipes where you cook the food uncovered. You want the low, consistent heat to glaze the cereal and crackers, but the moisture has to evaporate.

Stirring helps ensure that the crisp ingredients are evenly coated with the glaze and seasonings.

Ingredients

Fills a 3-litre bowl

1 litre cereal squares

1 litre square cheese crackers

500 ml small pretzel sticks

115 g cashew halves

115 g butter, melted

1 teaspoon dried basil

1 teaspoon dried Italian seasoning

1 teaspoon dried thyme

Pinch of cayenne pepper

Glazed Snack Mix

- In 3.5-litre slow cooker, combine cereal, crackers, pretzels and cashews.

- In small saucepan, melt butter over low heat. Remove from heat and add dried herbs and pepper.

- Drizzle herb mixture over cereal mixture in slow cooker; toss to coat. Cover and cook on low for 2 hours.

- Uncover; cook on low for 40–50 minutes longer, stirring once during cooking time, until mixture is glazed. Cool on paper towels; store in airtight container.

Sweet and Salty Snack Mix

Combine 1 litre cereal squares with 500 ml each pretzel sticks and small round pretzels and 115 g pecan halves in 3.5-litre slow cooker. Combine 115 g butter with 50 g brown sugar in saucepan; cook until smooth. Drizzle over mixture; cook uncovered 2 hours. Cool and stir in 350 g chocolate chips.

Caramel Corn

Place 2.5 litres air-popped corn and 350 g pecan halves in 3.5-litre slow cooker. Cook together 175 g butter, 350 g brown sugar, and 50 ml honey in saucepan. Drizzle over corn and nuts; stir to coat. Cook on low, uncovered, 2 hours, stirring every 30 minutes, until crisp.

Combine Ingredients

Prepare Butter Mixture

- As long as you keep the total volume the same, you can use any kind and combination of crisp foods.

- Small crackers, whole or half nuts, straight or round pretzels, bagel chips and plain cereals are good additions.

- Browse through the cereal and snack food aisles of the supermarket for more ideas.

- Store these mixes in airtight containers or heavy duty plastic bags at room temperature for up to a week.

- Dried herbs are used because they stand up better to the heat of the slow cooker.

- You can use any combination of herbs and spices to create your own snack mix.

- Sprinkle on some finely grated Parmesan or pecorino cheese at the end for more flavour.

- You can serve this mixture warm from the slow cooker; turn the appliance to low or keep-warm.

DRINKS & APPETIZERS

MEATBALLS

Meatballs flavoured with sauces and glazes make perfect appetizers

Meatballs are always among the most popular snacks at any party. And using the slow cooker, they are easy to prepare and serve.

With these types of recipes, make sure your slow cooker is attractive, because it should be used for serving. The slow cooker will keep the food warm and delicious up to 2 hours, if it lasts that long.

For best results, choose either fully cooked meatballs or sausages, or brown them thoroughly to make sure they are completely cooked before adding to the sauce in the slow cooker. You want to remove a good amount of the fat from the products before they cook in the sauce. And browning adds great flavour and eye appeal.

Ingredients

Serves 8–10

2 tablespoons butter

1 onion, chopped

3 cloves garlic, finely chopped

250 ml beef stock

120 ml apple jelly

1 star anise

Pinch of ground cloves

75 ml French mustard

50 g brown sugar

50 ml cider vinegar

Pinch of cayenne pepper

1/2 teaspoon hot pepper sauce

50 small frozen cooked Swedish meat-balls, thawed

1 tablespoon cornflour

Sweet and Hot Glazed Meatballs

- In small saucepan, heat butter and cook onion and garlic over medium heat for 5–6 minutes.

- Add 175 ml of the beef stock and bring to a simmer; add apple jelly and stir to melt. Pour into 3.5- or 4.5-litre slow cooker.

- Add star anise, cloves, mustard, sugar, vinegar, pepper and pepper sauce; stir; add meatballs. Cover; cook on low 7–9 hours.

- Remove star anise. Blend cornflour with remaining stock and add to slow cooker. Cover and cook on high until sauce thickens.

Sweet and Sour Sausages

Substitute 40–50 cooked cocktail sausages for the meatballs in this recipe. Omit cloves and star anise, and use chicken stock instead of beef stock. Omit cayenne pepper and hot sauce; increase vinegar to 75 ml.

Glazed Meatballs

Bake 48 regular meatballs until cooked through. Place in 3.5- or 4.5-litre slow cooker. In a pan, cook 1 chopped onion in 2 tablespoons butter for 5 minutes. Add 1 (450-g) can whole berry cranberry sauce, 2 tablespoons mustard, 2 tablespoons brown sugar and 250 ml barbecue sauce. Pour over meatballs; cover and cook on low 4–6 hours.

Chop Onions and Garlic

Stir Meatballs

- Onions and garlic should be chopped fairly finely so they melt into the sauce.

- Cut the onion in half, then peel off the papery skin. Place, cut side down, on work surface. Cut lengthwise through the onion 5–6 times, then cut crosswise to make dice.

- Smash the garlic cloves with the side of the knife, then remove skin and crush or chop finely.

- The onion and garlic flavour the butter so it permeates the sauce around the meatballs.

- Because the sauce has a lot of sugar from the apple jelly and brown sugar, you must stir fairly often to prevent burning.

- Use a wooden spoon, rubber spatula or scraper and gently stir the mixture.

- Scrape the sides firmly so the sauce doesn't stick and burn. These recipes work better when cooked on low heat.

- Other preserves would work well. Try pineapple jelly, apricot jam or raspberry seedless jam for a new flavour.

BREAKFAST EGGS
These rich and savoury egg dishes cook while you're asleep

Breakfast dishes are a great way to use your slow cooker. Put everything together the night before, leave the food to cook while you sleep and wake up to the wonderful aromas of breakfast cooking.

Eggs can be tricky in the slow cooker, and will sometimes curdle, so you need to add a stabilizer: in this case, a white sauce (either homemade or a bottled pasta sauce).

This sauce 'cushions' the eggs so they don't separate while cooking. It also adds great flavour to the dish.

Vary the recipe by choosing different herbs and cheeses. You can also use different cooked meats and vegetables.

Ingredients

Serves 8

450 g spicy pork sausagemeat

2 onions, diced

3 cloves garlic, finely chopped

1 (900-g) pack frozen rosti potatoes

14 eggs

500 ml white sauce

1 teaspoon dried tarragon

25 g grated Parmesan cheese

Sausage, Egg and Potato Casserole

- In large pan, cook sausage-meat, stirring to break up, until almost done. Pour off fat and add onions and garlic; cook until sausage is done.

- In 4.5-litre slow cooker, layer ⅓ of potatoes and ⅓ of sausage mixture; repeat twice.

- In large bowl, beat eggs with white sauce and tarragon until smooth; pour into slow cooker.

- Cover and cook on low for 7–9 hours until browned around edges. Sprinkle with Parmesan cheese and serve.

If you choose the overnight cooking option, you must know your slow cooker and how it cooks. To check this, half-fill the cooker with water. Cover and cook on low for 8 hours. If the water temperature is higher than 85°C, your slow cooker cooks 'hot' and you may need to reduce cooking times.

Eggs Florentine
Cook 225 g smoked streaky bacon until crisp; drain, crumble and set aside. Drain pan; cook 1 chopped onion. Add 1 (275-g) pack frozen spinach, thawed and drained, and 50 g soft breadcrumbs. Beat 12 eggs with 250 ml white sauce and 50 g Parmesan cheese; combine all in 3.5-litre slow cooker. Cover and cook on low 7–9 hours.

Beat Eggs with Sauce

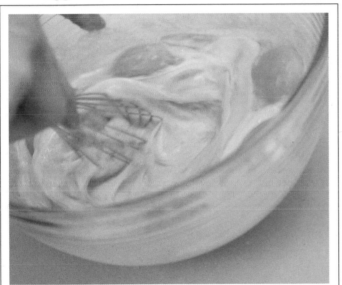

Pour Eggs into Slow Cooker

- It's important that you combine the eggs with another ingredient just before adding to the slow cooker.

- Otherwise, ingredients like cheese, milk, salty bacon or ham, tomatoes or salt will make the eggs separate before they are cooked.

- Beat with an eggbeater or wire whisk until smooth. You don't want to add too much air to the eggs.

- You can substitute a 450 g jar of creamy pasta sauce for the white sauce.

- Pour the egg mixture slowly into the slow cooker so it diffuses throughout the food.

- You want the casserole to be evenly soaked with egg so it will set well. Leave it to stand for 5 minutes before you turn the appliance on.

- If necessary, run a knife through the potato mixture before cooking to make sure the eggs have penetrated the layers.

- When serving the dish, use a large spoon to scoop through all the layers for each serving.

BREAKFAST & BRUNCH

VEGETABLE STRATA
Savoury vegetables add colour and nutrition to a classic strata

A popular American brunch dish, a strata is a layered dish, usually made with bread, that is held together with an egg custard mixture. When it's cooked in the slow cooker, the eggs need to be stabilized, so in this recipe a combination of evaporated milk and flour is used.

If the bread cubes float, you may want to spend a few minutes pushing them back into the custard. As the bread absorbs the custard it will sink. Then you can turn on the slow cooker.

Use your favourite combination of vegetables and cheeses in this easy recipe. Any kind of bread can be used: try cubes of leftover waffles or croissants, or whole-grain bread, to vary the dish. Be sure to check the strata at the end of the shortest cooking time.

Ingredients

Serves 6–8

1 onion, chopped

2 tablespoons butter

3 peppers, assorted colours, sliced

65 g grated carrots

1 (200-g) jar green pesto

14 slices sourdough bread

75 g grated Havarti cheese

8 eggs

1 (350-g) can evaporated milk

1 tablespoon plain flour

Salt and pepper to taste

Three-Pepper Pesto Strata

- Cook onion in butter over medium heat for 4 minutes. Add peppers and carrots and remove from heat.

- Spread pesto on bread, then cut bread into cubes. Layer ⅓ each bread, vegetable mixture and cheese in 4.5-litre slow cooker; repeat twice.

- Beat eggs with milk and flour and season with salt and pepper; pour into slow cooker.

- Cover and chill for 6–8 hours. Then cook on low for 6–8 hours until strata is puffed and temperature reads 75°C.

Loaded Hash Browns

Start recipe as directed, but substitute 1 (900-g) pack frozen hash brown or rosti potatoes, thawed, for the bread cubes. Omit pesto. Chop the peppers and add 115 g grated Cheddar cheese. Also add 6 rashers cooked, crumbled smoked streaky bacon.

Broccoli Strata

Cook onion in butter; add 3 cloves crushed garlic. Use 450 g broccoli florets in place of the sliced peppers; omit carrots. Substitute 115 g grated Emmental cheese for the Havarti. Sprinkle top with 2 tablespoons Parmesan cheese; cook as directed.

Prepare Vegetables

- To slice peppers, first cut them in half and pull out the stem, membranes and seeds.

- Then place the peppers on the cutting board. Slice 8 mm thick and repeat.

- It's important to cook the onions before adding them to the slow cooker to mellow the flavour.

- As you cook onions and garlic, the flavour becomes mild and sweet, perfect for the first meal of the day.

Layer Food

- Layer the food evenly in the slow cooker, to ensure that every serving gets some of the bread, cheese, vegetables and egg.

- Other vegetables that would work well include chopped spring onions or bottled mushrooms, drained.

- Vegetables high in water, like squash, courgettes or fresh mushrooms, must be sautéed until dry or they will add too much water.

- You may want to sprinkle the top with more grated cheese before serving; leave to stand 5 minutes, then serve.

BREAKFAST & BRUNCH

39

FRUIT STRATA

Sweet and tangy fruit makes this strata taste like sweet rolls

A sweet strata is comparable to a coffee cake or sweet roll, but it's healthier. The fruits you add will release their juice as they cook, flavouring the dish.

Cinnamon raisin bread is a good choice for this dish because it adds interest and flavour, but you can use other breads, like cracked wheat, croissants, multigrain or oatmeal bread.

It's best to use firm fruits such as apples or pears for this dish.

Soft fruits such as strawberries or raspberries will become mushy and add too much water to the mixture.

The fruit is tossed with lemon juice so it doesn't turn brown while it cooks. And for a topping that stays slightly crunchy, granola is a good choice; use your favourite variety. Serve the strata with maple syrup.

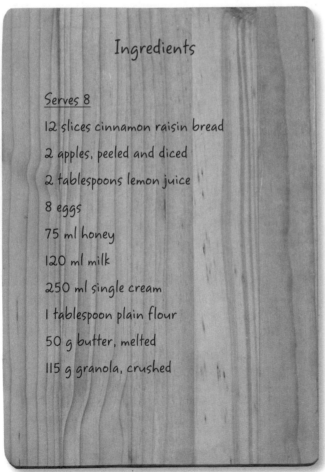

Ingredients

Serves 8

12 slices cinnamon raisin bread

2 apples, peeled and diced

2 tablespoons lemon juice

8 eggs

75 ml honey

120 ml milk

250 ml single cream

1 tablespoon plain flour

50 g butter, melted

115 g granola, crushed

Apple Strata

- Cut bread into cubes. Toss apples with lemon juice; layer in 3.5- or 4.5-litre slow cooker with bread.

- In large bowl, beat remaining ingredients except granola until smooth.

- Pour into slow cooker; cover and chill for 2–4 hours. Sprinkle with granola.

- Then cook mixture, covered, on low for 7–9 hours until strata is puffed and set.

40

Prepare Apples

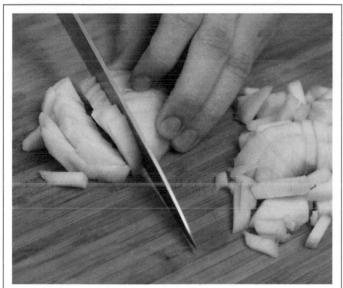

Layer Ingredients

- Choose an apple that is good for baking for this recipe. Some apples break down too much when exposed to heat.

- Eating varieties such as Russet, Worcester, Cox and Jonathan apples are good choices.

- Prepare the apples just before you are ready to turn on the slow cooker. Even when treated with lemon juice, they can turn brown.

- Peel the apples with a swivel-bladed peeler, then cut in half and core with a melon baller; then dice.

- It's important to layer the ingredients evenly in the slow cooker in the order described.

- Use more or less fruit and bread to fill the slow cooker ²/₃ full.

- When you pour the egg mixture over the layers,

the bread may float; just press it back down for a few minutes so it absorbs the liquid.

- You can cook the strata immediately without refrigerating, as soon as the bread has absorbed the egg mixture.

BREAKFAST & BRUNCH

PORRIDGE
Pinhead oats cook to creamy perfection overnight

Porridge is the ultimate comfort food for breakfast. It's possible to cook it in the slow cooker, but there are some special ingredients and tricks to keep it creamy.

Oatmeal, especially when cooked overnight, is one of those foods that burn easily. We can solve this by placing the oatmeal in a heatproof bowl inside the slow cooker to protect it from the heat at the bottom.

Pinhead oats are really necessary for this type of cooking. Even regular oatmeal, not the quick-cooking type, gets mushy when cooked this long.

Finally, toast the oats before cooking to create texture and bring out the flavour, as the heat releases aromatic oils.

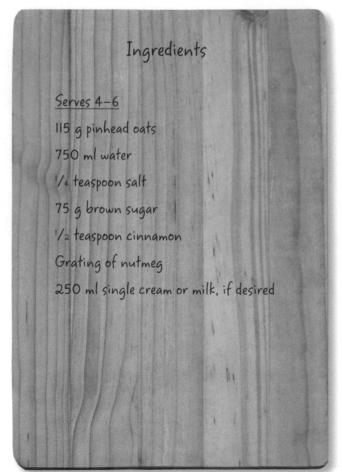

Ingredients

Serves 4–6

115 g pinhead oats

750 ml water

¼ teaspoon salt

75 g brown sugar

½ teaspoon cinnamon

Grating of nutmeg

250 ml single cream or milk, if desired

Brown Sugar Porridge

- Grease a 2-litre Pyrex bowl. Place on a trivet in a 3.5-litre slow cooker; pour 250 ml water into the slow cooker.

- In a medium pan, toast the oats until fragrant. Place in bowl and stir in remaining ingredients except cream.

- Cover and cook for 7–9 hours or until porridge is creamy and tender. Stir in cream, if using.

- Serve with warmed maple syrup, brown sugar or toasted nuts and granola.

Apple Granola Porridge

Toast oats as directed; place in greased bowl with water, salt and 75 g granulated sugar. Add 115 g granola, 1 apple, peeled and chopped, 50 g chopped walnuts and 115 g sultanas. Cover and cook on low for 6–8 hours. Stir in 120 ml whole milk and serve immediately.

Cranberry Porridge

Toast oats as directed; place in greased bowl with 500 ml water, 250 ml cranberry juice, salt and 75 g brown sugar. Add 115 g dried cranberries and 1 teaspoon vanilla extract. Cover and cook on low for 6–8 hours. Stir in 1 tablespoon butter and serve.

Toast Oats

- Toast the oats in a dry pan over low heat. Stir occasionally so they toast evenly.

- You can toast the oats ahead of time and keep them in an airtight container for up to 3 days.

- The oats are ready when they turn a slightly darker brown and you can smell the toasted aroma.

- If you can't find pinhead oats, toasting will help regular (not quick-cooking) oats keep their texture better in the slow cooker.

Combine Ingredients

- A pinch of salt brings out the flavour in the porridge, but add only a small amount.

- You can use granulated sugar, honey or maple syrup to flavour the porridge.

- If you choose maple syrup, reduce the water by 50 ml.

- If the oatmeal isn't sweet enough when it's done, just add more sugar to taste.

- You can substitute milk or cream for part of the water for a richer flavour and slightly thicker texture.

FRUIT COBBLER
Lots of healthy fruit cooks with a chewy topping in these fun recipes

Cobbler can be served as a delicious hot breakfast or brunch dish, or as a dessert. Hard fruits like apples and pears work best in this type of recipe, but peaches and blueberries would be nice additions.

There are two kinds of cobblers: those with a chewy or crisp topping and those with a cake-like topping. The main recipe has a chewy topping. The Peach Cobbler variation has a cake-like topping. Both are delicious and perfect for brunch.

For crunch, nuts, granola and some brown sugar make a good combination that holds up to the steamy environment of the slow cooker.

Serve these cobblers with ice cream, cream or yogurt for a cooling contrast.

Ingredients

Serves 6

3 Granny Smith apples, peeled

2 Kaiser pears, peeled

2 tablespoons lemon juice

125 g brown sugar

2 tablespoons flour

50 g dried cherries

1 teaspoon cinnamon

350 g granola cereal

115 g chopped walnuts

50 g butter

Mixed Fruit Caramel Cobbler

- Slice apples and pears into 1-cm slices; sprinkle with lemon juice as you work. Place in 3.5-litre slow cooker with 75 g of the brown sugar, flour and cherries.

- In large bowl, combine cinnamon, cereal, walnuts and remaining brown sugar.

- Drizzle melted butter over granola mixture and mix.

- Sprinkle granola mixture on top of fruit. Cover and cook on low for 7–8 hours or until fruit is tender. Serve with warmed caramel sauce, if desired.

Peach Cobbler

Sprinkle 4 peeled and sliced peaches with lemon juice. Place in 3-litre slow cooker with 75 g sugar and ¹/₂ teaspoon cinnamon. Mix 115 g plain flour, 75 g sugar, and ¹/₂ teaspoon baking powder; add 3 tablespoons melted butter and 175 ml evaporated milk; pour over peaches. Line lid with paper towels; cook on high 3–4 hours.

Pear Cranberry Cobbler

Omit apples and increase pears to 4; peel and toss with lemon juice as directed. Substitute 115 g dried cranberries for the dried cherries. Substitute 115 g chopped pecans for the walnuts. Cook as directed.

Prepare Fruits

Mix Topping

- The size you cut the fruits determines the texture of the final dish. The skin can stay on or be peeled off.

- Large slices will mean discrete pieces of fruit, while smaller slices or cubes will result in a sauce-like consistency.

- Choose fruits that are quite firm. In fact, underripe fruits work very well in this recipe.

- The heat and moisture will bring out their flavours and make them tender and juicy.

- You can mix the topping ahead of time; keep it in an airtight container up to 1 day. Sprinkle over fruit just before cooking.

- Use your favourite granola; the crunchier and chunkier the better. Homemade or bought are both fine.

- This cobbler can be served warm or cool, but it doesn't keep well for more than 12 hours.

- Vary the dried fruits, spices and nuts to create your own fruit cobbler.

BREAKFAST & BRUNCH

AMERICAN EGG CASSEROLES
Introduce different flavours to add variety to delicious egg dishes

Eggs are such a mild and versatile food: they combine with many different flavours. The eggs need stabilization in the long slow cooking time; a white sauce, bottled creamy pasta sauce or evaporated milk mixed with a little flour will all work.

A topping of cold chopped vegetables and herbs not only improves the appearance of these casseroles, but adds a great contrast of flavours and temperature as well.

Use your imagination to create other variations. For a Tex-Mex egg casserole, add chopped chorizo, Pepper Jack or Cheddar cheese and drained salsa. For a Spanish-style casserole, add paprika, roasted red peppers and oregano.

Ingredients

Serves 6

2 tablespoons butter

1 onion, chopped

225 g sliced mushrooms

1 red pepper, chopped

225 g French bread, cubed

225 g Brie cheese, cubed

400 g frozen hash brown or rosti
    potatoes, thawed

12 eggs

250 ml white sauce

1/2 teaspoon dried thyme

1/2 teaspoon dried herbes de Provence

40 g grated Parmesan cheese

French Breakfast Casserole

- Grease 3.5-litre slow cooker. In a frying pan, melt butter over medium heat and cook onion and mushrooms until tender; drain.

- Combine with peppers. Layer with bread, Brie cheese and potatoes in slow cooker.

- In large bowl, beat eggs with white sauce, thyme, herbes de Provence and Parmesan cheese. Pour into slow cooker.

- Cover and cook on high for 3–4 hours until set and puffed. Serve immediately.

All-American Egg Casserole

Use cracked-wheat bread, cubed and toasted in the oven. Omit red pepper and Brie cheese. Use 450 g breakfast sausages, browned, drained and chopped, in place of the potatoes, and 1 teaspoon dried basil in place of the thyme and herbes de Provence. Use Cheddar cheese; cook as directed.

Southwestern Egg Casserole

Add 1 (115-g) can chopped green chillies, drained, to the egg mixture. Omit mushrooms and red pepper; add 1 green pepper and 3 crushed garlic cloves. Add 1 tablespoon chilli powder; omit thyme and herbes de Provence. Omit Brie; use Pepper Jack cheese. Cook as directed.

Prepare Cheese

Assemble Casserole

- Cheese is a tricky ingredient in the slow cooker. It's usually added at the end of cooking time. But it can be included if there are lots of other ingredients to shield it from the heat.

- Brie cheese is easier to cube when it's very cold. Freeze it for 10–15 minutes before slicing.

- Don't prepare cheese ahead of time; it dries out very easily. Place in the freezer while cooking the onions.

- Pour the egg mixture slowly into the slow cooker so the bread absorbs it. The potatoes will help hold the bread in placè.

- Don't make the custard ahead of time; the egg mixture will separate and become runny.

- To accompany, combine 2 chopped tomatoes, 2 chopped spring onions and 1 tablespoon fresh thyme.

- Serve the mixture on the side, or spoon it on to the casserole as a topping when it's done.

BREAKFAST & BRUNCH

CHICKEN VEGETABLE PITTAS

This chicken and vegetable filling can be served hot or cold

Sandwich fillings are fun to make in the slow cooker. You can serve them hot or use the slow cooker to cook the ingredients, then combine with classic sandwich accompaniments like mayonnaise or mustard, and chill.

There are lots of wonderful flavours you can add to the classic chicken sandwich, and you can vary the vegetables you use. Just remember to place hard vegetables, like onion,

potatoes, carrots and garlic, in the bottom of the slow cooker and top with meats and tender vegetables. Cheeses and dairy products are stirred in at the end.

Serve these sandwich fillings in anything from croissants to crusty rolls to pitta breads. Or you can assemble the sandwiches, butter the outsides of the bread, and toast them in a dual-contact grill or a toasted sandwich maker.

Ingredients

Serves 6–8

1 onion, chopped

1 leek, rinsed and chopped

3 cloves garlic, finely chopped

6 boneless, skinless chicken breasts

1 teaspoon dried oregano

120 ml chicken stock

115 g crumbled feta cheese

Salt and pepper

4–5 whole-wheat pitta breads

Topping

1 green pepper, chopped

250 ml thick Greek yogurt

1 tablespoon chopped fresh mint

50 g seeded, diced cucumber

Greek Chicken Vegetable Pittas

- Place onion, leek and garlic in bottom of 3.5-litre slow cooker. Season chicken with salt and pepper, sprinkle with oregano and add to slow cooker.

- Pour stock into slow cooker; cover and cook on low for 5–7 hours until chicken is thoroughly cooked.

- Meanwhile, combine all topping ingredients, cover and refrigerate.

- When chicken is done, shred and stir into leek mixture with cheese. Make sandwiches with pitta bread and yogurt topping.

Tex–Mex Chicken Pitta Sandwiches
Increase onions to 2, and use 4 cloves garlic; omit leeks. Add 2 chopped jalapeño peppers and use 10 boneless, skinless chicken thighs; omit oregano and feta. Pour 250 ml salsa over; cover and cook 7–9 hours. Shred chicken; serve in pittas with guacamole and grated Monterey Jack or mild Cheddar cheese.

•••• YELLOW ● LIGHT ••••

Use your judgment and adjust accordingly if the filling is too liquid or too dry. You can add more liquid and cook on high for 10–15 minutes to heat through or you can remove the cover and cook on high for 15–20 minutes to reduce liquid.

Arrange Food

- Try to buy chicken breasts that are as evenly sized as possible. If they are very different in size, cut up the larger pieces so you can arrange them in an even layer over the vegetables.

- Place the chicken evenly over the onions and leeks,
sprinkling each with seasoning as you do.

- You could substitute boneless, skinless chicken thighs and give them a longer cooking time; cook for 6–8 hours on low.

Finishing Touches

- Make the yogurt topping ahead of time and keep it in the fridge so it stays cold.

- The chicken will shred very easily using two forks. As you work, return the chicken to the slow cooker.

- The shredded chicken will begin to absorb some
of the liquid in the slow cooker.

- At this point you can turn the slow cooker to keep-warm or low for another hour before adding the cheese.

CHICKEN TACO WRAPS

Tex-Mex flavours pair beautifully with tender chicken

Boneless chicken thighs are one of the best meats to cook in the slow cooker. When tender, they can be shredded with just a touch of a fork, and they pair beautifully with spicy Tex-Mex flavours.

This recipe is ideal for serving to a crowd. Just make a buffet with the slow cooker, additional ingredients and tortillas kept warm in some napkins; let everyone serve themselves.

You can make the dish as mild or as spicy as you like. Use habañero chillies in place of the jalapeños, add more chillies or chili powder, or reduce them.

This recipe can easily be made ahead of time. Shred chicken, mix with remaining ingredients and refrigerate. Then reheat on the hob or in the microwave just before you want to eat. Use the slow cooker to keep the filling warm.

Ingredients

Serves 8

6 boneless, skinless chicken thighs

1 tablespoon chilli powder

3 tablespoons plain flour

½ teaspoon cumin

1 onion, chopped

3 cloves garlic, finely chopped

2 jalapeño peppers, finely chopped

1 (425-g) can black beans, drained

250 ml salsa

200 g cherry tomatoes, halved

8 flour tortillas

115 g grated Pepper Jack cheese

1 avocado, sliced

Salt and pepper to taste

Spicy Chicken Taco Wraps

- Sprinkle chicken with chilli powder, flour, salt, pepper and cumin.

- Place onion, garlic, and jalapeño in 3.5-litre slow cooker; top with chicken.

- Add beans and salsa. Cover and cook on low for

- 7–9 hours until chicken is cooked.

- Remove chicken and shred; return to slow cooker; cook on high for 30 minutes until blended.

- Stir in cherry tomatoes. Make wraps with tortillas, cheese and avocado.

Chicken Enchiladas

Prepare chicken recipe as directed, shred meat and stir into remaining ingredients. Divide among 12 corn tortillas; sprinkle with 115 g grated Pepper Jack and 115 g grated Cheddar cheese. Arrange in 22 x 33-cm baking dish; cover with 1 (275-g) jar green salsa. Bake for 35–45 minutes.

BLT Chicken Wraps

Cook 5 rashers smoked streaky bacon until crisp; drain, crumble and set aside. Cook onion and garlic in bacon fat. Combine with chicken, salt and pepper, 1 (400-g) can chopped tomatoes, drained, and 250 ml white sauce; cook as directed; shred chicken. Make wraps with bacon, lettuce, 120 ml sour cream and flour tortillas.

Shred Chicken

Spoon into Tortillas

- The chicken will be very tender and will shred easily. Remove from the slow cooker with a slotted spoon.

- Using two forks, gently pull the chicken apart into long, thin pieces.

- Return the chicken and any accumulated juices to the slow cooker as you work.

- The mixture can be thickened at this point with 2 tablespoons cornflour blended with 50 ml water.

- To warm tortillas, wrap in foil and warm in a 180°C oven for 10–15 minutes.

- You can also wrap in microwave-safe paper towels and microwave on high for 10 seconds per tortilla.

- Prepare the avocado at the last minute so it doesn't turn brown. You can sprinkle it with lemon juice, but prepare it only about 20 minutes before serving.

- You can use corn or flour tortillas. Flour tortillas are usually larger.

HOT SANDWICHES

SLOPPY JOES

This classic American sandwich is easy to make in the slow cooker

Sloppy Joe sandwiches are the perfect slow cooker food. It's practically impossible to overcook or ruin this recipe.

The minced meat has to be browned before combining with the other ingredients, otherwise there will be too much fat and liquid in the mixture, which would render the finished sandwich too wet and greasy. Brown the beef (and the sausagemeat, too) and drain very well.

This is another recipe that's perfect to make ahead of time; in fact, the flavours mellow and improve if you store the filling in the refrigerator for several hours or overnight. Reheat in a saucepan on the stove, not in the slow cooker.

Season your Sloppy Joes any way you like. You can add spicy ingredients like chilli powder or jalapeños, or load up on cheese.

Ingredients

Serves 8

450 g lean minced beef

450 g spicy pork sausagemeat

2 onions, chopped

3 cloves garlic, finely chopped

50 ml tomato purée

250 ml barbecue sauce

120 ml tomato ketchup

50 ml mustard

2 tablespoons cider vinegar

Salt and pepper to taste

3 tablespoons butter

8 hamburger buns

Classic Sloppy Joes

- In large frying pan, cook beef with sausagemeat until almost done, stirring to break up. Pour off fat.

- Add onions and garlic; cook and stir 2–3 minutes longer. Place in 3-litre slow cooker.

- Add tomato purée, barbecue sauce, ketchup, mustard, vinegar, salt and pepper to pan; bring to the boil and pour into slow cooker.

- Cover and cook on low for 6–7 hours until blended. Toast and butter hamburger buns; serve mixture on buns.

Sloppy Janes

Make the recipe just as directed, but substitute 450 g minced turkey for the beef, and 450 g turkey sausage for the pork. Omit the ketchup and add 1 tablespoon Worcestershire sauce.

Vegetarian Joes

Make the recipe just as directed, but use 675 g Quorn mince in place of the beef and sausage. Add 1 teaspoon dried thyme and 1 teaspoon dried oregano.

Brown Minced Beef

Mix Ingredients

- Place the minced beef in a cold frying pan; turn the heat to medium.

- As the beef browns, break it apart with a fork or spoon so it crumbles and cooks evenly. Turn the beef so the uncooked parts are in contact with the pan.

- Choose lean minced meat. When the meat is cooked, spoon off and discard all of the fat.

- There will still be enough fat in the pan to cook the onions and garlic and add flavour.

- Because the meat is cooked, you don't need to layer ingredients in this recipe.

- Just combine everything and stir well. Cover and turn on the slow cooker. Stir again before serving.

- If the mixture needs to be thickened, add cornflour blended with water, or remove the cover and cook on high for 10 minutes.

- You can serve this mixture on buns, in buttered jacket potatoes, or with mashed potatoes or rice.

HOT SANDWICHES

MOROCCAN TURKEY WRAPS

Travel to North Africa with this exotic wrap sandwich

Moroccan food is rich and flavourful, full of spices. It is also characterized by the combination of meat with dried fruits, such as apricots and raisins. Other typical ingredients include fresh ginger, nuts, onions and garlic.

Turkey breast meat is like chicken breast in that it's easily overcooked in the slow cooker. It's very low in fat. Check on it after 5 hours of cooking.

If you want to cook this for a longer period of time, leave the turkey whole. Cook for 8–9 hours, then shred the meat and return it to the slow cooker.

Other dried fruits would be good additions to this recipe: try sultanas or chopped dates. For extra texture you could also add some cashews or chopped walnuts. Serve the turkey in flour tortillas or pitta breads.

Ingredients

Serves 8
1 onion, chopped
3 cloves garlic, finely chopped
1 tablespoon grated fresh ginger
900 g turkey breast
2 tablespoons flour
1/2 teaspoon salt
Pinch of cayenne pepper
1/2 teaspoon cinnamon
1 teaspoon ground cumin
115 g currants
115 g dried apricots, chopped
120 ml chicken stock
120 ml plain yogurt
2 tablespoons cornflour
8 flour tortillas
50 g chopped pistachios

Moroccan Turkey Wraps

- In 3-litre slow cooker, combine onion, garlic and ginger.

- Cut turkey into 5 cm cubes and toss with flour, salt, pepper, cinnamon and cumin. Place over vegetables in slow cooker. Add currants and apricots.

- Pour chicken stock over all. Cover and cook on low for 5–7 hours until turkey is thoroughly cooked.

- In small bowl, combine yogurt and cornflour; stir into slow cooker. Cover; cook on high for 20 minutes until thickened. Serve in tortillas with pistachios.

Thai Turkey Wraps

Use onion, garlic, ginger, turkey, flour, salt and pepper. Omit cinnamon, cumin, currants and apricots. Make sauce by mixing 75 g peanut butter, 120 ml barbecue sauce and 1 tablespoon soy sauce; pour over turkey. Cook as directed; make sandwiches with tortillas and 115 g goats' cheese.

Gyros Sandwiches

Start with onions, garlic and ginger. Add 900 g cubed trimmed lamb shoulder. Add remaining ingredients, but omit cinnamon, cumin, currants and apricots. Add 2 peeled, seeded, chopped tomatoes. Shred lamb, then make sandwiches with 115 g feta, olives and pitta breads.

Coat Turkey

Make Sandwiches

- Coat the turkey with flour and spices, so the spices penetrate the meat and the flour thickens the sauce.

- You can substitute cubed chicken breast (cook 5 hours on low) or chicken thighs (cook 7 hours on low) for the turkey.

- You can prepare all the ingredients ahead of time and refrigerate. Coat the turkey and layer the food when you're ready.

- Any leftover turkey mixture could be warmed and served on lettuce the next day as a salad.

- You don't have to add the yogurt mixture. If you like, you can just remove the ingredients from the slow cooker with a slotted spoon.

- Then make the wrap sandwiches with the drained turkey and fruits.

- You can make the filling mixture ahead of time; omit the yogurt mixture and serve it warm or cold.

- Think about using different types of bread in this and all of your sandwiches. Flatbread, pitta breads, ciabatta and French bread all work well.

HOT SANDWICHES

PULLED PORK SANDWICHES

A barbecue classic can come out of your slow cooker, too

Pork shoulder roast is an inexpensive cut of meat that cooks to perfection in the slow cooker.

Classic pulled pork was the original barbecued food of early settlers in the Southern States of America: a joint of pork cooked slowly over a smoky fire for a long time until the meat was so tender it could be pulled apart by hand. It is traditionally served in a sandwich with a sauce. In the slow cooker, the pork is cooked with the sauce, which adds flavour to the meat. There are several ways to eat pulled pork. It can be served alone on a bun or with coleslaw, which adds a great contrast in flavour, temperature and texture.

It's hard to overcook the meat in this recipe; the longer it cooks the more tender it will get. But you do have to watch out for the sauce burning; stir occasionally.

Ingredients

Serves 12

1.8-kg pork shoulder roast
1½ teaspoons salt
½ teaspoon pepper
1 tablespoon Cajun seasoning
2 tablespoons cider vinegar
1 (450 g) bottle barbecue sauce
12 crusty rolls, split

Coleslaw

450 g shredded white cabbage
2 Granny Smith apples, chopped
115 g sultanas
120 ml mayonnaise
2 tablespoons sugar
115 g chopped pecans

Carolina Pulled Pork Sandwiches

- Trim excess fat from pork. Sprinkle roast with salt, pepper and Cajun seasoning. Place in 4.5- or 5.5-litre slow cooker.

- Pour vinegar and barbecue sauce over all. Cover and cook on low for 8–9 hours until pork is falling apart.

- Shred pork using two forks; return to slow cooker. Stir mixture and cook on low for another hour.

- Meanwhile, combine coleslaw ingredients and chill. Split rolls and fill with pork mixture and coleslaw.

Classic Pork Sandwiches

Cook pork as directed, but add 1 (225-g) jar tomato sauce to the sauce and omit the vinegar. Omit the coleslaw. Shred pork, stir into sauce and serve on toasted and buttered onion buns.

Homemade Barbecue Sauce

Cook 1 chopped onion and 4 crushed garlic cloves in 1 tablespoon butter. Place in 2-litre slow cooker; add 250 ml tomato ketchup, 75 ml vinegar, 50 g brown sugar, 1 teaspoon salt and 2 chopped jalapeño peppers; cook on low for 7–8 hours. Refrigerate for up to 5 days.

Cook Pork

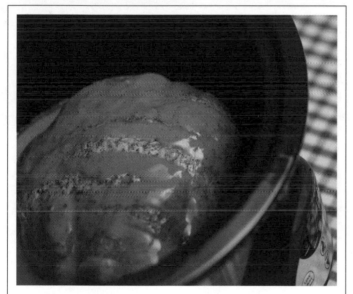

Shred Meat

- Make sure you trim any visible fat from the pork before adding it to the slow cooker.

- For a deeper flavour, you can brown the roast on all sides in some olive oil or butter for 6–8 minutes.

- The pork will start to fall apart after about 8 hours. You'll know it's done when you insert a fork and twist; the meat should split easily.

- This type of meat cooks to temperatures well past 70°C, so the fat and connective tissue melt.

- Use tongs to remove meat from the slow cooker. A fork will just slip right through the tender meat.

- Place the meat on a large plate. You can pull the meat apart with two forks, or wear heatproof gloves and use your fingers.

- As you work, return the shredded meat to the juices in the slow cooker.

- The meat will absorb some of the juice, adding more flavour and thickening the sauce.

HOT SANDWICHES

MU SHU PORK WRAPS
This Asian stir-fry can be served as a sandwich

Mu Shu pork originated in northern China, but it's been a staple of American Chinese cuisine since the 1960s. It's usually made as a stir-fry. Thin strips of pork are quickly cooked and combined with vegetables and a sauce, then served with rice or rolled up in thin steamed pancakes.

Traditional ingredients in the stir-fry version include lily buds, cloud ear mushrooms and hard-boiled or scrambled eggs, but these don't cook well in the slow cooker. Chinese cabbage is a staple ingredient in American Mu Shu pork.

The pork roast will fall apart at the end, making it very easy to shred. The pork mixture can be served hot or cold.

Onion, garlic, and ginger, along with hoisin sauce, add flavour and texture to the finished wraps. You can also serve these in Chinese pancakes or crêpes.

Ingredients

Serves 8

2 carrots, sliced

1 onion, chopped

900 g pork shoulder roast

2 tablespoons soy sauce

120 ml chicken stock

50 ml hoisin sauce

2 tablespoons grated fresh ginger

3 cloves garlic, finely chopped

350 g shredded Chinese cabbage

1 tablespoon cornflour

2 tablespoons oyster sauce

2 tablespoons water

2 teaspoons sesame oil

10 (25-cm) flour tortillas or Chinese pancakes

Mu Shu Pork Wraps

- Place carrots and onion in bottom of 3.5-litre slow cooker. Place joint on top.

- Mix soy sauce, chicken stock, hoisin sauce, ginger and garlic; pour over pork.

- Cover and cook on low for 7–8 hours or until pork is very tender. Shred pork and return to slow cooker. Combine with sauce.

- Add cabbage and cover. Cook on high 30 minutes.

- Mix cornflour, oyster sauce and water; add and cook on high 15 minutes. Add sesame oil. Fill tortillas or pancakes and wrap.

Mu Shu Chicken Wraps

Layer carrots and onion in slow cooker. Substitute 900 g boneless, skinless chicken thighs for the pork shoulder roast. Omit oyster sauce. Cover and cook on low for 6–8 hours until chicken is tender. Shred chicken, return to slow cooker. Make wraps with tortillas.

Chinese Pancakes

In blender, combine 115 g flour, 75 ml water, 75 ml milk, 2 eggs and 1 tablespoon melted butter. Brush 15-cm non-stick pan with unsalted butter and heat over medium heat. Add 2 tablespoons batter; spread evenly; cook 2 minutes. Turn and cook 1–2 minutes longer. Do not stack together; separate with greaseproof paper. Can be frozen.

Layer Ingredients

- You can brown the pork in some vegetable oil before placing in the slow cooker. Cook about 2 minutes per side on medium heat.

- Mu Shu Pork traditionally has some browner bits, and browning the meat would replicate this texture.

- Mushrooms could be added to this dish, but sauté them in a frying pan until browned first.

- Mushrooms release too much liquid to be added straight to the slow cooker in this recipe.

Shred Meat

- Remove meat from slow cooker with tongs and shred using two forks. Return to sauce in slow cooker and mix.

- The sesame oil is added at the very end so its flavour is pronounced. Heating this oil reduces its flavour.

- You can add some sliced spring onions to the sandwiches at the end, along with a small amount of hoisin sauce.

- This mixture is good hot or cold. It can be made ahead of time and reheated in a frying pan.

BEEF STEW

Chuck steak, cut into cubes, becomes very tender in this stew

Beef stew is the quintessential slow cooker recipe. The meats generally used for stews are inexpensive cuts of skirt or chuck steak, which become very tender when cooked for a long time at low heat.

Traditionally, onions, carrots and potatoes are added, but you can use any vegetable you like. Remember to add tender vegetables like peas and asparagus at the end of cooking time.

For liquid, beef stock makes a rich stew, but you can use water since the meat and vegetables add flavour to the gravy in the finished dish.

It's easy to thicken the stew if it needs it. Just add a mixture of 1 tablespoon cornflour blended to a paste with 50 ml dry red wine at the end of cooking time; cook on high for a further 15 minutes.

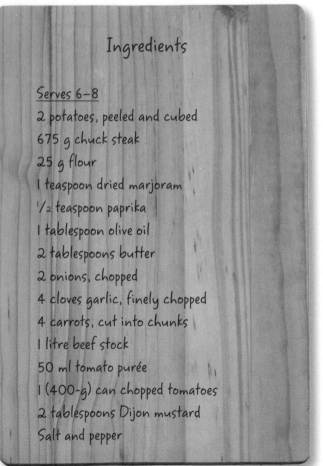

Ingredients

Serves 6–8

2 potatoes, peeled and cubed

675 g chuck steak

25 g flour

1 teaspoon dried marjoram

1/2 teaspoon paprika

1 tablespoon olive oil

2 tablespoons butter

2 onions, chopped

4 cloves garlic, finely chopped

4 carrots, cut into chunks

1 litre beef stock

50 ml tomato purée

1 (400-g) can chopped tomatoes

2 tablespoons Dijon mustard

Salt and pepper

Beef and Potato Stew

- Place potatoes in bottom of 3.5–4.5-litre slow cooker.

- Cut beef into 4-cm cubes and toss with flour, marjoram, paprika, salt and pepper.

- Cook beef in butter and oil in large pan for 5 minutes; remove to slow cooker.

- Add onions, garlic and carrot to pan; cook 4 minutes. Pour 250 ml of the stock into pan; bring to the boil and stir to deglaze pan.

- Pour into slow cooker along with remaining ingredients. Cover and cook on low for 7 hours, stirring once.

RECIPE VARIATIONS

French Beef Stew
Prepare stew as directed, but add 225 g chestnut mushrooms, sliced. Omit the marjoram and paprika; add 1 teaspoon dried thyme and $1/2$ teaspoon dried herbes de Provence. Add 50 g sliced black olives and 2 tablespoons orange juice.

Belgian Stew
Prepare as directed, but add 250 ml brown ale. Omit the potatoes; add 2 bay leaves and 2 tablespoons brown sugar. Reduce stock to 750 ml. When stew is done, remove bay leaves and serve.

Prepare Ingredients

- You don't have to brown the beef before adding it to the slow cooker, but it does add good flavour and colour to the stew.

- Cut the potatoes and carrots to about the same size so they cook through in the specified time.

- You can prepare the carrots, onions and garlic ahead of time, but prepare potatoes just before cooking.

- Potatoes can become brown when cut due to enzymatic browning in the vegetables' cells.

Place Ingredients in Slow Cooker

- Because all of the ingredients are covered with liquid, it isn't necessary to layer the root vegetables in the bottom and place the beef on top.

- If you don't brown the beef, be sure to trim off any visible fat before cutting the meat into cubes.

- The flour should thicken the stew sufficiently, but you can add a blend of cornflour during the last hour of cooking for a thicker stew.

- Add some fresh chopped marjoram at the very end of the cooking time for a punch of flavour.

BEEF BRISKET
The slow cooker makes all cuts of meat tender and juicy

Beef brisket comes from the breast of the animal and is one of the cuts traditionally associated with the Texas or 'cowboy' barbecue, with meat cooked over a smoky fire of mesquite. It can be tough if roasted, but it is full of flavour and most suitable for pot roasts and braises. For this reason it is perfectly suited to the slow cooker. The long, gentle cooking and the steamy atmosphere make it fork tender after 8 hours.

Brisket is a large cut and some parts of it can be quite fatty. Simply trim off the excess fat before cooking the meat.

You can brown the meat before cooking, which gives extra colour and flavour to the gravy, or place it straight in the slow cooker rubbed with spices and herbs.

Ingredients

Serves 8–10

2 teaspoons dried marjoram

1 teaspoon dried basil

2 teaspoons smoked paprika

1 1/2 teaspoons salt

1 teaspoon garlic pepper

1.8 kg beef brisket

2 onions, chopped

4 cloves garlic, finely chopped

250 ml barbecue sauce

120 ml tomato juice

1 bay leaf

Barbecue Brisket

- In small bowl, combine marjoram, basil, paprika, salt and garlic pepper.

- Trim excess fat from brisket and sprinkle marjoram mixture over; rub in.

- Place onions and garlic in 4.5- or 5.5-litre slow cooker; top with beef. Pour barbecue sauce and tomato juice over beef; add bay leaf.

- Cover and cook on low for 8–10 hours until beef is tender. Remove bay leaf, slice beef and serve with sauce from slow cooker.

••••• RECIPE VARIATION ••••

Mum's Brisket
Prepare as directed, but omit barbecue sauce and tomato juice. Place 4 cubed potatoes and 3 sliced carrots in slow cooker with onions and garlic. Top with beef; pour 1 cup beef stock over all. Cover and cook on low 8–10 hours until tender.

••••••• YELLOW ● LIGHT ••••••••

When you buy a large chunk of meat, you're spending a good amount of money. The beef should be firm and hold together well. There should be visible lines of fat running through it. The colour doesn't matter as much, as exposure to air can change the colour.

Add Herb Rub

Pour Sauce Over

- Use your fingers to rub the spice mixture well into the meat, so the flavours permeate as deeply as possible.

- When you create a spice or herb rub that you really like, make it in quantity.

- Store the rub in an airtight container for 3–4 months; don't forget to label it.

- When you use it, pour out the amount you want rather than dipping your fingers back into the rub as you work, to prevent contamination.

- You can use a bottled barbecue sauce or make your own. Make the sauce as mild or as spicy as you like.

- The sauce is very important in this recipe, so if you buy it get the best you can find, made with ingredients you would use yourself.

- To make your own sauce, cook onion and garlic in oil; add chopped tomatoes, tomato ketchup, mustard and vinegar.

- Simmer for 1–2 hours or until the flavours blend. Store in refrigerator for up to 4 days.

POT ROAST

This classic comfort food recipe cooks to perfection in the slow cooker

Nothing makes your home feel cosier than a simmering pot roast, and the slow cooker does such a good job with this way of cooking meat.

You can make any pot roast a one-dish meal by adding root vegetables: carrots, potatoes, parsnips, turnips and onions all cook very well and impart their flavour to the tender meat.

Use vegetables like tomatoes and celery to make wonderful gravy to serve with your pot roast. Just remove the meat and root vegetables – if you placed any under the roast – with tongs and a slotted spoon, then purée the remaining vegetables. Thicken the gravy further with cornflour blended to a paste with a little water if you like.

Ingredients

Serves 8–10

40 g plain flour

2 teaspoons paprika

I teaspoon salt

Pinch of pepper

1.8 kg beef silverside or brisket

I teaspoon dried oregano

I tablespoon butter

2 tablespoons olive oil

2 onions, chopped

2 tomatoes, peeled and chopped

4 cloves garlic, finely chopped

350 ml beef stock

50 ml tomato purée

Mum's Pot Roast

- On a plate, combine flour, paprika, salt and pepper. Dredge meat in this mixture.

- Brown joint in butter and olive oil over medium heat on all sides, about 10 minutes. Remove roast to 5.5-litre slow cooker.

- Add onions, tomatoes and garlic to pan; cook 4 minutes. Add beef stock and tomato purée; simmer and pour over meat.

- Cover; cook on low for 8–10 hours or until meat is falling apart. Remove meat from slow cooker; cover. Purée vegetables to make sauce.

Pot Roast and Vegetables

Make the recipe as directed, but use a 6.5-litre slow cooker. Place 4 potatoes and 4 carrots, scrubbed and cut into chunks, under and around the meat. Cook as directed. Remove meat and most of the vegetables to a serving platter when done; cover with foil to keep warm. Purée remaining mixture for gravy.

Tex-Mex Pot Roast

Cook recipe as directed, but add 2 finely chopped jalapeños to the onion mixture. Peel and cube 2 sweet potatoes; place under roast. Instead of paprika, rub 1–2 tablespoons chilli powder into the meat. Add 1 tablespoon chilli paste to the liquid along with the tomato purée.

Season Meat

- It's important to season large chunks of meat well. Enough salt is the secret to the best-tasting meat and gravy.

- Don't go overboard, but up to 2 teaspoons salt for a 1.8-kg piece of meat will work.

- Trim any excess fat off the meat before rubbing in the spices.

- Leftover pot roast makes wonderful sandwiches, or you can reheat it in the gravy to serve the next day.

Prepare Tomatoes

- To peel tomatoes, first bring a saucepan of water to the boil. Fill another bowl with iced water.

- Cut a small cross in the blossom end of each tomato (the side of the tomato without the stem).

- Drop the tomatoes into the boiling water for 5–10 seconds. Remove with a Chinese skimmer and plunge into iced water.

- Leave to cool for 2–3 minutes, then remove and slip off the skin; it should come off easily.

SAUERBRATEN
A German speciality, this hearty main dish is special enough for company

This German speciality results in tender meat served with a very flavourful, thick, sweet and sour gravy, perfect served over mashed potatoes or little dumplings.

Traditionally, Sauerbraten is made by marinating meat in a vinegar mixture for up to 4 days, then braising it in the oven. The slow cooker method is easier and just as delicious.

At the end of cooking, you'll need to taste the gravy several times, and add either gingernuts or vinegar until it is to your liking. Have extra gingernuts on hand for this purpose.

Sauerbraten is traditionally served with the tiny German noodles called *Spätzle* or with bread dumplings. It's also good with egg noodles and glazed carrots.

Ingredients

Serves 8

1.5 kg beef silverside

1 teaspoon paprika

25 g plain flour

1 teaspoon salt

Pinch of pepper

3 tablespoons butter

2 onions, chopped

4 cloves garlic, finely chopped

4 carrots, sliced

350 ml beef stock

50 ml cider vinegar

50 ml red wine vinegar

1 tablespoon Worcestershire sauce

50 g crushed gingernuts

50 g brown sugar

Sauerbraten with Gingernut Gravy

- Dredge beef in mixture of paprika, flour, salt and pepper. Brown in butter in large pan; remove to 4.5- or 5.5-litre slow cooker.

- Add onions and garlic to pan; cook, stirring, for 4 minutes. Add carrots, stock, vinegars and Worcestershire sauce; bring to boil.

- Pour over beef; cover and cook on low for 8–10 hours until tender.

- Add gingernut crumbs and sugar to slow cooker to taste. Cover and cook on high for 20–30 minutes until gravy is smooth.

66

Sauerbraten Stew
Instead of using the whole chunk of meat, cut it into 2.5-cm cubes. Add 115 g chopped celery. Cook as directed, but at the end, stir in 120 ml sour cream mixed with 2 tablespoons flour. Cover and cook on high for 15–20 minutes. Serve with egg noodles or rice.

········ GREEN ● LIGHT ·········

Sauerbraten is the type of recipe that you can make ahead of time if you wish. Get everything ready, then coat the meat, brown it, and assemble the food in the slow cooker. Cook as directed. Remove the meat, vegetables and gravy from the slow cooker, cover and refrigerate. Reheat in a saucepan on the hob until the food is hot and the sauce bubbling.

Brown Meat

- Browning meat means just that. You want to cook the meat in fat until the colour is deep and rich.

- You'll know when the meat has been sufficiently browned: it will release easily from the pan.

- Cook the joint on all sides, lifting and turning when the meat moves easily.

- Do not brown the meat ahead of time. For food safety reasons, you can't partially cook meat and then refrigerate it.

Add Gingernuts

- Homemade or purchased gingernuts work equally well in this recipe. They can be crisp or soft.

- The biscuits are used for their sweet taste and spices, and the way they thicken the gravy.

- If the gravy is too thick when the taste is right, thin it by adding more beef stock; cook on high 10–15 minutes to blend.

BEEF STROGANOFF

A smooth, rich sauce envelops tender beef cubes in this classic recipe

Beef stroganoff sounds rich, and it is. This is the perfect dish for entertaining. The food cooks all day while you're busy doing other things, and it's a very elegant dish.

Like Sauerbraten, beef stroganoff is usually made with marinated meat. Once again, the slow cooker comes to the rescue and obviates the need for a marinade. The beef is cut into fairly large cubes because it will fall apart slightly as you

stir in the sour cream mixture, and you want to see and taste discrete chunks of meat.

Sour cream and Worcestershire sauce are the usual seasonings for beef stroganoff. And it's served with egg noodles. Add a green salad and some roasted asparagus and you have a meal fit for a king.

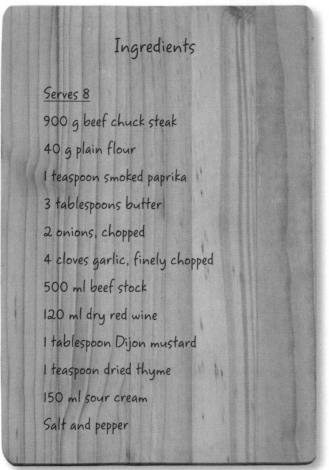

Ingredients

Serves 8

900 g beef chuck steak

40 g plain flour

1 teaspoon smoked paprika

3 tablespoons butter

2 onions, chopped

4 cloves garlic, finely chopped

500 ml beef stock

120 ml dry red wine

1 tablespoon Dijon mustard

1 teaspoon dried thyme

150 ml sour cream

Salt and pepper

Classic Beef Stroganoff

- Cut beef into 5-cm cubes. Toss with 25 g of the flour, paprika, salt and pepper. Brown in butter in saucepan; remove to 3.5- or 4.5-litre slow cooker.

- Add onion and garlic to pan; cook 4 minutes. Add stock, wine, mustard and thyme; bring to a simmer.

- Pour mixture over beef in slow cooker. Cover and cook on low 8–9 hours.

- Mix sour cream and remaining flour and stir into slow cooker; cover and cook on high for 20–30 minutes until thickened. Serve with noodles.

• • • • • • • • • • • • • • • RECIPE VARIATIONS • • • • • • • • • • • • • • •

Rich Beef Stroganoff
Prepare recipe as directed, but add 450 g baby carrots. Omit the sour cream and flour additions at the end. Cube 175 g cream cheese and stir in at the end of cooking time; cook on high 15–20 minutes until thickened.

Beef and Mushroom Stroganoff
Prepare recipe as directed, but cook 225 g mushrooms, sliced, in the fat left after the beef has browned. Add to slow cooker, then cook onions and garlic and proceed with the recipe. Serve with mashed potatoes made with sour cream.

Prepare Beef

- Trim off visible fat and cut beef into evenly sized cubes.

- Brown the beef cubes as you'd brown a large piece of meat. The meat will release from the pan when it's ready to be turned.

- Use tongs to turn the meat and place it in the slow cooker so you don't disturb the flavourful outer crust on the meat.

- You can use beef brisket, silverside or top rump for this recipe.

Add Sour Cream

- Make sure that the sour cream and flour are well combined before adding to the slow cooker.

- You can ladle a spoonful of the hot liquid into the sour cream mixture to temper it and bring it up to the temperature of the liquid.

- This will help prevent curdling, but as long as you stir thoroughly, it's not necessary.

- Don't make the sour cream mixture ahead of time. Stir it together just before you add it to the slow cooker.

SALT BEEF

Salt beef can be tough, but not when cooked for hours in the slow cooker

Curing in brine is an old method of preservation, which persists because it gives meat a distinctive flavour. In the USA and Canada, salt beef is still known as 'corned beef', a name that derives from the 'corns' of coarse salt used in the process, and it is traditionally eaten on St Patrick's Day. Because it uses cuts such as brisket and silverside, salt beef can be tough,

even when cooked correctly; the slow cooker is the perfect appliance for it. You should slice the meat very thinly, across the grain, for tender results. You can buy ready-made mixes of pickling spices in supermarkets and delicatessens to use as the basis of the spiced seasoning for the beef.

Serve salt beef with icy cold beer and a salad.

Ingredients

Serves 8

2 onions, chopped

4 cloves garlic, finely chopped

4 carrots, sliced

1.3 kg salt beef brisket

Salt beef seasoning (see next page)

250 ml beef stock

250 ml beer

1 bay leaf

Pinch of ground cloves

50 ml Dijon mustard

2 tablespoons sugar

2 tablespoons cornflour

50 ml water

Slow-Cooked Salt Beef

- Place onions, garlic and carrots in 3.5- or 4.5-litre slow cooker. Top with brisket; sprinkle with seasoning.

- In bowl, combine beef stock, beer, bay leaf, ground cloves, mustard and sugar; mix and pour into slow cooker.

- Cover and cook on low for 10–12 hours until beef is tender. Remove beef and bay leaf; cover beef.

- Slake cornflour with water; add to slow cooker, cover and cook on high for 30 minutes. Slice beef thinly across the grain and serve with vegetables and sauce.

RECIPE VARIATIONS

Salt Beef Seasoning
Mix 2 tablespoons mixed pickling spice, ground, with 2 teaspoons paprika and 1 teaspoon garlic powder. Add 1 teaspoon salt, 1/4 teaspoon pepper, 1/2 teaspoon mustard seeds and 1 teaspoon dried onion. Store in an airtight container up to 3 months. Rub into salt beef before cooking.

Salt Beef and Cabbage
Prepare recipe as directed, omitting carrots. When salt beef is cooked, remove from slow cooker and cover with foil to keep warm. Add 8 wedges red or green cabbage to slow cooker. Cover and cook on high for 25–35 minutes until cabbage is tender. Slice beef and serve with cabbage.

Place Food in Slow Cooker

Slice Beef

- You can vary the root vegetables you use in this recipe. Baby carrots are good, as are 1–2 peeled and cubed swedes.

- Try parsnips, turnips or potatoes for a change of pace.

- Small new potatoes can be added whole; cut larger potatoes into chunks. Just make sure they're all under the beef.

- Any kind of beer will work well in this recipe; non-alcoholic, light beer or a dark ale.

- To slice the beef, look carefully at the meat and you'll see the grain – thin lines running through the meat.

- Slice the meat across the grain; that is, perpendicular to the lines.

- Once the beef has been sliced, you can return it to the slow cooker and keep it warm for up to 1 hour on the keep-warm setting.

- Serve the meat with some grainy brown mustard and the juices from the slow cooker.

MEATBALLS

Meatballs, whether homemade or purchased, can be slow-cooked in many ways

Meatballs are easy to make, fun to eat and perfect to cook in the slow cooker.

As with minced meat, they do better if browned first in butter, oil or bacon fat. The meatballs can also be baked on a tray in the oven or browned under the grill before adding to the slow cooker. This forms a crust on the meatballs, which gives extra flavour and texture. Alternatively, you can drop the meatballs, unbrowned, directly into a sauce in the slow cooker, but in this case you must use very lean meat so the dish doesn't become too fatty.

Serve these meatballs with mashed potatoes, rice or pasta, or on a crusty roll for a great sandwich.

Ingredients

Serves 6

3 tablespoons olive oil

1 onion, chopped

2 cloves garlic, finely chopped

1 egg, beaten

25 g cracker crumbs

1 teaspoon dried marjoram

115 g grated Emmental cheese

675 g 85 per cent lean minced beef

1 (750-g) jar tomato sauce for pasta

Salt and pepper

Classic Meatballs

- In large frying pan, heat 1 tablespoon of the olive oil; cook onion and garlic for 5 minutes. Remove to large bowl.

- Add egg, crumbs, marjoram and cheese, and season with salt and pepper; mix well. Add beef and mix gently but thoroughly.

- Form into 2.5-cm meatballs. Heat remaining 2 tablespoons oil in same pan; brown meatballs; drain.

- Combine meatballs with sauce in a 3.5-litre slow cooker. Cover; cook on low 6–8 hours until done.

- Serve with pasta or rice.

Meatballs in Gravy

Follow recipe as directed, but substitute 475 ml beef stock for the pasta sauce; cook as directed. Remove meatballs with slotted spoon; set aside. Mix 3 tablespoons cornflour with 50 ml water; add to slow cooker; cook on high 15–20 minutes until thickened. Return meatballs to gravy; cook 10 minutes longer.

Mexican Meatballs

Follow recipe as directed, but use 25 g tortilla crumbs in place of the cracker crumbs. Omit marjoram; add 2 teaspoons chilli powder. Add 2 chopped jalapeño peppers with onions. Omit pasta sauce; add 2 (450-g) jars salsa. Cook as directed.

MINCED BEEF

Mix Meatballs

Add Meatballs

- You can make the meatball mixture ahead of time; refrigerate until you brown and add to the slow cooker.

- You can use breadcrumbs or crushed cereal instead of the cracker crumbs.

- When you're making meatballs, it's important to mix all ingredients except the meat first.

- Add the meat and work gently with your hands just until combined. Overhandling will result in tough meatballs.

- Place about a cup of the pasta sauce in the slow cooker and add a layer of meatballs.

- Repeat until all sauce and meatballs are used. The meatballs are quite tender and have to be handled gently.

- You can make this entire recipe ahead of time; after cooking, refrigerate until ready to eat.

- Then place the sauce and meatballs in a saucepan and heat gently for 15–20 minutes until bubbling.

BEEF CURRY

Inexpensive minced beef is the base for this rich and elegant dish

'Curry' is an Anglicized form of the Tamil word *kari*, originally meaning 'gravy' or 'sauce', which came into general use during the British Raj to mean any spiced Indian dish, and was then transplanted to Britain and the West.

All curries are flavoured with a combination of spices, and in India every family makes its own unique spice blends. You can make your own curry by combining different amounts of

spices. The most common include cinnamon, paprika, cumin, mustard, turmeric, coriander and cloves.

The British occupation of India gave rise to a distinctive Anglo-Indian cuisine, of which this beef curry is an example. It uses ready-made curry powder, whose pungent flavours are well matched to the rich meat. The mince must be fully cooked before combining with the other ingredients.

Ingredients

Serves 6

1 parsnip, peeled and diced

675 g 85 per cent lean minced beef

2 onions, chopped

4 cloves garlic, finely chopped

1 tablespoon grated fresh ginger

½ teaspoon salt

1 tablespoon curry powder

2 tablespoons plain flour

Pinch of cayenne pepper

50 ml tomato purée

250 ml beef stock

200 g crushed tomatoes

50 g sultanas

120 ml mango chutney

50 g toasted flaked almonds

Beef Curry

- Place parsnips in bottom of 3.5-litre slow cooker.

- In large frying pan, cook minced beef, onion, garlic and ginger until meat is browned, stirring to break up meat; pour off fat.

- Add salt, curry powder, flour and cayenne; cook 3

minutes. Add tomato purée and stock; simmer and pour into slow cooker with tomatoes and sultanas.

- Cover and cook on low for 6–7 hours until sauce is blended. Stir in chutney. Topped with toasted almonds and serve with rice.

Brown Minced Beef

- Start by adding the minced beef to the frying pan. As it begins to sizzle, break up the meat with a fork.

- Add onion, garlic and ginger when some of the fat has been rendered from the meat.

- Cook and stir until no pink meat remains. Pour off the surplus fat.

- There will still be enough fat and liquid in the meat mixture to cook the curry powder and flour.

Add Chutney

- Curry powder tastes better after it's been heated. The heat brings out the aromatic oils in the spices.

- Chutney, however, tastes better when it hasn't been cooked for a long period of time.

- Add the chutney at the end of cooking time, then serve the curry immediately.

- If you want to make this ahead of time, don't add the chutney. Refrigerate the curry; reheat and add chutney just before serving.

COTTAGE PIE

A pie without a crust, this traditional dish is great for a cold night

Cottage pie is made from a minced beef and vegetable mixture that is topped with mashed potatoes. The pie doesn't have a bottom crust.

You can use mashed potatoes made from scratch, ready-prepared chilled mashed potatoes, or instant mash made from dried potatoes. The minced beef mixture should be hot when the potato topping is added so the whole dish starts cooking immediately. Sweet potatoes and cheese give the topping plenty of flavour.

You can make the dish with lamb (when it becomes shepherd's pie) or other minced meats. And it can be varied with flavours from around the world. A Middle Eastern shepherd's pie could use allspice and pine nuts, while a Cajun pie might have jalapeños, green peppers and Tabasco with chicken.

Ingredients

Serves 8

250 g mashed potatoes

115 g mashed sweet potatoes

40 g grated Asiago cheese

675 g 85 per cent lean minced beef

2 onions, chopped

3 cloves garlic, finely chopped

4 carrots, sliced

2 tablespoons plain flour

1 tablespoon Worcestershire sauce

250 ml beef stock

120 ml tomato ketchup

3 tablespoons mustard

25 g grated Parmesan cheese

Salt and pepper

Easy Cottage Pie

- Heat mashed potatoes and sweet potatoes, blend together and stir in Asiago cheese; set aside.

- In large saucepan, cook beef with onions, garlic and carrots until beef is browned. Add flour and season to taste with salt and pepper; simmer.

- Add Worcestershire sauce, stock, ketchup and mustard; simmer for 3 minutes, then pour into 3.5-litre slow cooker.

- Top with potato mixture and sprinkle with Parmesan. Cover and cook on low for 7–9 hours until hot.

Tex-Mex Cottage Pie

Make as directed, but add 2 chopped jalapeños with the onions. Omit carrots; add 350 g frozen sweetcorn. Omit ketchup; use 250 ml salsa. For topping, combine 350 g mashed potatoes with 250 ml sour cream, 1 tablespoon chilli powder and 25 g grated Parmesan cheese. Pour over hot meat mixture; cook as directed.

Greek Cottage Pie

Prepare as directed, but add 1 peeled and chopped courgette in place of the carrots. Omit sweet potatoes; add 50 g crumbled feta cheese to the potato topping. Omit ketchup; use 120 ml yogurt plus 1 tablespoon cornflour in its place.

Simmer Mixture

- The minced beef mixture can be made ahead of time. Just refrigerate it, and when you're ready to cook, heat in a saucepan until bubbling.

- Because the beef is fully cooked, you can prepare the dish in advance up to this point.

- You can add other vegetables to the beef mixture if you like: mushrooms or peppers would be good.

- Grease the slow cooker before adding the food to make washing up easier.

Add Potatoes

- Chilled prepared mashed potatoes are a very high quality product and easy to use.

- They usually just involve reheating, in the microwave or in a saucepan. You can add other ingredients to them, like sour cream or cheese.

- Adding sweet potatoes to the mash not only changes the colour, but provides great flavour and lots of vitamin A.

- You could also add 120 ml sour cream or softened cream cheese to the potatoes for a richer taste.

MEATLOAF

Meatloaf 'bakes' to a moist and tender finish in the slow cooker

Meatloaf is an easy dish that's easy to make badly. Everyone has eaten a meatloaf that is dry, chewy or bland and lacking in flavour.

To make the best meatloaf, follow a few rules. First, always precook any additions to the meatloaf, like onions or shallots. Then, combine all the binding and flavouring ingredients – breadcrumbs, egg, ketchup and seasonings – thoroughly

first. Then add the minced meat and mix gently. Overmixing at this stage will make the meatloaf rubbery.

The slow cooker's steamy environment will ensure the meatloaf is always juicy. Let it stand for 10 minutes after you take it out of the slow cooker, then enjoy the perfect meatloaf.

Ingredients

Serves 6–8

1 onion, chopped

3 cloves garlic, finely chopped

1 tablespoon olive oil

50 g chopped kalamata olives

25 g fresh breadcrumbs

50 g ground almonds

50 g grated Manchego cheese

1 egg, beaten

1 teaspoon smoked paprika

675 g 85 per cent lean minced beef

25 g grated Asiago cheese

Salt and pepper

Spanish Meatloaf

- Cook onion and garlic in olive oil. Mix with olives, breadcrumbs, almonds, Manchego cheese, egg and paprika, and season with salt and pepper.

- Add beef; mix and form into round loaf. Fold two long foil strips and crisscross in 3.5-litre slow cooker.

- Place meatloaf in slow cooker. Cover; cook on low for 6–8 hours or until meat thermometer registers 70°C.

- Lift meatloaf out of slow cooker using foil strips, sprinkle with Asiago cheese, cover and leave to rest for 10 minutes before slicing.

Home-Style Meatloaf
Make recipe as directed, but increase breadcrumbs to 50 g. Omit almonds, olives and Manchego cheese; increase eggs to 2 and add 75 ml tomato ketchup. Omit Asiago cheese; instead, mix 50 ml tomato ketchup and 2 tablespoons mustard; spread over meatloaf; cook as directed.

Tex-Mex Meatloaf
Make recipe as directed, but add 1 (115-g) jar chopped green chillies, undrained, in place of the olives. Omit almonds; add 25 g yellow cornmeal and 1 tablespoon chilli powder along with 50 ml salsa to meatloaf mixture. Cook as directed; sprinkle with Parmesan cheese.

Add Minced Beef

- It's important to mix all of the other ingredients before adding the minced beef.

- This ensures that the ingredients will be evenly mixed throughout the meatloaf, making it tender and flavourful.

- The more you handle minced beef, the tougher the final product will be. Handle gently.

- Form the meatloaf into a round if you have a round slow cooker; into an oval shape for an oval slow cooker.

Place Meatloaf in Slow Cooker

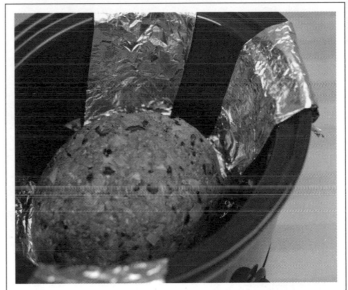

- Make sure the foil strips are crossed and placed centrally in the slow cooker.

- The ends of the foil strips should extend beyond the slow cooker edges so you can grab them to lift the meatloaf.

- After the meatloaf has been removed from the slow cooker, cover it with foil and leave to rest for 10 minutes.

- This will give the juices time to redistribute so the meatloaf is tender and juicy.

STUFFED CABBAGE
Old-fashioned comfort food is easy to prepare in the slow cooker

Stuffed cabbage is a comforting, old-fashioned dish. It is delicious when well seasoned and cooked in the slow cooker.

Green cabbage is usually used because it's milder than red cabbage and the finished product has a nice colour. Choose a head of cabbage that is heavy and firm, with no soft spots or brown edges. For food safety reasons, it's best to cook the beef completely before you fill and cook the cabbage rolls.

Traditionally, the beef is mixed with rice. Barley is a less common filling, but it has lots of nutrition and fibre and adds a wonderful nutty taste to the cabbage rolls.

Ingredients

Serves 6

1 (225-g) jar tomato sauce

1 (400-g) can chopped tomatoes

3 tablespoons Dijon mustard

3 tablespoons brown sugar

2 tablespoons lemon juice

1 teaspoon dried thyme

1 head green cabbage

450 g lean minced beef

1 onion, chopped

3 cloves garlic, finely chopped

150 g cooked barley

1 egg

Salt and pepper to taste

Old-Fashioned Stuffed Cabbage

- Combine tomato sauce, tomatoes, mustard, sugar, lemon juice, thyme, salt and pepper; set aside.

- Cut core out of cabbage. Remove 8 outer leaves; set aside. Chop rest of cabbage.

- Cook minced beef with onion and garlic; pour off fat. Stir in barley, chopped cabbage, egg, and 120 ml of the tomato mixture.

- Fill cabbage leaves with beef mixture; roll up and place in 3.5-litre slow cooker.

- Pour remaining tomato sauce over all. Cover and cook on low for 8–9 hours.

Rice-Stuffed Cabbage

Make recipe as directed, but omit barley. Add 150 g cooked brown, basmati, white long-grain or wild rice. For sauce, omit mustard; add 2 tablespoons cider vinegar and 75 ml tomato ketchup. Cook rolls as directed.

Mushroom-Stuffed Cabbage

Make recipe as directed, but add 175 g chopped mushrooms to the minced beef mixture. Cook with onions and garlic until browned. Add 1 teaspoon marjoram in place of the thyme. At the end of cooking time, stir in 120 ml sour cream blended with 1 tablespoon cornflour; cook 10 minutes on high.

Add Filling

Place in Slow Cooker

- For 150 g cooked barley, cook 60 g medium barley in 150 ml beef stock or water for 25–30 minutes until tender.

- Core the cabbage before removing the largest leaves. You can soak the cabbage leaves in very hot water for 5–6 minutes to soften them and make them easier to roll up.

- Don't pack the filling tightly in the leaves because it will expand when heated.

- Roll the leaves up gently, folding in the sides. Place the rolls seam side down in the slow cooker.

- You don't need to use cocktail sticks to secure the rolls. The cabbage will cook around the filling and stay in place.

- If you like, you can substitute your favourite pasta sauce for the tomato mixture.

- To make ahead of time, make the filling, stuff the rolls and refrigerate. Then put everything in the slow cooker and cook as directed.

TAMALE PIE

With a few extra steps, you can make this dish in a slow cooker

A tamale pie, named after the traditional Mexican steamed, stuffed corn dough parcel, is a popular baked dish from the American Southern States. It consists of a well-seasoned combination of beef and vegetables with a cornbread topping.

Cornbread mix or corn muffin mix works well in this recipe. It's just a combination of flour, cornmeal, some seasonings and baking powder. Adding sweetcorn kernels to the topping imparts a wonderful fresh flavour and texture. The pie usually contains beans, for added texture and nutrition. You can use pinto beans, black beans or kidney beans. They must be cooked before combining with the other ingredients.

You can make this dish as mild or as spicy as you like. Add more or less jalapeños; use a mild or spicy salsa. Serve with guacamole and sour cream for cooling contrast.

Ingredients

Serves 8

675 g minced beef

2 onions, chopped

3 cloves garlic, finely chopped

1 jalapeño pepper, chopped

2 (425-g) cans black beans, drained

250 ml tomato salsa

120 ml barbecue sauce

1 (175-g) pack corn muffin mix

75 g frozen sweetcorn

1 egg, beaten

120 ml double cream

120 ml green tomatillo salsa

40 g grated Parmesan cheese

250 ml sour cream

1 (115-g) jar chopped green chillies, drained

Tex-Mex Tamale Pie

- Cook minced beef with onions, garlic and jalapeño; pour off fat. Add beans, tomato salsa and barbecue sauce; simmer.

- While sauce simmers, combine muffin mix, corn, egg, cream, green salsa and cheese; mix.

- Pour hot beef mixture into 3.5-litre slow cooker. Immediately top with corn muffin mixture.

- Top with folded paper towels; cover and cook on low for 6–8 hours until topping is done. Combine sour cream and chillies; serve with pie.

Refried Bean Tamale Pie

Make recipe as directed, but substitute 1 (450-g) can refried beans and 1 (450-g) can of kidney beans for the 2 cans of black beans. For the topping, combine muffin mix with 1 egg; 1 (115-g) jar chopped green chillies, undrained; and 3 tablespoons oil. Cook as directed.

Homemade Cornbread Topping

Instead of the cornmeal muffin mix, combine 115 g cornmeal, 50 g plain flour, 1 teaspoon baking powder, $^1/_2$ teaspoon bicarbonate of soda and $^1/_2$ teaspoon salt. Add 175 ml buttermilk and 1 beaten egg with 2 tablespoons double cream. Mix; pour over hot mixture in slow cooker.

Add Cornbread Topping

- The meat filling has to be hot when the cornbread mixture is added so the bread starts to cook immediately.

- If the meat filling isn't hot, there will be an uncooked layer of cornbread mixture right on top of the filling.

- If you want to make the filling ahead of time, you must bring it back to a simmer on the hob. Then pour it into the slow cooker and add the cornbread topping.

Paper Towels

- Do not make the cornbread mixture ahead of time; the leavening will be activated before it should and the topping will collapse.

- After the mixture has cooked for 3–4 hours, you can remove the paper towels.

- At this point, the cornbread mixture will have risen to cover the beef mixture and there will be less condensation on the lid.

- This pie can be served with salsa, guacamole or a mixture of sour cream and chilli powder.

CHICKEN CACCIATORE
Shorter cooking time ensures chicken breast is tender and juicy

Cacciatore literally means 'hunter' in Italian. This doesn't mean food prepared with game, but made 'hunter-style', traditionally using onions, mushrooms and wine. These days tomatoes are often added to the dish.

Chicken is probably the meat most commonly associated with this cooking method, because its mild taste blends well with the assertive flavours of the other ingredients. You can use chicken breasts or thighs. For thighs, use boneless, skinless meat and cook for 7–9 hours on low.

You can vary the type of mushrooms you use, and the vegetables to some extent, but to be true to the basic flavours of the dish, keep tomatoes, onions and wine in the recipe.

Serve this hearty dish with pasta or a rice pilaf to soak up the wonderful sauce, and a spinach salad.

Ingredients

Serves 6

1 onion, chopped

3 cloves garlic, finely chopped

225 g chestnut mushrooms, sliced

2 tablespoons olive oil

2 tablespoons plain flour

1 teaspoon dried oregano

1 teaspoon dried thyme

1 (400-g) can chopped tomatoes

1 (175-g) can tomato purée

120 ml red wine

6 boneless, skinless chicken breasts

1 green pepper, chopped

Salt and pepper to taste

Chicken Cacciatore

- In saucepan, cook onion, garlic and mushrooms in oil until tender. Add flour, oregano, thyme, salt and pepper; cook 3 minutes.

- Add tomatoes, tomato purée and wine; simmer 4 minutes.

- Sprinkle chicken with salt and pepper to taste and place chicken in 3.5- or 4.5-litre slow cooker. Top with green peppers; pour sauce over the top.

- Cover and cook on low for 5–7 hours until chicken registers 75°C on a meat thermometer. Serve with pasta or rice.

Chicken Cacciatore on the Bone

To cook this meal using bone-in, skin-on chicken breasts, first brown the meat, skin side down, in 2 tablespoons olive oil, then cook as directed, but increase cooking time to 7–8 hours. For chicken thighs, brown the meat and cook on low for 8–9 hours.

Triple Mushroom Cacciatore

Make recipe as directed, but add 65 g sliced button mushrooms and 65 g sliced shiitake mushrooms. Omit the green pepper at the end; instead, add 250 g frozen green beans. Cook 15–20 minutes on high and serve with pasta.

Sauté Onion Mixture

Mix Sauce

- When you cook onions, they become sweet and tender. The sugars in the onion develop in the heat.

- The sulphur compounds that are harsh and make your eyes run will evaporate as the onions cook.

- When cooking mushrooms in the slow cooker, you must sauté them first. Otherwise the mushrooms can add a lot of water, which dilutes the dish.

- Cook the onion and garlic mixture until the liquid evaporates. This concentrates the flavour, too.

- You can make the sauce ahead of time. Cook the onion, garlic and mushrooms, and add the flour and seasonings.

- Stir in the tomatoes and wine and simmer. Then refrigerate the sauce.

- When you're ready to cook, heat this mixture to a simmer again and assemble the recipe in the slow cooker, layering as directed.

- Serve this dish with plain rice, a rice pilaf, mashed potatoes or pasta.

SLOW-COOKED CHICKEN

EASY DRUMSTICKS
The kids' favourite can be flavoured in many ways

Drumsticks are many children's favourite kind of chicken. They are easy to hold and eat and come with a built-in handle!

Chicken drumsticks cook very well in the slow cooker, but the meat tends to fall off the bone unless the drumsticks are browned first. Grilling them is an easy way to brown them, adding flavour and colour without adding fat. You can remove the skin from the drumsticks before cooking if you

prefer; in that case, don't brown them first. Just grasp the skin firmly with a paper towel and pull it off.

If you cook with the skin on, and then remove the skin at serving time, the chicken will be moist and juicy. Removing the skin after cooking also removes most of the fat.

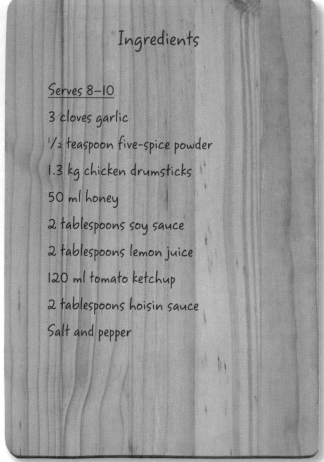

Ingredients

Serves 8–10

3 cloves garlic

½ teaspoon five-spice powder

1.3 kg chicken drumsticks

50 ml honey

2 tablespoons soy sauce

2 tablespoons lemon juice

120 ml tomato ketchup

2 tablespoons hoisin sauce

Salt and pepper

Sticky Drumsticks

- Crush garlic and work together with ½ teaspoon salt using the back of a spoon. Add pepper and five-spice powder; set aside.

- Place drumsticks under preheated grill for 5–7 minutes, turning once, until browned. Rub with garlic mixture.

- Combine honey, soy sauce, lemon juice, ketchup and hoisin sauce. Layer drumsticks and honey mixture in 3.5- or 4.5-litre slow cooker. Stir to coat.

- Cover and cook on low for 7–9 hours until chicken registers 75°C on a meat thermometer.

Barbecue Drumsticks

Make recipe as directed, but add 120 ml barbecue sauce and 1 teaspoon chilli powder. Omit five-spice powder, soy sauce and hoisin sauce. Grill the drumsticks, rub with the garlic mixture, then cook as directed.

Sweet and Sour Drumsticks

Make recipe as directed, but add 75 ml cider vinegar and 75 g sugar to the honey mixture. Omit five-spice powder, soy sauce and hoisin sauce. Grill, rub and cook drumsticks as directed.

Make Sauce

Layer Drumsticks

- One of the nice things about slow cooking is that you can vary proportions in a recipe and it will still work beautifully.

- You can use more or less honey or ketchup, or substitute other sauces for the ketchup.

- Add your favourite herbs to this recipe, too. Some dried oregano and thyme would be nice.

- You can make the sauce ahead of time; just store it covered in the refrigerator. Layer with the chicken when you're ready.

- Even if you are making part of this recipe ahead of time, don't grill the drumsticks until you are ready to put them in the slow cooker.

- Whenever you partially cook meat, whether it's grilled or browned in a pan, you must fully cook it immediately.

- If you don't follow this rule, bacteria could grow on the meat. Be safe, not sorry.

- Because of the high sugar content of this sauce, it can burn easily. Check the food after 5 hours.

SLOW-COOKED CHICKEN

STUFFED CHICKEN BREASTS
Chicken breasts are easy to stuff and are delicious with any filling

Stuffed chicken breasts are such an elegant entrée. They impress guests and the flavour combinations are really delicious. And they're easier to make than you might think.

There are a few ways to stuff chicken. One is to pound the boneless, skinless breasts so they are thin enough to wrap around the filling. For a second method, you can cut a pocket in the side of the breast and fill it. Or, if you use chicken breasts with their skin on you can stuff the filling mixture between the skin and the flesh.

Invent your own fillings by using these basic proportions, and then combine your favourite ingredients and flavours. When you create a masterpiece, write it down so you don't forget it.

Ingredients

Serves 6

4 rashers smoked streaky bacon

1 tablespoon butter

2 shallots, chopped

2 cloves garlic, finely chopped

175 g chopped ham

175 g grated Emmental cheese

6 boneless, skinless chicken breasts, flattened

50 ml sour cream

250 ml white sauce

120 ml chicken stock

40 g grated Parmesan cheese

Chicken Cordon Bleu

- Cook bacon until crisp; crumble and set aside. Pour off fat; add butter to pan. Cook shallots and garlic.

- Remove to bowl; add ham and bacon; cool 10 minutes. Add Emmental cheese.

- Divide mixture among breasts; roll up, enclosing filling; use cocktail sticks to secure. Place chicken in 3.5- or 4.5-litre slow cooker.

- Mix sour cream, white sauce and chicken stock; pour over chicken. Cover; cook on low for 7–8 hours until done.

- Sprinkle with Parmesan and remove sticks. Serve.

Easier Chicken Cordon Bleu

Make recipe as directed, but use boneless, skin-on chicken breasts. Make the filling and stuff it between the skin and the flesh. Dredge chicken in flour; brown in 2 tablespoons oil, skin side down. Place in slow cooker, add sauce and cook on low 8 9 hours.

Tex-Mex Cordon Bleu Chicken

Make recipe as directed, but add 2 chopped jalapeño peppers to the garlic mixture. Omit shallot; add 1 chopped onion. Omit ham; use 175 g chopped cooked chorizo. Use Pepper Jack cheese instead of Emmental. And use 250 ml salsa in place of the chicken stock for the sauce.

Pound Chicken

Fill Chicken

SLOW-COOKED CHICKEN

- To pound chicken, place smooth side down on cling film; top with a second piece of cling film.

- Gently pound the chicken using the smooth side of a meat mallet or a rolling pin. Don't pound too hard or you'll tear the flesh.

- When the breasts are 6 mm thick, remove the top sheet of cling film and add filling.

- You can pound the chicken ahead of time; wrap well and store in the refrigerator.

- Divide the filling among the chicken breasts, but don't overstuff them; you want the filling to stay enclosed.

- Use the cling film to help you roll the chicken around the filling. (But don't wrap the plastic into the chicken!)

- Use cocktail sticks to hold the seam together, or tie up the chicken parcels with kitchen string.

CHICKEN MEATBALLS

Meatballs made with chicken are tender and delicate

Meatballs aren't generally made of chicken, but when properly seasoned and cooked, they can be meltingly tender.

These meatballs are naturally lower in fat than beef or pork meatballs. For best results, use mixed dark and white chicken meat, minced. If you use all white meat, the meatballs can dry out easily. In meat dishes, the fat not only carries the flavour, but conserves moisture.

As with beef and pork meatballs, combine all the additional ingredients – fillers, binders and seasoning – before you add the chicken. Then, when the other ingredients are well blended, add the chicken and work gently with your hands to incorporate everything.

Flavour your meatballs any way you like: with Asian ingredients, Tex-Mex flavours or Mediterranean ingredients.

Ingredients

Serves 6

1 onion, finely chopped

1 tablespoon chopped fresh ginger

2 cloves garlic, finely chopped

1 tablespoon butter

1 teaspoon salt

Pinch of cayenne pepper

1 egg

40 g soft breadcrumbs

675 g minced chicken,
    dark and white meat

475 ml white sauce

120 ml chicken stock

115 g grated Havarti cheese

Creamy Chicken Meatballs

- In medium saucepan, cook onion, ginger and garlic in butter; remove to large bowl.

- Add salt, cayenne, egg and breadcrumbs; mix. Add chicken and mix gently.

- Form into 2.5-cm meatballs. Gently brown in butter in frying pan; remove to 3- or 3.5-litre slow cooker.

- To the frying pan, add white sauce, stock and grated cheese; pour over meatballs. Cover and cook for 5–7 hours on low until chicken registers 75°C.

90

Greek Chicken Meatballs

Cook onion and garlic in butter; omit ginger. Add salt, pepper, egg and breadcrumbs. Add $1/2$ teaspoon dried oregano, 25 g grated Parmesan cheese and $1/2$ teaspoon grated lemon zest. Add chicken; brown as directed. Add 120 ml lemon juice and 75 g sliced olives to white sauce; omit cheese.

Tex-Mex Chicken Meatballs

Cook onion and garlic in butter; add 1 chopped jalapeño. Omit ginger. Add 25 g grated Cotija or Parmesan cheese and 2 teaspoons chilli powder to breadcrumbs. Brown meatballs; place in slow cooker with white sauce and 250 ml salsa. Omit stock and Havarti.

Form Meatballs

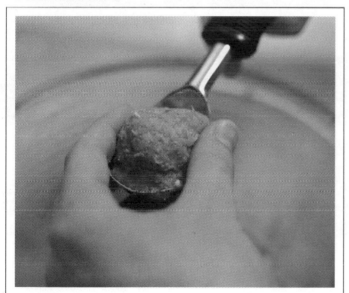

- For perfectly sized meatballs, use a small ice-cream scoop. This tool won't compact the mixture, so the meatballs stay tender.

- Wet the scoop so the meatballs don't stick to it. You can roll them lightly between your hands so they are perfectly round.

- You can make the meatballs ahead of time and refrigerate them until you're ready to cook.

- The meatballs are very delicate, so handle with care. Don't press down on them as they cook.

Layer Meatballs and Sauce

- The tender meatballs will hold together well if they are first browned, either in a pan or under the grill.

- Still, be careful when you layer them in the slow cooker. If some break apart, that's OK. The dish will still taste wonderful.

- When testing the final temperature, make sure that the thermometer probe sits in the middle of a meatball.

- You can also break one of the meatballs in half and test it with a thermometer.

SLOW-COOKED CHICKEN

MOROCCAN CHICKEN SALAD
A hearty and nutritious chicken salad

Chicken salads, made with ingredients cooked in the slow cooker, are a real treat, especially when the weather is hot. Use root vegetables along with the chicken; this is a fancy variation on the theme of potato salad.

The characteristic foods of Morocco include couscous, lemon, cumin and coriander. Fresh vegetables are used in great quantity.

This salad uses the liquid in the slow cooker to soften the couscous. Not only is this easy, but it imbues the couscous with all the flavours of the other ingredients that cooked in that liquid.

Regular plain yogurt works well, but if you can find thick Greek yogurt, use it. It has a fabulous tang and texture that will set the salad apart.

Ingredients

Serves 6–8
1 sweet potato, peeled and cubed
1 onion, chopped
3 cloves garlic, chopped
1 (425-g) can chickpeas, drained
4 boneless, skinless chicken breasts, cubed
1 teaspoon cumin
1/2 teaspoon caraway seed
1/2 teaspoon salt
Pinch of cayenne pepper
350 ml chicken stock
250 ml plain yogurt
50 ml extra virgin olive oil
3 tablespoons lemon juice
15 g chopped fresh coriander
175 g precooked couscous
1 red pepper, chopped
2 sticks celery, chopped

Moroccan Chicken Salad

- In 3.5-litre slow cooker, layer potato, onion, garlic, and chickpeas; top with chicken.

- Sprinkle with cumin, caraway, salt and pepper; add chicken stock. Cover and cook on low 7–8 hours.

- Mix yogurt, olive oil, lemon juice and fresh coriander. Remove chicken mixture from slow cooker with slotted spoon; add to dressing.

- Add couscous to liquid in slow cooker; leave to stand 5 minutes, then add to salad with pepper and celery. Stir and chill for 3–4 hours before serving.

Chicken Potato Salad

Use 4 peeled, cubed waxy potatoes in place of the sweet potato. Omit chickpeas, cumin and caraway. Add 1 teaspoon each dried basil and thyme. For dressing, combine 120 ml each mayonnaise and yogurt, 3 tablespoons mustard and 50 ml milk. Add chicken, potatoes, celery and peppers and toss gently.

Wild Rice Chicken Salad

Place 250 g wild rice in slow cooker. Add 500 ml chicken stock, onion, garlic and 1 teaspoon dried marjoram; season with salt and pepper. Omit sweet potatoes, chickpeas, cumin and caraway. Add chicken and cook. Add chicken mixture to 250 ml yogurt, 120 ml mayonnaise, 3 tablespoons mustard and 115 g cubed Havarti cheese.

Layer Ingredients

Mix Salad

- It's important that the potatoes are in the liquid, so place them in the bottom of the slow cooker.

- You can substitute chicken thighs for the breasts; in this case increase cooking time to 8–9 hours.

- The combination of potato, chickpeas and couscous is classically Middle Eastern.

- This salad should be made ahead of time. Add the chicken to the dressing while it's hot, so it will stay juicy.

- By adding the hot ingredients to the salad dressing, the food will absorb the flavours of the dressing.

- Make sure you use quick-cooking couscous, which will absorb the liquid without additional cooking.

- It's a good idea to make extra dressing. After the salad has chilled in the refrigerator, you may want to add more.

- Or you can pass additional dressing at the table, letting your guests dress their own salads.

CHICKEN THIGHS
Dark meat combines beautifully with sweet cherries in this rich dish

Chicken thighs cook very well in the slow cooker. They have more fat than the breast, so they won't dry out or become tough, as can happen with white meat.

The only difference between preparing chicken thighs and chicken breasts in the slow cooker is the cooking time. The thighs do take a bit longer. Remember that boneless meat always needs to cook for a shorter time than bone-in cuts.

Chicken thighs have a stronger flavour than breasts, so they can stand up to more intense accompanying flavours. Think about incorporating assertive ingredients, such as chillies, peppers, strong cheeses and herbs such as oregano or rosemary.

Serve this dish, or any chicken dish with a sauce, with rice or pasta.

Ingredients

Serves 6

2 onions, chopped

8 boneless, skinless chicken thighs, cubed

1 teaspoon salt

Pinch of cayenne pepper

1 teaspoon dried tarragon

250 ml chicken stock

1 (425-g) can black cherries, drained

2 tablespoons cornflour

75 ml cherry jam

2 tablespoons lemon juice

40 g flaked almonds, toasted

Cherry Chicken Thighs

- Place onion in bottom of 3.5-litre slow cooker. Sprinkle chicken with salt, pepper and tarragon; add to slow cooker.

- Pour chicken stock over all. Cover and cook on low for 6–8 hours, until chicken is done.

- Add drained cherries to slow cooker. Combine cornflour, cherry jam and lemon juice; stir into slow cooker.

- Cover and cook on high for 20–30 minutes until sauce has thickened. Sprinkle with toasted almonds and serve with rice.

Italian Chicken Thighs

Cook recipe as directed, omitting tarragon, cherries, jam, lemon juice and almonds. Add 1 (400-g) can chopped tomatoes, 50 ml tomato purée, 3 crushed garlic cloves and 1 teaspoon dried Italian seasoning. Thicken mixture with 1 tablespoon cornflour slaked with 50 ml water.

Lemon Chicken

Place 2 chopped onions and 3 cloves garlic in slow cooker. Add chicken, sprinkle with salt, pepper and tarragon. Add stock, 75 ml lemon juice and 50 ml honey. Cook as directed. Thicken mixture with 1 tablespoon cornflour slaked with 50 ml water.

Season Meat

Cherries and Cherry Jam

SLOW-COOKED CHICKEN

- Make sure that you trim off any visible fat, especially if the meat isn't browned before it is added to the slow cooker.

- It's important to season the meat well. This brings out the flavour of the meat.

- You can use purchased or homemade chicken stock. Fresh chilled stocks are usually of higher quality than bottled stocks.

- For bone-in, skin-on thighs, brown first, then cook for 8–9 hours on low.

- Make sure that you use plain cherries, not pie filling. They are found in the canned fruit aisle of the supermarket.

- Check the cherries carefully before adding to the slow cooker to make sure there are no stones.

- The cherry jam will also contain pieces of whole fruit.

- Serve this dish, which is intensely flavoured, with plain white or brown rice.

CHICKEN DUMPLING STEW
Slow cookers were made for stews; the aroma is irresistible

Dumplings are a very old-fashioned food that is pure comfort. Dumplings and chicken are a classic combination.

The dumplings in this dish, which are basically soft scones, cook well in the slow cooker as long as you follow a few rules. Mix the batter very gently; overworking makes tough dumplings. Make sure the liquid is bubbling when you add the dumplings. Don't lift the lid while the dumplings are cooking.

You can use these dumplings in soup or stew, with beef or pork. Make them just before you want to cook them; the batter doesn't keep well.

This one-dish meal needs just a fruit or spinach salad for a perfect evening.

Ingredients

Serves 6
1 onion, chopped
3 cloves garlic, finely chopped
4 carrots, cut into chunks
2 sticks celery, chopped
8 boneless, skinless chicken thighs, cubed
1 litre chicken stock
250 ml apple juice
500 ml water
1 teaspoon dried thyme
2 tablespoons lemon juice
225 g pudding and dumpling mix
75 ml sour cream
50 ml milk
25 g grated pecorino cheese
20 g chopped flat-leaf parsley
Salt and pepper

Grandma's Chicken Dumpling Stew

- In 3.5- or 4.5-litre slow cooker, place onion, garlic, carrots and celery. Top with chicken thighs.

- Pour over chicken stock, apple juice, water and thyme. Season with salt and pepper, cover and cook on low for 8–9 hours. Stir in lemon juice.

- Place dumpling mix in medium bowl. Add sour cream, milk and cheese; stir just until mixed.

- Drop dumplings on to bubbling chicken mixture; cover; cook on high 20–30 minutes until dumplings are cooked. Sprinkle with parsley and serve.

Bacon Chicken Dumpling Soup
Cook 5 rashers bacon until crisp; drain, crumble and refrigerate. Drain all but 2 tablespoons of fat from pan; cook onion and garlic 5 minutes. Combine all stew ingredients in slow cooker as directed; omit apple juice. Mix dumplings as directed. Add bacon to soup, then dumplings; cook as directed.

Be sure that your dumpling mix is fresh. There should be a 'best before' date stamped on the package. If it's too old, the baking powder won't react with the liquid and your dumplings will be hard and flat.

Prepare Ingredients

- To chop garlic, first hit with the side of a knife to loosen the peel. Remove peel and discard.

- Slice garlic into strips, then cut across. Gather the pieces together and cut through again until pieces are fine and even.

- Cut carrots into 4-cm chunks. Peel the carrots before cutting them.

- Remove visible fat from the chicken thighs and then cut into even pieces about 2.5 cm square.

Add Dumplings

- Follow the pack instructions when mixing the dumpling batter.

- Stir the mixture lightly just until dry ingredients are moistened.

- Work quickly when dropping the dumplings into the stew. Use a tablespoon and drop batter from the side of the spoon.

- Don't lift the lid until 20 minutes have passed. Cut a dumpling in half to check doneness; the dumplings should not be doughy, but evenly cooked through.

POULTRY STEWS

MULLIGATAWNY STEW

Chicken cooked with curry and vegetables makes a classic English stew

The word 'mulligatawny' comes from a Tamil expression meaning 'pepper water' and it is the name of a thick, chunky stew-like Anglo-Indian soup flavoured with curry spices and containing chicken or lamb and rice with vegetables.

Other traditional ingredients for the dish include apples, coconut milk, onions and leeks. This version uses brown rice;

if you want to use white rice, stir in 50 g along with the apple and cook until tender.

Ready-made curry powder blends contain turmeric, which provides a strong yellow colour that is characteristic of mulligatawny. For a more intense flavour, you can use a few teaspoons of curry paste instead of curry powder.

Ingredients

Serves 6–8

2 onions, chopped

4 cloves garlic, finely chopped

3 carrots, cut into chunks

1 leek, chopped

75 g brown rice

5 boneless, skinless chicken thighs, chopped

2 boneless, skinless chicken breasts

1 teaspoon salt

Pinch of cayenne pepper

1 tablespoon curry powder

1/4 teaspoon allspice

2 tablespoons chopped fresh ginger

1.75 litres chicken stock

1 Granny Smith apple, chopped

120 ml coconut milk

120 ml sour cream

1 tablespoon lemon juice

2 tablespoons cornflour

Mulligatawny Stew

- In 4.5- or 5.5-litre slow cooker, place onions, garlic, carrots, leek and rice.

- Sprinkle chicken with salt, cayenne, curry powder and allspice; add to slow cooker. Add ginger and chicken stock.

- Cover and cook on low for

6–8 hours or until chicken is thoroughly cooked. Shred chicken breasts and return to slow cooker.

- Add apple; turn slow cooker to high. In bowl, combine remaining ingredients and mix; add to slow cooker. Cover and cook on high for 30–40 minutes.

Lentil Mulligatawny Soup

Cook as directed, but omit rice. Add 115 g dried green lentils in place of the rice. Use 8 boneless, skinless chicken thighs, cubed; omit chicken breasts. Omit curry powder and allspice; use 2 teaspoons red curry paste dissolved in 50 ml chicken stock. Omit sour cream; increase coconut milk to 250 ml.

Coconut milk is not the liquid found inside a fresh nut, but is made by blending pulverized coconut flesh with hot water. It is about 20 per cent fat. The fat rises to the surface and forms a solid layer in canned coconut milk; shake the can well to combine the fat and liquid before using. Coconut milk is good for you: it contains antibacterial agents and healthy fats.

Layer Ingredients

Combine Ingredients

- To prepare the leek, trim off tough green parts and the root. Cut the leek in half lengthwise.

- Place the leek in a sink of cold water and separate into layers. As the leek grows, it traps sand in between the layers.

- Make sure all the sand and grit are removed, then slice the leek crosswise and chop.

- Prepare the chicken breasts as directed so they cook through, but don't overcook.

- The chicken will be so tender it should fall apart. To shred it, place on a plate and pull apart using two forks.

- Return the chicken and any juices to the slow cooker.

- The apple will cook quickly; you want to make sure it

- doesn't turn into applesauce, but remains in discrete pieces.

- If the coconut milk has a solid layer on top, that's fine. Add it to the stew and stir a few times to dissolve.

POULTRY STEWS

TURKEY AND SWEET POTATO STEW

Sweet potatoes and other root vegetables add colour and nutrition to this easy stew

The richness of sweet potato adds wonderful flavour, texture and nutrition to this easy stew. Turkey is available all year round, but this is a perfect dish to serve during the Christmas season, or in any of the cold winter months.

Sweet potatoes have to be peeled before they are cooked in the stew. Use a swivel-bladed peeler to remove the skin, then cut the hard potatoes into evenly sized cubes.

Turkey breast is very low in fat and tender. There may be a tendon running along the meat; just cut through it, then cut the turkey into bite-sized cubes.

Serve this hearty stew with a spinach salad made with apples and dried cherries, and some crunchy breadsticks.

Ingredients

Serves 6–8

2 sweet potatoes, peeled and cubed

3 carrots, cut into chunks

1 onion, chopped

4 cloves garlic, finely chopped

900 g turkey breast, cubed

1/2 teaspoon cinnamon

Pinch of freshly grated nutmeg

3 tablespoons plain flour

1.5 litres chicken stock

1 teaspoon dried thyme

175 g frozen peas

Salt and pepper

Turkey and Sweet Potato Stew

- In 4.5- or 5.5-litre slow cooker, place sweet potatoes, carrots, onion and garlic.

- Season turkey with salt and pepper and toss with cinnamon, nutmeg and flour; add to slow cooker. Add stock and thyme.

- Cover and cook on low for 7–9 hours until sweet potatoes are tender and turkey is done.

- Add peas; cover and cook on high for 20–30 minutes until hot. Stir and serve.

Turkey Potato Stew
Use 4 potatoes, peeled and cubed, in place of the sweet potatoes. Omit cinnamon and nutmeg; add 1 teaspoon dried basil to the flour mixture. Cook as directed. Omit thyme.

African Sweet Potato Stew
Cook as directed, but omit carrots, cinnamon and nutmeg. Add 1 teaspoon ground cumin and 1 tablespoon grated fresh ginger. Omit peas, add 50 g peanut butter mixed with 75 ml chicken stock; cook on high 15 minutes. Sprinkle with 50 g chopped peanuts.

Prepare Ingredients

Toss Turkey with Spices

- You can prepare the potatoes, carrots, onion and garlic ahead of time; just cover tightly.

- Make sure that the sweet potatoes and carrots are at the bottom of the slow cooker, because they take longer to cook.

- The turkey breast shouldn't have any visible fat. Cut into even 2.5-cm pieces so the turkey cooks in the right time.

- You can substitute chicken breasts or thighs for the turkey; cook 6–7 hours for breasts, 7–8 hours for thighs.

- Don't prepare the turkey ahead of time. Once tossed with the flour and spices it should be placed in the slow cooker with the stock.

- You can vary the spices used in this recipe. Use allspice and cardamom instead of cinnamon and nutmeg.

- Other ingredients that would work well in this recipe include peppers or sliced mushrooms.

- This stew reheats well. Remove from the slow cooker when done and place in a shallow container to cool.

POULTRY STEWS

CHICKEN FRUIT STEW

Dried fruits are a delicious addition to this easy chicken stew

Add some dried fruit to a chicken stew for a delightful change of pace. Dried fruits cook exceptionally well in the slow cooker, becoming plump and succulent.

The fruits add a remarkable depth of flavour to this easy stew. Choose high quality fruits that are packaged with little or no preservative. You can also use dates, prunes, dried cranberries or dried cherries in this recipe.

This combination of flavours and textures is reminiscent of the Middle East, so the spices used in the recipe – cinnamon and cardamom – are from that region as well.

You could make this recipe with chicken breasts; cook them whole and cook for 5–7 hours on low.

Serve the stew with couscous or basmati rice pilaf for the perfect finishing touch.

Ingredients

Serves 6

2 onions, chopped

4 cloves garlic, finely chopped

1 tablespoon grated fresh ginger

900 g boneless, skinless chicken thighs, cubed

25 g plain flour

4 teaspoons curry powder

1 teaspoon salt

Pinch of cayenne pepper

1.75 litres chicken stock

250 ml apple juice

150 g sultanas

115 g currants

50 g chopped dried apricots

250 ml sour cream

50 g pomegranate seeds or chopped cherries

Chicken Fruit Stew

- In 4.5-litre slow cooker, combine onions, garlic and ginger. Toss chicken with flour, 2 teaspoons of the curry powder, salt and cayenne; add to slow cooker.

- Pour chicken stock and apple juice over; add raisins, currants and dried apricots.

- Cover and cook on low for 6 hours; stir. Cover and cook on low for another 1–2 hours or until chicken is thoroughly cooked.

- Combine sour cream, remaining curry powder, and pomegranate seeds. Top stew with sour cream mixture to serve.

Mexican Chicken Fruit Stew

Cook recipe as directed, but add 1 tablespoon chilli powder to onion mixture. Omit ginger, cinnamon, cardamom, sultanas, currants and apricots. Add 2 poblano chillies, chopped, and 1 (225-g) can pineapple pieces. In last 20 minutes, stir in 1 chopped apple and 1 chopped banana.

Chicken Tagine

Make recipe as directed, but add 75 g kalamata olives and 75 g sliced black olives to onion mixture. Omit ginger, cinnamon, cardamom, sultanas and currants. Add 1 teaspoon dried marjoram, 75 ml cider vinegar and 50 g brown sugar. Omit sour cream topping.

Prepare Chicken

Sour Cream Topping

- Trim excess fat off the chicken thighs. Because they aren't browned before cooking in this recipe, this is a necessary step.

- You can increase the spice level in this dish, or add other warm spices, including nutmeg or allspice.

- Make sure the chicken is evenly coated with the flour. If there's any flour mixture left over, just add it to the slow cooker.

- The fruits will plump up in the liquid as they cook, absorbing the other flavours in the dish.

- The flour coating the chicken will thicken the stew as the recipe cooks.

- If you want a thicker stew, stir in 2 tablespoons cornflour dissolved in 50 ml water; cook on high 15 minutes.

- You can make the topping ahead of time and keep it in the refrigerator until you're ready to eat.

- To remove pomegranate seeds, cut fruit in half and hit the rounded side of each half with a spoon.

POULTRY STEWS

RICH TURKEY STEW
Double cream and melted cheese make this stew special

This rich stew is really a meal in a bowl. Classic flavours like bacon, onion and garlic complement the turkey, cooked in a thickened sauce that's full of cheese.

You can use your own favourite cheeses in this dish; grated Pepper Jack or Havarti would also be delicious. Just be sure that the cheese is evenly grated, and add it at the end of the cooking time.

Cooking in bacon fat is a traditional way to flavour poultry recipes. The flavour will permeate the whole dish if you cook the onions and garlic in the fat rendered from the crisply fried rashers of bacon.

This stew will be even better the second day, if there's any left. Refrigerate it, then place it in a saucepan. Heat on the stove until the soup bubbles, and serve.

Ingredients

Serves 6–8

5 rashers smoked streaky bacon

1 onion, chopped

3 cloves garlic, finely chopped

450 g baby carrots

2 potatoes, peeled and cubed

900 g turkey breast, cubed

25 g plain flour

1 teaspoon dried marjoram

500 ml white sauce

1 litre chicken stock

275 g frozen green beans

115 g frozen peas

165 g grated Gouda cheese

Salt and pepper

Rich Turkey Stew

- Cook bacon until crisp; drain, crumble and refrigerate. In the bacon fat, cook onion and garlic 5 minutes.

- In 4.5-litre slow cooker, combine onion, garlic, carrots and potatoes. Toss turkey with flour, marjoram, salt and pepper.

- Add turkey to slow cooker with white sauce and stock; stir. Cover and cook on low for 7–9 hours.

- Add green beans and peas; cover and cook on high for 20 minutes. Add cheeses and bacon; cover and cook on high for 20–30 minutes.

Tex-Mex Turkey Stew
Cook as directed, but add 2 finely chopped jalapeños with the onion and garlic. Omit bacon; use 2 tablespoons olive oil. Omit potatoes and baby carrots; use 2 cubed sweet potatoes and 3 sliced carrots. Add 2 tablespoons chilli powder. Omit peas; use grated Cheddar cheese in place of Gouda.

Tuscan Turkey Stew
Cook as directed, but use turkey bacon. Omit potatoes; use 225 g chestnut mushrooms, sliced. Omit marjoram; use 1/2 teaspoon fennel seed and 1 teaspoon dried Italian seasoning. Add 1 (425-g) can cannellini beans in place of frozen peas.

Add White Sauce

- The white sauce can be made ahead of time and frozen. Thaw it in the refrigerator overnight before using.

- The chicken stock can be homemade or purchased. Chilled stocks in cartons are the highest quality.

- Stir gently but thoroughly, so the white sauce is well incorporated with the stock.

- You may want to stir once or twice during cooking time; add another 20 minutes to the time if needed.

Add Cheeses

- Don't grate the cheeses ahead of time; they should be freshly grated so they don't dry out.

- Packaged grated cheeses can be used, but they are coated with anti-caking agents that can prevent smooth melting.

- If you can find a pre-grated cheese that doesn't have any other ingredients, it will work well.

- This recipe won't work well with the keep-warm feature after you add the cheese – serve it immediately.

POULTRY STEWS

CHICKEN VEGETABLE STEW

Add tender vegetables at the end of the cooking time so they are perfectly cooked

Greek flavours and ingredients are the perfect companions for tender chicken in this easy stew. Typical Greek ingredients include lentils, olive oil, lemon, oregano, garlic and olives. Chicken, with its mild flavour, blends very well with these ingredients. You can substitute cubed chicken thighs for the breasts; the cooking time will be the same.

You can vary the vegetables to your own taste. Use parsnips instead of potatoes, baby carrots in place of regular carrots, add sliced portobello or shiitake mushrooms in place of the celery: this is an easy way to make a recipe your own.

Serve with a mixed green salad with a creamy herb dressing, some grilled garlic toast, and rice pudding for dessert.

Ingredients

Serves 6–8

3 potatoes, peeled and cubed

4 carrots, cut into chunks

3 sticks celery, chopped

1 onion, chopped

4 cloves garlic, finely chopped

225 g green lentils

900 g boneless, skinless chicken breasts

1.2 litres chicken stock

250 ml dry white wine

1 teaspoon dried basil

1 teaspoon dried oregano

½ teaspoon dried thyme

75 g sliced olives

115 g frozen peas

2 tablespoons lemon juice

Greek Chicken Stew

- In 4.5-litre slow cooker, combine potatoes, carrots, celery, onion, garlic and lentils.

- Top with chicken breasts; pour over stock and wine and sprinkle with basil, oregano and thyme.

- Cover and cook on low for 6–8 hours, until chicken is done and vegetables are tender. Remove chicken and shred; set aside.

- Using a potato masher, mash some of the vegetables. Add chicken, olives, peas and lemon juice; stir well, cover, and cook on high 15 minutes.

Moroccan Chicken Stew
Make as directed, but use 2 peeled and cubed sweet potatoes in place of the potatoes. Omit celery, basil, oregano, thyme and olives. Add ½ teaspoon each turmeric and cinnamon and a pinch of ground cloves. Add 1 (400-g) can chopped tomatoes and 1 (425-g) can chickpeas, drained.

French Chicken Stew
Make as directed, but cook 6 rashers smoked streaky bacon; drain and refrigerate. Cook onion and garlic in bacon fat. Omit lentils, oregano and olives. Add 1 (400-g) can chopped tomatoes, 1 teaspoon dried tarragon and 12 new potatoes.

Prepare Ingredients

Add Vegetables

- Pick over the lentils, removing any extraneous material. Rinse them well, then drain and add to the recipe.

- The chicken breasts are cooked whole and shredded later so they don't overcook by the time the vegetables are tender.

- You can omit the wine if you like. The alcohol will not cook out of the stew. The flavour isn't crucial to the recipe.

- Substitute apple juice, or just use more chicken stock or water.

- Mashing and puréeing vegetables is an easy and low-fat way to thicken any stew.

- Turn the slow cooker off before you use the potato masher, for safety reasons.

- You can also remove some of the vegetables and purée

them in a food processor or blender, then return them to the stew.

- When you return the chicken to the slow cooker, add any juices that may have accumulated on the plate during shredding.

POULTRY STEWS

107

CARNITAS

Shredded pork flavoured with Mexican spices is tender and crisp

Carnitas are made of slowly cooked pork, which is then shredded and fried to make crispy edges. This full-flavoured recipe can be served as it is, added to a chilli or barbecue, or used as a filling for enchiladas or burritos.

This is a great recipe to make ahead of time. Cook the pork completely, shred it, then combine with some of the cooking liquid. Leave to stand for 15 minutes, then freeze.

When you want to use the pork, leave it to stand in the refrigerator overnight to thaw. Then place in a roasting tin and roast the meat as directed, adding about 10 minutes to the cooking time.

You can make your own version of carnitas as mild or spicy as you like. Add chilli peppers for more heat.

Ingredients

Serves 6–8

1.8 kg boneless pork shoulder

6 cloves garlic, slivered

1 teaspoon salt

1 teaspoon paprika

½ teaspoon turmeric

2 teaspoons ground cumin

1 teaspoon ground coriander

2 onions, chopped

1 bay leaf

500 ml chicken stock

3 tablespoons lime juice

Carnitas

- Cut the pork into 6 pieces. Cut slits in the pork and insert slivers of garlic.

- In small bowl, mix salt, paprika, turmeric, cumin and coriander; rub on pork. Place with onions in 3.5-litre slow cooker.

- Add bay leaf and chicken stock. Cover; cook on low for 9–10 hours until pork is tender. Shred pork.

- Place pork in large roasting tin; top with 250 ml of the cooking liquid and the lime juice. Stir, then bake at 200°C 20 minutes, until edges are crisp.

Carnitas Enchiladas
Make the carnitas as directed. Mix 1 (275-g) jar enchilada sauce with 250 ml salsa. Place 120 ml of this sauce in 22 x 33-cm dish. Divide carnitas among 12 flour tortillas; add 115 g grated Pepper Jack cheese; roll up. Place in dish; add remaining sauce. Bake at 190°C for 35–45 minutes.

Carnitas Tamales
Make carnitas as directed. Make tamale dough using a corn flour masa mix. Spread dough on cleaned and soaked corn husks. Spoon pork mixture on top of the dough; fold up and tie with kitchen string. Place in steamer; steam 40 minutes.

Shred Pork

Brown Pork in Oven

- Evenly space the garlic slivers in the pork. Press the garlic completely into the pork so it disappears.

- The garlic will flavour the pork and slowly mellow to become sweet as it cooks.

- You can use your own spice blend, or choose a Mexican or Tex-Mex packaged spice blend to season the pork.

- Use two forks to shred the pork; it should fall apart very easily as you work.

- You can skip the step of browning the pork in the oven if you prefer it to be soft and tender.

- But the crisp edges, contrasting with the tender interior, are part of the appeal of the dish.

- You can make the pork mixture ahead of time, shred it, combine with some liquid and refrigerate.

- Then when you're ready to eat or make enchiladas, brown the pork in the oven as directed.

PORK & LAMB ENTRÉE...

STUFFED CANNELLONI
This elegant recipe is flavourful and so easy

Cooking pasta in the slow cooker can be problematic. The transition from al dente to mushy can occur in minutes, if not seconds. Most slow-cooker recipes tell you to cook pasta in a separate pan and add it to the slow cooked recipe at the end of the cooking time.

However, some pasta will cook fairly well in the slow cooker. Just like brown rice, whole-grain pastas stand up better to the long, moist cooking environment. And large pasta shapes like cannelloni tubes or large shells, can turn out well.

It's important to only partially cook the shells before draining and filling with the sausage mixture. Don't cook them completely or they will fall apart as you serve the dish.

Ingredients

Serves 8

450 g spicy pork sausagemeat

1 onion, chopped

3 cloves garlic, finely chopped

115 g baby spinach leaves

2 tablespoons tomato purée

120 ml chicken stock

1 teaspoon dried oregano

16 cannelloni shells

1 (725-g) jar tomato pasta sauce

115 g grated mozzarella cheese

25 g grated Parmesan cheese

Salt and pepper

Stuffed Cannelloni

- Bring a large pan of salted water to the boil. Meanwhile, cook sausage-meat with onion and garlic in frying pan; pour off fat.

- Add spinach, tomato purée, stock and oregano to pan; season. Simmer 5 minutes.

- Cook shells for 5 minutes; drain, rinse with cold water, and drain again. Fill shells with pork mixture.

- Place 120 ml pasta sauce in bottom of 4.5-litre slow cooker. Top with shells. Pour pasta sauce over. Cover and cook on low for 7–8 hours. Top with cheeses, leave to stand until melted.

Pesto Cannelloni

Make recipe as directed, but omit pork sausage, spinach, tomato purée and chicken stock. Cook onions in 1 tablespoon olive oil; mix with 450 g ricotta cheese, 75 g cream cheese and 1 (200-g) jar basil pesto. Stuff shells with this mixture; proceed.

Tex-Mex Cannelloni

Make recipe as directed, but omit spinach leaves. Add 1 (425-g) can refried beans and 1 finely chopped jalapeño to sausagemeat mixture. Add 250 ml salsa to pasta sauce. Top with grated Pepper Jack and Cotija cheeses in place of the mozzarella and Parmesan cheeses.

Cook Pork

Fill Shells

- You can usually find pork sausagemeat in the supermarket, sold by the kilogram.

- However, for the best sausagemeat it's better to buy very good quality sausages. Just slit the side of each sausage and remove the meat; discard casings.

- There are lots of different levels of spicing in pork sausages. They range from hot to sweet to mild; choose your favourite.

- Work the sausagemeat with a fork as it cooks so it breaks into small pieces.

- Don't cook the shells ahead of time; they will dry out if not filled immediately.

- The water the shells cook in should be well salted. Some cooks throw in a handful of salt; Italians say the water should be as salty as the sea.

- When the shells have cooked for 5 minutes in the boiling water, rinse them with cold water.

- This will stop the cooking and make the shells easier to handle. Drain well and fill using a small spoon.

PORK & LAMB ENTRÉES

STUFFED PORK CHOPS
Pork chops are stuffed with an apple and raisin filling

Pork chops are an excellent choice for the slow cooker. Chops can be tough if overcooked or cooked in very dry heat. The slow cooker keeps them moist and renders them fork tender.

To stuff, pork chops have to be cut at least 3 cm thick. These might only be available if you ask your butcher, and you may have to order them ahead of time. Boneless chops are easier

to work with, but bone-in chops have more flavour. If you choose bone-in chops, cook for 8–10 hours on low.

You can stuff pork chops with any type of stuffing; use your favourite ingredients. Just don't overstuff them, or they may split during cooking.

Ingredients

Serves 6

6 (4-cm-thick) boneless pork loin chops

2 tablespoons butter

1 onion, chopped

2 cloves garlic, finely chopped

1 Granny Smith apple, peeled and chopped

150 g raisins

50 g soft fresh breadcrumbs

1 teaspoon dried thyme

250 ml chicken stock

500 ml white sauce

Salt and pepper

Apple Stuffed Pork Chops

- Cut a pocket in each of the pork chops, cutting almost to the other side. Sprinkle chops with salt and pepper.

- In small pan, cook onion and garlic in butter until tender. Remove from heat; add apple, raisins, bread-crumbs, thyme and 50 ml of the chicken stock.

- Stuff chops with this mixture. Layer into 3.5- or 4.5-litre slow cooker.

- In bowl, combine remaining stock and white sauce; pour over chops. Cover and cook on low for 7–9 hours until pork is cooked.

Cornbread Stuffed Pork Chops

Make recipe as directed, but add 75 g crumbled cornbread in place of breadcrumbs. Omit apple and raisins; add 4 rashers crisply cooked crumbled smoked streaky bacon. You may need to add more chicken stock to the stuffing mixture to make it moist. Cook as directed.

Vegetable Stuffed Chops

Make recipe as directed, but omit apple and raisins. Add 175 g frozen sweetcorn, thawed, and 1 red pepper, chopped, to the stuffing mixture. Omit white sauce; use 1 (425-g) jar tomato sauce, seasoned with 1 teaspoon dried Italian seasoning.

Cut Pocket in Chops

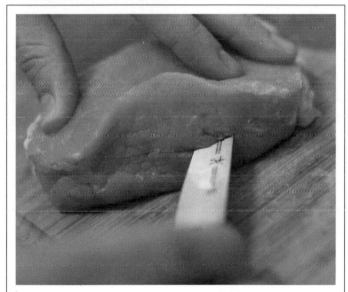

- Use a small, sharp knife to cut the pocket in the chops and work slowly and carefully.

- Be sure that your knife stays parallel to the chops so you don't poke holes or make weak spots in the meat.

- Make the opening as small as you can, and move the knife back and forth to enlarge the pocket.

- Sprinkle the chops inside and out with salt and pepper. And don't pack the stuffing into the chops.

Layer Chops in Slow Cooker

- As you layer the chops and the sauce in the slow cooker, be sure that there is a bit of sauce in between the layers.

- This will help keep the pork moist and will help the chops cook evenly.

- You can flavour the white sauce any way you like. Add some more herbs, add some cheese for richness or add spices.

PORK & LAMB ENTRÉES

BARBEQUE RIBS

Glazed and tender pork ribs are easy to make in the slow cooker

Most people have only eaten spare ribs cooked on the barbecue. They are, of course, delicious, but there's nothing as meltingly tender as ribs cooked slowly and gently in the slow cooker.

There are a few steps to take before the ribs are ready to put in the slow cooker. The ribs are very fatty; you have to remove some of that fat.

There are several ways to do this: grill the ribs, bake them in the oven, or boil in water or stock.

Grilling and baking not only remove fat, but also add flavour through browning and caramelization The proteins and sugar in the meat combine to form complex compounds that create rich flavour. Use your favourite barbecue sauce, whether homemade or purchased, and enjoy.

Ingredients

Serves 6

1.8 kg spare ribs

1 teaspoon five-spice powder

2 tablespoons olive oil

2 onions, chopped

250 ml barbecue sauce

50 ml hoisin sauce

3 tablespoons honey

3 tablespoons soy sauce

2 tablespoons Dijon mustard

3 cloves garlic, finely chopped

1 tablespoon finely chopped fresh
    ginger

Salt and pepper

Asian Glazed Ribs

- Preheat oven to 190°C. Place ribs in roasting tin. Sprinkle with salt, pepper and five-spice powder; drizzle with olive oil.

- Roast ribs for 1 hour; remove and drain. Place onions in 3.5- or 4.5-litre slow cooker; top with ribs.

- Combine remaining ingredients in bowl and pour over ribs.

- Cover and cook on low for 8–9 hours, or on high for 4–5 hours, until ribs are very tender.

Classic Barbecue Ribs
Make recipe as directed, but omit five-spice powder, hoisin sauce, soy sauce and ginger. Add 1 teaspoon dried oregano and 1 teaspoon dried basil. Add 250 ml tomato ketchup to the sauce mixture. Bake ribs, then cook as directed.

Spicy Barbecue Ribs
Make recipe as directed, but add 2 finely chopped jalapeños to onion mixture. Omit five-spice powder, hoisin sauce and soy sauce. Add 250 ml hot salsa to the sauce mixture. Bake ribs as directed, then cook in slow cooker with sauce.

Brown Ribs

Add Sauce

- The ribs are seasoned before they are browned to bring out as much flavour as possible.

- There will be quite a bit of fat in the pan when you roast the ribs; be careful removing it from the oven.

- Do not roast the ribs ahead of time. Never partially cook meat then hold it for later cooking.

- You can place the ribs in large racks; just be sure they fit in the slow cooker.

- Substitute your own favourite homemade barbecue sauce, or use a purchased sauce instead of this recipe if you'd like.

- Create your own sauce by varying the ingredients. Add herbs, more tomato products like salsa, or fresh tomatoes.

- The ribs will be so tender they will probably fall off the bone. Be careful removing them from the slow cooker.

- Serve these ribs with fresh, crisp coleslaw and lots of napkins; they're messy but fun to eat.

PORK & LAMB ENTRÉES

LAMB RAGOUT
Tender lamb cooks beautifully in the slow cooker

This classic ragout pairs lamb with lots of tender root vegetables and spices.

A ragout is a simple French stew of meat and vegetables, seasoned with herbs and spices. It can be made with any meat, but typically is made from lamb or beef.

The flavours blend and meld beautifully in the slow cooker. If you want to punch up the flavour even more, you can add a few stems of fresh oregano to the dish just before serving.

Serve this delicious ragout with rice or pasta to soak up the flavourful juices, and a spinach salad.

Ingredients

Serves 6–8

900 g lamb shoulder,
    cut into 5-cm cubes

1 teaspoon salt

1 teaspoon paprika

1 teaspoon cinnamon

1/4 teaspoon pepper

1 teaspoon dried oregano

3 tablespoons flour

2 tablespoons olive oil

2 sweet potatoes, peeled and cubed

1 parsnip, peeled and cubed

2 onions, chopped

4 cloves garlic, finely chopped

120 ml dry red wine

500 ml beef stock

15 g chopped parsley

Middle Eastern Lamb Ragout

- Toss lamb cubes with salt, paprika, cinnamon, pepper, oregano and flour. Brown in olive oil in large frying pan.

- Place potatoes, parsnip, onions and garlic in bottom of 3.5- or 4.5-litre slow cooker. Add lamb as it browns.

- Add wine to pan; bring to the boil and deglaze pan. Add stock and pour over food in slow cooker.

- Cover and cook on low for 8–9 hours or until lamb is very tender. Shred lamb, using two forks; stir ragout, sprinkle with parsley, and serve.

French Lamb Ragout
Make recipe as directed, but use 675 g small red potatoes and 1 turnip, peeled and chopped, in place of the sweet potatoes. Omit paprika, cinnamon and oregano; use 2 teaspoons fresh rosemary.

Layer Ingredients

- Leave any visible fat on the lamb as you cut it into cubes. Unlike other red meats, lamb fat is delicate and carries much of the flavour.

- When you brown the lamb, don't cook it too long. Just brown it on both sides; this adds colour and flavour.

- Prepare the vegetables and place them in the slow cooker before browning the lamb.

- Be sure to thoroughly scrape up the residue in the pan with the wine; there's lots of flavour in those brown bits.

Shred Lamb

- The lamb should fall apart when the recipe is done, but you may need to pull some pieces apart.

- You can use two forks to shred the lamb, or your fingers if you're careful.

- Return the lamb and any juices to the ragout and stir

to incorporate. If you are adding fresh oregano, stir it in at this time.

- Keep the lamb in fairly large pieces to provide a texture and flavour counterpart to the dish.

PORK & LAMB ENTRÉES

LAMB SHANKS

This classic dish is topped with gremolata, a mixture of garlic, lemon and parsley

The lamb shank is a very flavourful cut of meat that contains bone. Shanks can be tough if not cooked correctly; they have to be braised for a long period of time. So the slow cooker is the ideal choice. Pairing the shanks with haricot beans makes this the perfect one-dish meal.

The lamb shanks you buy from the butcher or supermarket should be 'cracked'. This means the butcher makes some cuts in the meat so the shanks don't curl up tightly while cooking. You can place garlic cloves in those slits.

Serve this dish with garlic toast to soak up the juices, and a spinach salad.

Ingredients

Serves 4

350 g dried haricot beans

25 g plain flour

1 teaspoon dried thyme

1 teaspoon dried marjoram

4 lamb shanks

2 tablespoons olive oil

1 onion, chopped

3 cloves garlic, finely chopped

2 carrots, sliced

500 ml chicken stock

250 ml dry red wine

1 (400-g) can tomatoes, undrained

Salt and pepper

Gremolata (see next page)

Lamb Shanks with Haricot Beans

- Pick over beans; cover with cold water and soak overnight. Drain and rinse.

- Combine flour, thyme, marjoram, salt and pepper; sprinkle over lamb shanks. Brown in oil over medium heat. Add onion to the lamb after lamb is browned; cook 2 minutes.

- Place beans in 3.5-litre slow cooker. Add lamb, onion, garlic and carrots; pour stock over. Cover and cook on low for 8–9 hours.

- Add wine and tomatoes; cook, uncovered, on high for 40 minutes. Sprinkle with gremolata and serve.

Gremolata

Finely chop 25 g flat-leaf parsley. In small bowl, place 3 peeled garlic cloves. Add ½ teaspoon salt; work with back of spoon until paste forms. Add 2 teaspoons lemon juice, parsley and 1 teaspoon grated lemon zest; mix and refrigerate.

Greek Lamb Shanks

Make recipe as directed, but chop together 1 clove garlic and ½ onion; press into slits in lamb. Omit marjoram; add 1 teaspoon dried oregano and ½ teaspoon dried mint. Omit beans; increase onions to 2 and carrots to 4. Cook as directed.

Brown Lamb

Add Stock

- It's important to brown the lamb well, to add colour and flavour to the recipe.

- When browning the lamb, don't move the shanks until they release easily from the pan.

- When they do, turn them and brown on the second side. Cooking the onions will help deglaze the pan.

- The brown bits stuck to the pan bottom have a lot of flavour and you don't want to lose them.

- The wine and tomatoes are added after the beans are cooked because their acidity will prevent the beans from softening.

- If you use 2 (425-g) cans cannellini beans, drained, instead of dried beans you can add the wine and tomatoes right away.

- The dish is cooked uncovered at the end to help evaporate some of the liquid.

- This also concentrates the flavour of the juices. Serve this dish in a bowl, not a plate.

PORK & LAMB ENTRÉES

FISH AND POTATOES
Cook potatoes for hours, then steam fish in the slow cooker

Seafood isn't commonly cooked in the slow cooker, and for good reason. Fish fillets, prawns, salmon steaks and other fish take only minutes to cook, and that just doesn't translate to the slow cooker.

But with a few tricks you can cook seafood to perfection in this appliance. The low, moist heat is really ideal for producing tender, melting fish and seafood dishes.

Cook a base for the fish first. Cook potatoes, root vegetables, or wild rice or other grains, then add the fish during the last hour or so of cooking time.

The fish will be perfectly cooked, and will pick up some of the other flavours in the dish.

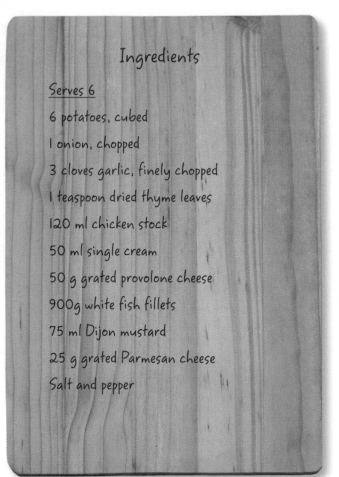

Ingredients

Serves 6

6 potatoes, cubed

1 onion, chopped

3 cloves garlic, finely chopped

1 teaspoon dried thyme leaves

120 ml chicken stock

50 ml single cream

50 g grated provolone cheese

900g white fish fillets

75 ml Dijon mustard

25 g grated Parmesan cheese

Salt and pepper

Cheesy Smashed Potatoes with Fish

- In 3.5-litre slow cooker, combine potatoes, onion and garlic. Sprinkle with thyme and season with salt and pepper.

- Pour chicken stock over. Cover and cook on high for 4 hours or until potatoes are tender.

- Turn off slow cooker and mash potatoes, leaving some pieces. Stir in cream and provolone cheese.

- Turn slow cooker to high and add fish fillets. Mix mustard and Parmesan cheese; spread over fish. Cover and cook for 45–60 minutes until fish flakes.

RECIPE VARIATIONS

Fish and Sweet Potatoes

Make recipe as directed, but use 4 sweet potatoes, peeled and cubed, in place of the potatoes. Add ½ teaspoon cinnamon along with the thyme leaves. Use 120 ml double cream in place of the single cream. And spread the fish fillets with 50 ml Dijon mustard; omit Parmesan cheese.

Fish with Fluffy Mashed Potatoes

Make recipe as directed, but reduce chicken stock to 120 ml. Peel the potatoes before cubing them. When potatoes are done, add 50 g softened butter and mash until smooth. Beat in cream, then top with fish fillets and Dijon-Parmesan mixture. Omit provolone cheese.

Potatoes in Slow Cooker

- Cut all the potatoes to the same size so they cook in the same time.

- You want the potato pieces to be fairly large, about 2.5 cm in width, because this is a rustic dish.

- Leave the skins on for more nutrition and fibre and an even more rustic dish!

- Mash the potatoes using a potato masher, a large spoon, or other handheld tool. For safety, turn off the slow cooker while you do this.

Add Topping

- You can spread the topping individually on each fish fillet, or just pour it over the top of the fish in the slow cooker.

- The topping will help keep the fish moist, and gives the dish a pretty appearance.

- Use other types of mustard if you like; a coarse mustard with visible seeds gives a nice look.

- Sprinkle the dish with chopped parsley or some fresh thyme sprigs when done to add colour.

POACHED SALMON

Salmon steaks, which are sturdy and thick, cook well on low in a few hours

Poached fish is slowly simmered in a pan. The poaching liquid never comes to the boil; in fact, the French say the liquid is 'smiling'. But you can also poach fish in a slow cooker, with very little liquid. Low, moist heat, rather than a lot of liquid, achieves the poached effect. And that describes the slow cooker environment to a tee.

Still, you have to keep an eye on the fish. When testing the fish, lift off the first layer with a large spatula and set aside. Test the fish in the middle of the stack. If the flesh flakes easily when a fork is inserted and twisted, it's done.

Ingredients

Serves 6

6 salmon steaks (or fillets)

2 teaspoons dried dill

75 ml coarse mustard

1 onion, chopped

3 cloves garlic, finely chopped

2 tablespoons butter

250 ml chicken stock

Salt and pepper

Dill Poached Salmon

- Season salmon with salt and pepper and sprinkle with dill. Spread thinly with mustard. Cook onion and garlic in butter until tender in small pan.

- Place five crumpled foil balls in the bottom of the slow cooker, or insert a wire rack.

- Top with two salmon steaks and sprinkle with some onion and garlic; repeat layers twice.

- Pour chicken stock over all. Cover and cook on low for 3¹/₂–4¹/₂ hours, or until salmon flakes when tested with fork.

Layer Salmon

- It's important to have some of the onion and garlic mixture between the salmon steaks so they cook evenly.

- If you just plopped the salmon into the slow cooker, the mass would cook like a single piece of fish.

- And that would mean that the salmon steaks around the edges and on the bottom and top of the stack would overcook by the time the middle was done.

- So carefully layer the steaks with the vegetables for the best results.

How to Test if Fish is Done

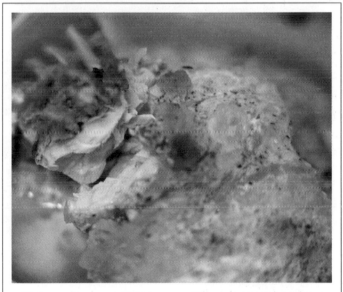

- There are two ways to test that fish is cooked. You can insert a fork directly into the flesh of the fish, and twist.

- When the salmon is done, it will flake. That means it will easily separate into long, thin fibres.

- Or you can test the salmon by temperature. Use an instant-read meat thermometer in the centre of a fish steak.

- When done, the salmon will register 60–63°C. Remove the salmon from the slow cooker immediately.

SEAFOOD STEW
Fish and shellfish combine to make this delicious stew

Seafood stew is cooked like fish fillets and shellfish: the fish is added at the end of cooking time for perfect results. When you cook a seafood stew on the stove, you do the same thing. The base of the stew – the vegetables and seasonings – cook until tender and blended, then you add the fish.

You can add any seafood to any slow cooker soup or stew recipe, as long as you follow these basic rules. Cut the fish fillets into cubes and cook for 30–40 minutes on high. Prawns and scallops will cook on high for 15–20 minutes. And whole fillets cook for about an hour on high heat.

Serve this hearty dish with a mixed green salad tossed with apples and pears.

Ingredients

Serves 6
3 tablespoons olive oil
1 onion, chopped
4 cloves garlic, finely chopped
2 tablespoons grated fresh ginger
225 g sliced mushrooms
2 sticks celery, chopped
Handful celery leaves, finely chopped
2 tablespoons soy sauce
Pinch of pepper
½ teaspoon five-spice powder
1 (400-g) can chopped tomatoes,
250 ml white wine
1.2 litres seafood stock or clam juice
750 ml water
2 salmon steaks
6 scallops
12 medium raw prawns

Asian Seafood Stew

- In 5.5-litre slow cooker, combine olive oil, onion, garlic, shallot, ginger, mushrooms, celery and celery leaves.

- Add soy sauce, pepper and five-spice powder; pour tomatoes, wine, stock and water over. Cover and cook on low 7–8 hours.

- Stir soup. Cut salmon into 2.5-cm pieces; add to soup. Cover and cook on low for 20 minutes.

- Add scallops and prawns. Cover and cook on low for 15–20 minutes or until prawns and scallops are done.

• • • • • • • • • • • RECIPE VARIATIONS • • • • • • • • • • •

Italian Seafood Stew
Cook onion and garlic in olive oil; omit ginger, celery leaves, soy sauce and five-spice powder. Add 1 teaspoon dried thyme, $1/2$ teaspoon dried oregano and 1 teaspoon grated lemon zest. Omit salmon steaks; add cleaned mussels with prawns and scallops.

Greek Seafood Stew
Cook onion and garlic as directed; omit ginger, celery and leaves, soy sauce and five-spice powder. Add 1 chopped leek, 1 small fennel bulb, chopped, 1 teaspoon dried oregano and 1 bay leaf. Substitute white fish fillets for salmon. Stir in 2 tablespoons lemon juice and 15 g chopped parsley before serving.

Cook Soup Base

- A good soup base uses lots of fresh vegetables and good olive oil.

- As they cook, the vegetables release their flavour into the stock, flavouring the whole soup.

- You can use your favourite vegetables for this stew.

Add sliced or baby carrots, leeks or fresh chopped tomatoes.

- The soup base can cook for a longer period of time without overcooking. Cook for 8–9 hours with no problem.

Prepare Seafood

- To prepare the salmon steaks, cut off the skin, or peel it off using a sharp knife.

- Remove the bones and feel the flesh with your fingers. There may be tiny pin bones in the flesh.

- Remove these bones with tweezers, then cut the salmon into chunks.

- The prawns can be peeled or unpeeled, depending on whether you want an elegant or a rustic dish.

JAMBALAYA
Spicy sausage and tender prawns cook in a velvety tomato sauce

Jambalaya is a festive dish – a combination of highly seasoned vegetables and lots of seafood. The original came from Louisiana, a blend of French, Spanish and Creole influences.

This dish is one of the original one-pot meals, traditionally served with rice. Classic jambalaya combines sausages, chicken, tomatoes and spices, but there are countless variations on the recipe.

You can make your jambalaya as mild, hot or smoky as you wish. Add crisply cooked smoked bacon, andouille or boudin sausage, or any type of seafood.

The rice cooked in the jambalaya soaks up all the delicious juices of the seafood, meat and vegetables and makes it a complete meal. All you need to go with it is a simple green salad and some nice white wine.

Ingredients

Serves 6

225 g smoked sausage, sliced
2 tablespoons butter
2 onions, chopped
4 cloves garlic, finely chopped
1 teaspoon salt
Pinch of cayenne pepper
2 tablespoons plain flour
1 bay leaf
3 sticks celery, chopped
1 green pepper, chopped
1 red pepper, chopped
200 g long-grain brown rice
350 ml chicken stock
2 (400-g) cans chopped tomatoes
3 tablespoons tomato purée
250 ml clam juice or fish stock
250 ml dry white wine
675 g raw medium prawns

Prawn Jambalaya

- In large frying pan, cook sausage until browned, then drain; pour off fat.

- Add butter to pan and cook onion and garlic until tender. Add salt, pepper and flour; cook until flour begins to brown.

- Add bay leaf, celery, peppers, rice and chicken stock; stir thoroughly. Pour into 3.5- or 4.5-litre slow cooker; add sausage.

- Add tomatoes, tomato purée, clam juice and wine. Cover and cook on low 6–8 hours. Add prawns and cook on high 15–20 minutes until prawns are pink.

Mixed Seafood Jambalaya

Make jambalaya as directed, but start with 225 g smoked streaky bacon, cooked crisp. Drain and crumble the bacon; pour fat out of pan but don't wipe. Add butter; cook onions and continue with the recipe. Add 450 g prawns, 450 g mussels and 450 g clams for last 20 minutes.

Rice for Jambalaya

You can add cooked rice directly to the Jambalaya during the last 5 minutes of cooking time so it absorbs some of the liquid. Or cook white rice in chicken or seafood stock in a 1:2 ratio. You can add herbs to the rice for green rice, or saffron for yellow rice.

Cook Vegetables

Add Prawns

- If you have a slow cooker with a flameproof insert made of metal, cook the bacon and vegetables in that to save washing up.

- Using the same pot for cooking the sausage and for finishing the dish also ensures you don't lose a drop of flavour.

- Vary the proportion and combination of vegetables as you wish. Add mushrooms, carrots or fennel.

- The 'holy trinity' of onion, celery and green pepper is traditional in jambalaya.

- You can add the prawns peeled or unpeeled. Peeling them makes the jambalaya easier to eat.

- But using unpeeled prawns is very pretty and looks rustic.

- To peel prawns, remove the legs and pull the shell from

the body. If the vein along the back is visible (a dark line), remove it.

- To remove the vein, make a shallow cut down the back and rinse, or remove it by hand.

SALMON WITH PILAF

A rice pilaf cooks in the slow cooker, then is topped with salmon fillets

This dish is perfect for entertaining. Not only do you get perfectly cooked, tender, and flavourful salmon fillets, but a creamy and cheesy wild and brown rice pilaf to serve with it.

Wild rice and brown rice are the types that cook best in the slow cooker. Long-grain white rice will become mushy, and short-grain rice is too sticky.

A rice pilaf consists of rice with other vegetables. Sometimes a sauce is added, and the pilaf is highly seasoned.

When you're ready to serve the dish, remove the salmon carefully with a large spatula to a serving plate and cover with foil to keep warm. Remove the rice and pile in a bowl. Serve with crusty rolls and a salad.

Ingredients

Serves 6

2 shallots, finely chopped

2 cloves garlic, finely chopped

2 tablespoons butter

200 g long-grain brown rice

250 g wild rice

1 teaspoon dried marjoram

225 g mushrooms, sliced

750 ml chicken stock

375 ml white sauce

115 g grated Emmental cheese

6 salmon fillets

25 g grated Parmesan cheese

2 tablespoons chopped fresh parsley

25 g ground almonds

Salt and pepper

Salmon with Cheesy Rice Pilaf

- Cook shallot and garlic in butter over medium-low heat until soft.

- Add both kinds of rice; cook and stir for 3 minutes. Place in 3.5-litre slow cooker with marjoram and mushrooms; add salt and pepper.

- Pour chicken stock and

white sauce into pan; simmer. Pour into slow cooker; cover; cook on high 3–4¹/₂ hours, until rice is tender.

- Add Emmental cheese to pilaf. Mix Parmesan, parsley and almonds; sprinkle on salmon. Place salmon on pilaf; cover; cook on high 20–30 minutes until done.

• • • • • • • • • • • • • • • RECIPE VARIATIONS • • • • • • • • • • • • • • •

Salmon with Wild Rice Pilaf
Make recipe as directed, but use 450 g wild rice instead of combination of wild and brown rice. Substitute 1 teaspoon dried thyme for the marjoram, and use 225 g chestnut mushrooms, sliced. Sprinkle salmon with a combination of parsley and chopped spring onions.

Salmon with Brown Rice Pilaf
Make recipe as directed, but use 450 g long-grain brown rice instead of the combination of wild and brown rice. Substitute 1 teaspoon dried oregano for the marjoram. Add 175 g sliced carrots. Top the salmon with a combination of chopped coriander and pecorino cheese.

Cook Pilaf

- Look for wild rice that was naturally harvested, with very long grains. Some rice is mechanically harvested.

- If you use grains that are short or broken, the finished pilaf will be mushy.

- Gently stir the pilaf before adding the salmon. Add more white sauce if the mixture seems dry.

Add Salmon

- Try to arrange the salmon in a single layer, or overlap just a little bit, so it cooks evenly.

- If you'd prefer to use steaks instead of fillets, increase the cooking time to 50–60 minutes.

- Watch the cooking time carefully and remove the salmon when it flakes. Check after 20 minutes to see if it is done.

- For a more casual dish, when the salmon is done stir it into the rice mixture for a salmon pilaf.

BACCALÀ STEW

This old-fashioned stew is made with salt or dried cod for lots of flavour

Baccalà is salt cod, an unusual dried and salted fish that becomes very tender when it is soaked and cooked.

You may need to order baccalà (spelled *bacalhau* in Portuguese) from your fishmonger; it's not a common ingredient. And you must follow soaking and rinsing times exactly or the dish will be too salty.

Baccalà is cooked in many different ways, depending on region and local traditions. Use your favourite vegetables, or take a chance and try something different: a combination of olives, prunes and cauliflower in place of the tomatoes and potatoes. Serve with crisp garlic toast, a fresh salad and some red wine to savour.

Baccalà Stew

Ingredients

Serves 6

450 g dried salted cod

2 onions, chopped

3 cloves garlic, finely chopped

5 potatoes, peeled and cubed

2 tomatoes, peeled, seeded and diced

1 (225-g) jar tomato sauce

2 tablespoons plain flour

Pinch of pepper

250 ml white wine

750 ml seafood stock

75 g sliced green olives

1 tablespoon fresh thyme

- Place cod in large bowl; cover with water. Refrigerate for 12–18 hours, changing water 3 times.

- When ready to cook, remove the skin and pick out bones with tweezers. Cut into chunks.

- Place onions, garlic and potatoes in 3.5-litre slow cooker. Top with fish and tomatoes. Mix tomato sauce, flour, pepper and wine in bowl; pour over fish.

- Add stock. Cover and cook on low for 6–8 hours, until vegetables are tender. Add olives and thyme; stir.

ZOOM

Baccalà (or *bacalhau*) is dried and salted cod. It's used in Portuguese cooking, and was once a staple during the winter months. When you choose baccalà, make sure that the piece is uniformly thick and the flesh is pliable, not hard. Soak for 12 hours, changing the water 3 times.

• • • • • RECIPE VARIATION • • • • •

Classic Baccalà Stew
Make recipe as directed, but use 12 small red potatoes in place of the potatoes. Add 4 prunes, chopped, and 1 head cauliflower, cut into florets. Omit tomatoes and tomato sauce; add 1 (400-g) can chopped tomatoes. Cook recipe as directed.

Prepare Baccalà

- Make sure that you completely change the water when soaking the baccalà.

- The fish is too salty to eat as it is, and even after a simple soaking in water it will be too salty.

- To make sure that the fish isn't too salty, you can cook a small piece in a bit of butter until flaky, then try it.

- If it's still salty, change the water again and soak for another 1–2 hours.

Add Other Ingredients

- The tomatoes must be peeled because the tomato skins can have an unpleasant texture when cooked for a long period of time.

- You can use other types of olives. Authentic olives would be kalamata, or wrinkled oil-cured olives.

- Be careful with the amount of olives you add; the stew is already salty. Taste before adding.

- You can add other fresh herbs at the end; some chopped parsley or coriander would be nice.

CHILLI WITH BEANS
True chilli doesn't use beans, but this hybrid version is rich and delicious

Chilli with beans might not be authentic, but it is very satisfying. And the inexpensive beans add nutrition and fibre.

Using canned beans in the slow cooker is much easier than using dried. Dried beans can be tricky to cook, especially when salt and tomatoes are used in the recipe. These ingredients stop the beans from softening properly. But canned beans are very high in salt, so they have to be drained and rinsed before using.

This recipe is for a fairly mild chilli. Jalapeño peppers are hot, but on the mild end of the chilli heat range. For more heat, use habañero chillies or Scotch bonnets. Season to taste!

Ingredients

Serves 6

450 g beef skirt, cubed

2 tablespoons plain flour

1 teaspoon salt

Pinch of cayenne pepper

2 tablespoons olive oil

2 onions, chopped

3 cloves garlic, finely chopped

1–2 jalapeño chillies, finely chopped

1 (175 g) can tomato purée

2 (400-g) cans chopped tomatoes

1 (225-g) jar tomato sauce

250 ml beef stock

2 tablespoons Dijon mustard

2 tablespoons chilli powder

1 teaspoon ground cumin

2 (425-g) cans kidney beans, drained

Tex-Mex Chilli with Beans

- Toss beef with flour, salt and cayenne. Brown in olive oil in large frying pan; drain and place in 3.5- or 4.5-litre slow cooker.

- Add onions, garlic and jalapeños to fat remaining in pan; cook and stir for 1 minute. Add 2 tablespoons tomato purée; leave to brown for 3–4 minutes.

- Pour 1 can chopped tomatoes into pan and bring to simmer to deglaze pan. Add to slow cooker along with remaining ingredients.

- Cover and cook on low for 8–9 hours or until chilli is thick and blended.

Minced Beef Chilli

Make as directed, but use 450 g minced beef in place of the beef skirt. Omit flour; reduce salt to ½ teaspoon. Brown the minced beef with the onions and garlic; drain and combine with remaining ingredients. Cook as directed.

Beefier Chilli

Make recipe as directed, but use 900 g of beef. Add another 250 ml of beef stock; keep other ingredients the same, except add 1 (115-g) jar diced green chillies, undrained.

Brown Beef

Stir Chilli

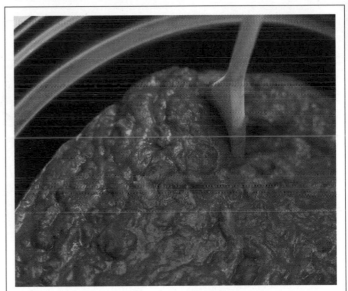

- As the beef browns, the flour will cook too. This releases the starch in the flour, which will help thicken the chilli.

- Letting the tomato purée brown for a few minutes also adds great depth of flavour to the mixture.

- Don't let the tomato purée burn; you're looking for a dark brown colour.

- Then scrape up the bits on the bottom of the pan with the juice from the chopped tomatoes and mix everything together in the slow cooker.

- If necessary, you can thicken the chilli with cornflour blended with a little water. About 2 tablespoons cornflour to 50 ml water or beer is perfect.

- Or you can thicken the chilli by cooking it on high for 20–30 minutes with the lid removed.

- Mashing some of the beans will thicken the chilli by releasing starch. Do this about 30 minutes before serving.

- Sprinkle the chilli with grated cheese; top with sour cream, crushed tortilla chips or guacamole.

133

CLASSIC BEEF CHILLI
Classic chilli includes chunks of tender beef in a luscious red sauce

While most people know that true chilli is made without beans, many don't know that true chilli is also made without tomatoes. The red colour of this authentic kind of chilli comes from dried red chillies.

The chillies are soaked in water and chopped, or just crushed and added to the mixture. They will soften in the long cooking time. You can find dried red chillies in larger

supermarkets or good delicatessens. Use an inexpensive cut of beef for this recipe. Chuck steak, topside or silverside are good choices. These meats benefit from the moist environment and long slow cooking time. The meat should fall apart when done.

Ingredients

Serve 6

900 g braising steak

2 tablespoons chilli powder

1 teaspoon cumin

3 tablespoons plain flour

1 teaspoon dried oregano

4 rashers smoked streaky bacon

2 onions, chopped

4 cloves garlic, finely chopped

2 jalapeño chillies, finely chopped

2 dried ancho chillies, crushed

250 ml water

1 litre beef stock

Salt and pepper

A Bowl of Red

- Cut steak into 5-cm cubes; trim excess fat. Toss with chilli powder, cumin, flour, oregano, salt and pepper.

- In large frying pan, cook bacon until crisp; remove, drain, crumble and refrigerate. Brown beef cubes in bacon fat.

- Place beef in 3.5-litre slow cooker. Cook onions and garlic in remaining fat until tender; add to slow cooker.

- Add all remaining ingredients. Cover and cook on low for 8–9 hours until chilli is thick and beef is very tender; stir in bacon and serve.

ZOOM

There is chilli powder, and there is ground chilli powder. Chilli powder is a combination of ground chillies, cayenne pepper, cumin, paprika and oregano or garlic powder. Ground chilli powder is made of just the dried chilli, finely ground. Both of these powders are hot and spicy, but their flavours do vary. Buy several kinds and experiment to find your favourites.

Brown Beef

- The beef is cut into large cubes so, after it falls apart in the chilli, you'll still be able to see it and bite into a chunk of meat.

- When the beef is browned in the bacon fat, it will pick up that authentic smoky flavour.

- The onions and garlic add juices to the pan to help release the caramelized brown bits of meat.

Combine Ingredients

- You can add the bacon at the end of cooking time so it keeps its texture, or stir it in at the beginning, when it will melt into the chilli.

- Make sure that the dried and crushed chillies are covered with liquid as they cook.

- The chillies will rehydrate and add great flavour along with heat to the chilli.

- Top this chilli with some sour cream mixed with chopped tomatoes and avocados for a cooling contrast.

WHITE CHILLI

White chilli uses chicken or turkey along with green chillies

Not all chilis have to be tomato-based. When they don't include tomatoes or red chillies, these stews are called white or green chillies. These hearty dishes are made with chicken or pork, completing the 'white' theme. They can be just as spicy as red chilli.

White beans used in white or green chilli include butter beans, cannellini beans, pinto beans, black-eyed peas, navy beans and small haricot beans – you can choose either dried or canned. Chilli can be thickened by adding cornflour blended with water, coating the meat in flour before cooking, or puréeing or mashing some of the beans. The thickness and texture are up to you.

Serve chilli with cornbread or tortilla chips, and some cold Mexican beer.

Ingredients

Serves 6

6 boneless, skinless chicken thighs, cubed

2 tablespoons plain flour

1/2 teaspoon dried thyme

1/2 teaspoon dried basil

2 onions, chopped

5 cloves garlic, finely chopped

2 green peppers, chopped

2 jalapeño peppers, finely chopped

1 (425-g) can pinto beans, drained

2 (425-g) cans cannellini beans, drained

1 litre chicken stock

2 tablespoons cornflour

1 (115-g) jar chopped green chillies, undrained

Salt and pepper

White Chicken Chilli

- Toss chicken with flour, thyme, basil, salt and pepper. Place onions and garlic in 3.5- or 4.5-litre slow cooker.

- Top with chicken; add green peppers, jalapeño peppers, pinto beans and 1 can cannellini beans.

- Puree second can of cannellini beans and add to slow cooker with stock. Cover and cook on low for 7–8 hours.

- In small bowl, combine cornflour and green chillies; stir into slow cooker. Cover and cook on high for 20–30 minutes until thickened.

Green Pork Chilli

Make recipe as directed, but substitute 450 g boneless pork shoulder, cut into 2.5-cm cubes, for the chicken thighs. Instead of the pinto beans, add 250 ml green enchilada sauce and 250 ml green salsa. Finish the chilli with 2 tablespoons lime juice and a handful of fresh coriander, chopped.

Creamy White Chicken Chilli

Make chilli as directed, but use 4 whole boneless, skinless chicken breasts instead of thighs. Do not purée beans. To thicken chilli, combine 2 tablespoons cornflour with 250 ml single cream instead of the green chillies. Cook on high 20–30 minutes until thickened. Top with chopped fresh coriander.

Prepare Chicken

- For more heat, add 1–2 teaspoons ground chilli powder to the mixture used to coat the chicken.

- You can brown the chicken in some olive oil or butter before adding it to the slow cooker for more flavour.

- If you want to use chicken breasts in this recipe, do not cube them; keep them whole and shred after cooking.

- Reduce the cooking time to 5–7 hours if you use chicken breasts so they don't overcook.

Layer Food in Slow Cooker

- It's important to layer the food as directed. The onions take longest to cook, so have to be placed at the bottom of the slow cooker.

- You may not need to add the cornflour mixture if you think the chilli is thick enough.

- You can stay with the green and white theme and garnish the chilli with sour cream and chopped avocados.

- Or to add a pop of colour, texture and flavour, top with fresh chopped tomatoes, spring onion and coriander.

FOUR-PEPPER CHILLI
Vegetarian chilli is rich, thick and delicious

Chilli is a perfect choice for a hearty vegetarian stew. All the peppers and onions add lots of flavour and heat, and beans add protein, fibre, B vitamins and texture.

Chillies and peppers can be added as they are, just chopped, diced or sliced. But for more flavour and a silky texture, roast them and remove the skin. This is easy to do, and takes just a few extra minutes.

Adapt the recipe by using your own favourite combination of chillies, other vegetables and beans in vegetarian chilli. And for toppings, cheeses, guacamole, salsa and tortilla chips are good choices.

Ingredients

Serves 6

2 onions, chopped
4 cloves garlic, finely chopped
I jalapeño pepper, finely chopped
I red pepper, cut in half
I green pepper, cut in half
I poblano chilli, cut in half
I (425-g) can black beans, drained
I (425-g) can aduki beans, drained
I (425-g) can haricot beans, drained
500 ml vegetable stock
2 tablespoons chilli powder
I teaspoon dried oregano
I teaspoon dried marjoram
I bay leaf
Salt and pepper

Four-Pepper Chilli

- Place onion and garlic in 3.5- or 4.5-litre slow cooker. Preheat grill.

- Place peppers on grill rack, skin side up. Grill for 7–8 minutes until skin browns. Remove and wrap in foil; leave 5 minutes to steam. Remove and discard skins.

- Chop peppers and add to slow cooker with all remaining ingredients.

- Cover and cook on low for 7–8 hours until chilli is thickened. Remove bay leaf and thicken with cornflour blended with a little water, if needed; serve.

Dried Bean Chilli

Make recipe as directed, but use 115 g each dried aduki beans, black beans and haricot beans in place of the canned beans. Soak beans overnight and place in bottom of slow cooker; top with remaining ingredients. Cook on low for 8–9 hours.

Vegetarian Mince Chilli

Make chilli as directed, but add 350 g vegetarian mince to the slow cooker. This product is safe to cook from frozen. Omit the white beans and the marjoram.

Grill Chillies

Remove Blackened Skins

- When you grill or cook chillies over high heat, the skin blackens and wrinkles and the flesh starts to cook.

- This process gives the peppers a smoky flavour that adds greatly to the chilli.

- Rearrange the peppers often while grilling. The skin should turn dark brown or even black.

- But you want to make sure just the skin is black, not the flesh. Then place the chillies in a paper bag or wrap them in foil to steam.

- As the chillies steam, the skin loosens from the flesh and becomes easy to peel away.

- Peel using your fingers or tweezers. Remove as much of the skin as you can; you don't have to remove all of it.

- Never rinse chillies that have been roasted and peeled; you'll rinse away all the flavour you've added.

- When the chillies are cool enough to handle, discard the stalk and seeds, then slice or chop according to the recipe.

BLACK BEAN CHILLI

Kidney beans, while classic, aren't the only legume used in chilli recipes

Black beans, also sometimes called turtle beans, are shiny and black on the surface, but brown or red inside. They look like the back of a turtle shell, which is how they got their name.

Black beans taste very nutty, with a perfect creamy texture. They pair beautifully with grains like wild rice or barley, to add more flavour and nutrition to the chilli.

In chilli, canned beans work better than dried ones. Dried beans won't soften in the presence of tomatoes, and tomatoes are now an integral part of most chilli recipes. Look for low-salt and flavoured black beans in the supermarket.

Top black bean chilli with grated cheese if you wish, and serve with sour cream and chopped chives.

Ingredients

Serves 6

175 g wild rice, rinsed

2 onions, chopped

3 cloves garlic, finely chopped

1 jalapeño pepper, finely chopped

3 (425-g) cans black beans, drained

2 (400-g) cans chopped tomatoes

1 (225-g) jar tomato sauce

750 ml water

1 tablespoon chilli powder

1 teaspoon dried basil

1 teaspoon dried marjoram

1 bay leaf

1 tablespoon cornflour (optional)

Black Bean Wild Rice Chilli

- Place wild rice in bottom of 3.5- or 4.5-litre slow cooker. Top with onions, garlic and jalapeño.

- Rinse black beans and drain again. Add to slow cooker with remaining ingredients.

- Cover and cook on low for 7–9 hours, stirring halfway through cooking time, until wild rice is tender.

- Remove bay leaf and thicken chilli with cornflour blended with water if desired. Serve with sour cream and chopped chives.

Barley Black Bean Chilli

Make recipe as directed, but add 175 g medium pearl barley in place of the wild rice. Omit the tomato sauce and add 250 ml beef or chicken stock, or water or vegetable stock for a vegetarian chilli. Omit basil; add 1 teaspoon dried oregano.

Super-Spicy Black Bean Chilli

Make recipe as directed. Add 1 chopped habanero chilli and 1 (115-g) jar diced green chillies, undrained, to the slow cooker. Add 1 roasted and peeled poblano chilli, and increase chilli powder to 2 tablespoons. Add 2 teaspoons dried ancho chilli powder with other ingredients.

Rinse Black Beans

- To rinse black beans, open the can and pour the contents directly into a sieve or colander placed in the sink.

- Run cold water over the beans, gently stirring them with your fingers or shaking the colander.

- You want to remove the thick, sweet liquid the beans are packed in.

- You can add a small amount of that sweet liquid to thicken the chilli, but no more than 50 ml.

Stir Chilli

- Stir the chilli only once during cooking time. Remember, every time you lift the lid you should add 20 minutes to the total cooking time.

- Stir quickly but gently, and be sure to scrape the sides of the slow cooker.

- A heatproof rubber spatula or wooden spoon are good tools to use. Stirring will clean the sides and mix all the ingredients.

- Stir the chilli once again when it's done, just before you serve it, to mix all the ingredients and flavours.

BEEF AND BEAN CHILLI

Minced beef makes an inexpensive and hearty chilli

The least expensive and heartiest of all the chillies, this recipe uses a special ingredient: seasoned canned beans. In the supermarket, you'll find all kinds of seasoned canned beans, ranging from mild to super hot chilli beans.

Add these beans, liquid and all, to the slow cooker. Don't drain this type of bean, because the liquid includes ingredients like chillies and garlic and provides lots of flavour.

Think about using other forms of meat: spicy pork sausages, andouille or mortadella. Remove the sausages from their casings and break up, then brown with the onions and garlic.

Enjoy this easy chilli with a green salad and tortilla chips.

Ingredients

Serves 6

450 g minced beef

1 onion, chopped

2 cloves garlic, finely chopped

1 (115-g) jar chopped green chillies, undrained

1 (225-g) jar salsa

2 (425-g) cans kidney beans, drained

1 (425-g) can kidney beans in chilli sauce

1 tablespoon chilli powder

1/2 teaspoon ground cumin

1/2 teaspoon pepper

500 ml beef stock

1 tablespoon cornflour

120 ml tomato juice

Thick Beef and Bean Chilli

- In large frying pan, brown minded beef with onion and garlic until beef is done; drain and add to 3.5-litre slow cooker.

- Add all remaining ingredients except for the cornflour and tomato juice.

- Cover and cook on low for 8–9 hours, or on high for 4–5 hours, until chilli is blended.

- In small bowl, combine cornflour with tomato juice; stir into slow cooker. Cover and cook on high for 20 minutes before serving.

Mixed Bean and Beef Chilli
Make recipe as directed, but use 2 (425-g) cans kidney beans in chilli sauce and 1 (425-g) can pinto beans in sauce in place of the kidney beans and beans in chilli sauce. You could also use spicy pinto beans or chilli beans with jalapeño and red pepper.

Keep a good supply of canned beans in your store cupboard and you'll be able to put together a chilli at a moment's notice. Nothing's easier than opening some cans, pouring them into the slow cooker, adding some spices, and turning it on. You can prepare dinner in 5–10 minutes before you leave for work in the morning.

Brown Minced Beef

- You can brown the minced beef ahead of time, as long as it's fully cooked before you refrigerate it.

- In fact, when there's a supermarket offer on minced beef, stock up and have a marathon cooking session.

- Cook the mince with onions and garlic, then pack in freezer containers.

- You can use this mixture to start a multitude of recipes, including chilli and pasta sauce.

Thicken with Cornflour

- Slaked cornflour is the best way to thicken this type of chilli.

- Use care when mixing the cornflour with water. Make sure the cornflour is completely dissolved before adding it to the chilli.

- And stir the chilli thoroughly while you're adding the liquid. You don't want to come upon a congealed lump of cornflour.

- If the chilli gets too thick, just add some more stock or tomato juice to it.

QUINOA STEW

Quinoa is a delicious and nutritious ancient grain

Vegetable stews cooked in your slow cooker are among the healthiest meals on the planet. The sealed slow-cooking environment traps all the vitamins and nutrients, and the low, slow heat prevents the formation of harmful compounds that can form when food is cooked at a high heat.

Quinoa has some special properties that must be noted. It is gluten-free, so is a good choice for people with coeliac disease or wheat allergies. And it is a great source of B vitamins and minerals such as zinc and potassium.

The tiny, round seeds become tender when cooked, but retain a slightly crunchy coating, resulting in a dish with an interesting texture.

Enjoy this savoury stew using this ancient South American grain; serve with a crisp salad.

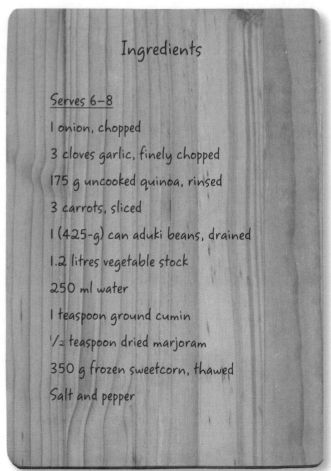

Ingredients

Serves 6–8

1 onion, chopped

3 cloves garlic, finely chopped

175 g uncooked quinoa, rinsed

3 carrots, sliced

1 (425-g) can aduki beans, drained

1.2 litres vegetable stock

250 ml water

1 teaspoon ground cumin

½ teaspoon dried marjoram

350 g frozen sweetcorn, thawed

Salt and pepper

Quinoa Vegetable Stew

- In 3.5-litre slow cooker, combine onion, garlic, thoroughly rinsed quinoa and carrots.

- Top with rinsed and drained aduki beans, stock, water, cumin and marjoram; season with salt and pepper.

- Cover and cook on low for 7–8 hours or until quinoa and vegetables are tender.

- Stir in frozen sweetcorn. Cook on high for 20–30 minutes until stew is hot and blended.

Quinoa (pronounced 'keen-wah'), is an ancient grain that is a complete source of high quality protein. Most grains are missing one or more of the amino acids your body needs, so they have to be combined; not so with quinoa. It was a staple food of the Incas and has been harvested in the Andes for hundreds of years.

Curried Quinoa Stew
Make recipe as directed, but add 1 tablespoon curry powder and 1 tablespoon grated ginger to onion mixture. Omit red beans; add 1 red pepper, chopped, and 115 g chopped celery. Stir 120 ml mango chutney into stew just before serving.

Rinse Quinoa

- It's important to rinse quinoa before you use it because the grain has a natural coating of saponin, which is bitter.

- The coating is easily removed by a thorough rinsing.

- To tell if the saponin is all rinsed off, place the quinoa in a bowl and add water; swish a bit.

- If you do not see suds, the saponin is removed and you can proceed with the recipe.

Add Vegetables

- Find quinoa in health food stores and in the grains aisle of the supermarket.

- Add more vegetables to this stew if you like. Chopped peppers, green or yellow courgettes or mushrooms would be good additions.

- You'll know the quinoa is done when you bite into it. There will be a slightly crunchy coating, with a tender centre.

- Make sure that the sweetcorn is completely heated through before you serve the stew.

BEAN STEWS

Dried beans cook perfectly in the slow cooker along with seasonings and vegetables

Cooking dried beans so they are evenly tender can be a challenge. Here's the trick: avoid ingredients that prevent softening – which means salty foods and acidic ingredients.

Salty foods include salt, olives, capers, fermented black beans, bacon and smoked sausages. High-acid foods include tomatoes, citrus juices, sour cream, buttermilk and wine.

Soaking the dried beans before you cook them is an important step. The beans should be soaked overnight, or you can boil them for a few minutes then leave them to stand for 1–2 hours; cook as directed.

Make sure the beans are completely covered with liquid in the slow cooker so they cook evenly.

Ingredients

Serves 6

150 g dried haricot beans

150 g dried black beans

150 g dried pinto beans

1 onion, chopped

4 cloves garlic, finely chopped

1 teaspoon celery salt

1 teaspoon dried oregano

Pinch of pepper

3 carrots, sliced

2 potatoes, peeled and diced

2 litres vegetable stock

175 g frozen sweetcorn, thawed

1 (400-g) can chopped tomatoes

Many Bean Stew

- Pick over beans to remove extraneous material and rinse well. Place in large saucepan and cover with cold water.

- Bring to the boil; boil for 2 minutes, then cover, remove from heat, and leave to stand for 2 hours.

- Drain and place in 4.5- or 5.5-litre slow cooker with all other ingredients except sweetcorn and tomatoes.

- Cover and cook on low for 8–10 hours until beans are tender. Mash some of the beans. Add sweetcorn and tomatoes; cook on high for 20 minutes.

Mediterranean Bean Stew
Make recipe as directed, but use lima beans in place of pinto beans. Omit oregano; add 1 teaspoon dried thyme. Add 1 chopped red pepper with the beans. Omit sweetcorn; add 50 g sliced green olives.

Tex-Mex Bean Stew
Make recipe as directed, but increase onions to 2. Add 2 finely chopped jalapeño peppers with the onions and garlic. Omit frozen sweetcorn; add 250 g baby corn, blanched and drained, instead. Stir 120 ml single cream into stew before serving.

Pick Over Beans

- Pick over beans to remove any twigs, leaves or bits of dirt that processing left behind.

- Beans are, after all, a natural product, and processing doesn't remove every bit of extraneous material.

- Rinse the beans well to remove dust or dirt; drain and add fresh water for soaking.

- You can often find prepared bean mixes that are already cleaned and blended.

Boil Beans

- If you choose to boil the beans for 1–2 minutes, make sure the water comes to a complete boil.

- This means the water is bubbling furiously, and the bubbling doesn't subside when the mixture is stirred.

- If you'd rather soak the beans, just cover them with cold water, cover the bowl, and let stand overnight.

- In the morning, drain the beans, rinse again, and use as the recipe directs.

VEGETABLE STEWS

VEGETABLE RAGOUT

Winter squash adds colour, flavour and nutrition to a vegetable stew

A ragout or, in Italian, *ragù* (derived from a French word meaning 'to stimulate the appetite'), means a stew or sauce that is heavy with slow-cooked vegetables. This type of food is perfect for the slow cooker.

This is where root vegetables shine. Think about using less common types of vegetable, like turnips, swedes and parsnips, in these recipes.

A ragout is a very comforting dish, inexpensive and warming on cold winter days. You can serve it as a stew, accompanied by rice, barley or mashed potatoes, or use it as a chunky sauce for pasta.

Flavour the ragout well using dried herbs during cooking, and stir in fresh herbs just before serving for an extra pop of fresh flavour.

Ingredients

Serves 6–8

1 butternut squash, peeled, seeded and cubed

2 onions, chopped

4 cloves garlic, finely chopped

4 carrots, sliced

225 g chestnut mushrooms, sliced

1 (400-g) can artichoke hearts, drained

1 teaspoon dried thyme

1 teaspoon dried oregano

1.2 litres vegetable stock

2 tablespoons lemon juice

25 g chopped parsley

25 g chopped coriander

40 g grated pecorino cheese

Salt and pepper

Vegetable Ragout

- Layer vegetables in order in 4.5- or 5.5-litre slow cooker. Sprinkle with salt, pepper, thyme and oregano.

- Pour stock over all. Cover and cook on low for 8–10 hours until vegetables are tender.

- You can also cook this on high for 4–5 hours. For a thicker ragout, partially mash some of the vegetables about 30 minutes before serving.

- Add lemon juice just before serving. Serve topped with a mixture of parsley, coriander and pecorino cheese.

Root Vegetable Ragout

Make recipe as directed, but add 1 peeled, cubed sweet potato and 2 peeled, cubed potatoes. Omit mushrooms and artichoke hearts. Add 1 (425-g) can drained haricot beans with the vegetables. Serve with rice.

Greek Vegetable Ragout

Make recipe as directed, but omit mushrooms. Add another can of artichoke hearts, and add 350 g cauliflower florets. Omit thyme; add 1 teaspoon dried marjoram. Stir in 75 kalamata olives at end; use crumbled feta cheese in topping mixture.

Prepare Squash

Mix Herb Topping

- To prepare squash, cut it in half using a chef's knife. Be careful with this process; hold the knife with both hands so you don't cut yourself.

- Then use a metal spoon to scrape out the seeds and membranes from the cavity.

- At this point, you can peel the squash. Then cut it into strips, and cut those strips into chunks.

- Any squash, whether butternut, acorn or buttercup, is prepared the same way.

- When you use sturdy herbs like parsley and coriander, you can prepare the herb topping ahead of time.

- You could repeat the flavours used in the stew and choose fresh oregano and thyme leaves.

- But beware: fresh oregano is very strong, so only use about 2 tablespoons of it. Thyme is milder, so you can use more.

- Pull the leaves from the stems and coarsely chop with a chef's knife. Refrigerate until ready to serve.

PUMPKIN STEW

A fresh pumpkin is easy to prepare and cook in this colourful stew

Pumpkins are the essence of autumn. Their colour, texture and flavour are evocative of the cooler months, when we start craving heartier and more filling foods.

If you've never had pumpkin in a soup or a stew, you're in for a treat. Pumpkin's smooth texture, rich flavour and beautiful colour make a spectacular stew. Look for small, sweet pumpkins, not the giants you carve for Halloween. These smaller

pumpkins are sweeter with a less dense flesh. Once you've learned how to work with pumpkins, the sky's the limit. Make a pumpkin bisque or a spicy pumpkin soup with the flavours of autumn and winter.

Serve these rich stews and soups with crusty bread and salads of winter leaves.

Ingredients

Serves 6–8

900 g pumpkin, seeded, peeled and cubed

2 onions, chopped

4 cloves garlic, finely chopped

1 red pepper, chopped

1 teaspoon dried thyme

1 teaspoon dried marjoram

1 teaspoon dried basil

1.2 litres vegetable stock

1 tablespoon lemon juice

250 ml single cream or milk

2 tablespoons cornflour

2 teaspoons fresh thyme

15 g chopped parsley

Salt and pepper

Herby Pumpkin Stew

- Layer pumpkin, onions, garlic and pepper in 4.5- or 5.5-litre slow cooker.

- Season with salt and pepper and sprinkle with dried herbs. Pour vegetable stock over all. Cover and cook on low for 8–10 hours until pumpkin is tender.

- Partially mash some of the pumpkin and stir in the lemon juice.

- Mix cream and cornflour and stir into stew with fresh thyme and parsley. Cover and cook on high for 15–20 minutes.

Pumpkin Bisque

Make recipe as directed, but don't add red pepper to slow cooker. Cook as directed. Then turn off slow cooker; mash vegetables until smooth. Turn slow cooker to high. Add pepper and cream and cornflour mixture; cook 30–40 minutes on high.

Curried Pumpkin Stew

Make recipe as directed, but add 115 g chopped celery along with the red pepper. Omit thyme and marjoram; add 1 tablespoon curry powder and 1/2 teaspoon cinnamon. Cook as directed, but omit thyme and parsley; garnish with mango chutney.

Prepare Pumpkin

Layer Ingredients

- Choose a pumpkin that's heavy for its size, smooth and firm, with no soft spots.

- To prepare pumpkin, cut into quarters then scoop out seeds. Peel the pumpkin with a swivel-bladed vegetable peeler.

- Then cut the pumpkin into lengths and chunks. You can reserve the seeds if you like.

- Wash the seeds and leave to dry overnight. Toss with oil, spread on a baking sheet, and then toast in 140°C oven for 70–80 minutes, stirring every 20 minutes.

- Cut the pumpkin into evenly sized cubes so it cooks thoroughly.

- You could add other vegetables to this recipe: sliced mushrooms or carrots would be good.

- Many recipes for pumpkin stew include meat. You could brown 450 g of cubed stewing beef and add it with the pumpkin.

- Or choose chicken thighs or breasts, or cubed pork shoulder. Don't brown these – just add them to the slow cooker.

151

POTATO KALE STEW

This simple, rustic stew is delicious and nutritious

Potato stew is one of the most nutritious and least expensive stews you can make. And it's so easy when you make it in your slow cooker.

The best potatoes to use in stews are varieties good for baking and mashing, such as King Edward or Maris Piper. Or you can use sweet potatoes. Red potatoes are too waxy and won't melt into the stew the way the floury varieties will.

To give the stew some deep flavour and gorgeous colour, along with another texture, add sturdy greens toward the end of cooking time.

Greens that stand up to the slow-cooker treatment include mustard greens, kale, turnip greens and chard. These slightly bitter greens add a punch of flavour to the mild potato mixture. Garnish with chopped chives or parsley.

Ingredients

Serves 6

2 tablespoons butter

2 onions, chopped

4 cloves garlic, finely chopped

900 g potatoes, cubed

1.2 litres vegetable stock

½ teaspoon caraway seeds

Pinch of grated nutmeg

450 g kale, chopped

2 tablespoons cornflour

120 ml single cream or milk

15 g chopped coriander

Salt and pepper

Potato and Kale Stew

- Melt butter in medium pan. Add onions and garlic; cook and stir 4 minutes.

- Place potatoes in 3.5-litre slow cooker; top with onion mixture. Add stock, caraway, nutmeg, salt and pepper.

- Cover and cook on low for

7–9 hours until potatoes are tender. Partially mash potatoes.

- Add kale to slow cooker; cover and cook on low 30 minutes. Combine cornflour with cream; stir into slow cooker. Cover; cook on high 15 minutes. Sprinkle with coriander.

Creamy Vegetable Potato Stew

Make recipe as directed, but peel the potatoes before you cube and add them to the slow cooker. Add 115 g sliced celery and omit the nutmeg and caraway seeds. Omit the kale. Add 250 ml single cream mixed with 2 tablespoons cornflour at the end; stir in 115 g grated Havarti cheese.

Tex-Mex Potato Stew

Make recipe as directed, but add 2 finely chopped jalapeño peppers with the onions. Omit caraway seeds, nutmeg and kale. Add 1 teaspoon dried oregano, 1 teaspoon dried basil and 2 tablespoons chilli powder. Stir in 115 g grated Pepper Jack or Cheddar cheese at end.

Chop Kale

Add Stock

- Kale is a member of the cabbage family, with all of the health benefits that implies.

- It has powerful antioxidant compounds, including beta-carotene, vitamin K and vitamin C.

- Kale should be dark green, with firm leaves and no browned, soft or wet spots.

- To prepare, swish in a sink full of cool water, then shake off. Chop the leaves roughly, discarding thick stems and ends. Other dark greens are prepared the same way.

- If you don't peel the potatoes, the stew will be more rustic and have an earthier flavour. Most of the potato's nutrients are found just under the skin. The stew will also have more fibre.

- Peel the potatoes for a more elegant stew or a creamier finish.

- For a richer stew, you can use chicken or beef stock in place of the vegetable stock.

- Top the stew with chopped parsley, gremolata or grated cheese.

ROOT VEGETABLE STEW

Wheat berries become chewy and nutty in this hearty stew

Root vegetables have sustained populations for generations, and for good reason. They are filling, hearty, easy to store and use, and combine into sublime stews and soups for warming, nourishing winter meals.

Root vegetables include onions, garlic, carrots, potatoes, sweet potatoes, parsnips, turnips and swedes. They all keep well provided they are stored in a cool, dark place. Prepare

them by peeling and cutting out any rough spots or eyes, then cut into slices and cube or chop.

Fresh herbs, including oregano, thyme, basil, marjoram or rosemary, are great complements to root vegetables. Choose your favourite.

Serve these stews with crusty bread hot from the oven and a chopped fruit or vegetable salad.

Ingredients

Serves 6

175 g wheat berries, rinsed

1 onion, chopped

2 cloves garlic, finely chopped

225 g mushrooms, sliced

3 carrots, sliced

1.5 litres vegetable stock

2 teaspoons finely chopped fresh
  rosemary

1 bay leaf

Salt and pepper

Wheat Berry Vegetable Stew

- Place wheat berries, onion, garlic, mushrooms and carrots in a 3.5- or 4.5-litre slow cooker.

- Top with stock, season with salt and pepper, and add rosemary and bay leaf.

- Cover and cook on low for 8–10 hours or on high for

4–5 hours, until wheat berries are tender.

- Remove bay leaf. Cover and cook on low for 30–40 minutes longer until soup is hot and blended. You can partially mash some of the root vegetables to thicken the stew if you like.

Roasted Root Vegetable Stew

Toss all the prepared root vegetables with olive oil and spread in a single layer on a large baking sheet. Roast in the oven at 200°C for 15 minutes. Add all vegetables to slow cooker; omit wheat berries. Add stock; cook as directed.

Creamy Root Vegetable Stew

Make recipe as directed. When done, remove bay leaf and purée vegetables using an immersion blender or potato masher. Add 120 ml single cream with 115 g grated Cheddar cheese tossed with 1 tablespoon cornflour. Cover and cook on high 20–30 minutes longer.

Prepare Wheat Berries

Layer in Slow Cooker

- Wheat berries are actually the entire kernel of wheat. The hull has been removed so the wheat will cook.

- They're easy to prepare; just rinse and add to the recipe. Their texture will become nutty while still retaining a little crunch.

- You can find wheat berries in health food stores and some large supermarkets.

- Store them in an airtight container in a cool, dark place; a glass jar is ideal. Label with date of purchase.

- Make sure that the wheat berries are completely covered with liquid in the slow cooker.

- The berries are very nutritious and add a great texture to the soup.

- Peel all the root vegetables, cut out any eyes or soft spots, and cut into cubes of equal size.

- You could use other root vegetables, including swedes and turnips, in this easy stew.

VEGETABLE STEWS

SWEETCORN

Cornmeal and sweetcorn are delicious baked into a soft and moist Southern-style 'spoon bread'

Side dishes are where your slow cooker really shines. No matter what kind of main dish you're planning, you can find a side dish recipe that beautifully complements it and cooks all by itself in your slow cooker.

Most hearty vegetables cook well in the slow cooker, but need to be placed at the bottom of the insert. More tender vegetables such as sweetcorn, peas and mushrooms also work well; however, they should be handled a bit differently.

Corn or maize is a whole grain that is available in many different forms. Frozen sweetcorn is ideal for use in the slow cooker. It retains its texture when cooked from frozen and thaws and cooks perfectly in a relatively short time.

Corn Spoon Bread

Ingredients

Serves 6

3 tablespoons butter

1 onion, chopped

3 cloves garlic, finely chopped

175 g plain flour

115 g yellow cornmeal

1 teaspoon baking powder

4 eggs, beaten

250 ml sour cream

350 g frozen sweetcorn

Salt and pepper

- In small pan, melt butter on medium heat. Add onion and garlic; cook until tender, about 6 minutes.

- Season with salt and pepper and set aside. In large bowl, combine flour, cornmeal and baking powder; mix well.

- Add eggs and sour cream; stir until combined. Fold in onion mixture and frozen sweetcorn.

- Pour into greased 3-litre slow cooker. Partially cover and cook on high 2–3 hours until knife inserted in centre comes out clean. Spoon from slow cooker to serve.

Scalloped Corn

Cook 1 chopped onion in 50 g butter. Add 675 g frozen sweetcorn; remove from heat. Add 1 chopped red pepper, 250 ml sour cream, 2 beaten eggs, 1 teaspoon dried thyme, 3 tablespoons plain flour, 50 g cornmeal and 25 g cracker crumbs. Cover and cook on high 2–3 hours.

Creamed Corn

Cook 1 chopped onion and 1 clove finely chopped garlic in 3 tablespoons butter. Add 225 g cream cheese, cubed, 500 ml white sauce, 1 kg frozen sweetcorn and 115 g grated Cheddar cheese. Place in 4.5-litre slow cooker; cook on low 3 hours, stirring twice.

Make Batter

Fold in Sweetcorn

- It's important to cook the onion and garlic before adding to the batter because it won't cook surrounded by batter.

- Stir the dry ingredients together using a wire whisk, then beat in the eggs and sour cream.

- Don't make the batter ahead of time; the baking powder will react with the liquid too soon.

- You can add other vegetables to this mixture. Precook mushrooms until brown, or add chopped, seeded tomatoes.

- You can use thawed frozen sweetcorn in this recipe, just drain it before adding it to the batter; you don't want to add too much water.

- You can use fresh corn cut off the cob instead of the frozen corn if you like.

- Husk the corn and stick one end in the hole in the middle of a ring mould. Cut down the cob: the kernels will fall into the cake tin. Then scrape the cob with your knife to remove any bits of corn.

- Serve this recipe hot from the slow cooker.

VEGETABLE SIDES

157

CARROTS

Carrots become sweet and tender when cooked in the slow cooker

Nearly everyone loves carrots, and both regular carrots and baby carrots cook very well in the slow cooker. These root vegetables become tender and sweet when cooked for a longer period of time.

When using large carrots, peel them first. Use a swivel-bladed vegetable peeler and remove all the dull skin. Then cut off the tips and slice the carrot into 1-cm slices.

Baby carrots don't need any special preparation once they've been cleaned; just pour them straight into the slow cooker, add the other ingredients and turn it on.

It's fun to cook carrots using lots of different foods and flavours. They can be sweet, savoury, sweet-and-sour or hot and spicy. Use your imagination to create your own special recipes.

Ingredients

Serves 6

2 tablespoons butter

1 onion, chopped

3 cloves garlic, finely chopped

8 large carrots, sliced

1 (225-g) can crushed pineapple, undrained

3 tablespoons tomato purée

120 ml water

75 g sugar

75 ml cider vinegar

1 tablespoon mustard

Salt and pepper

Sweet and Sour Carrots

- In small pan, melt butter and cook onion and garlic until tender, about 6 minutes.

- Add carrots and pineapple and transfer to 3-litre slow cooker.

- Add tomato purée and water to saucepan; cook and stir until blended and pour into slow cooker. Stir in remaining ingredients.

- Cover and cook on low for 6–7 hours, or until carrots are tender. Serve hot or cold.

Honey Glazed Carrots

Make recipe as directed, but increase butter to 3 tablespoons and omit pineapple, tomato purée, sugar, vinegar and mustard. Add 75 ml honey; reduce water to 120 ml. Cook as directed. During last 30 minutes, cook on high with lid off to glaze carrots.

Spicy Baby Carrots

Make recipe as directed, but use 900 g baby carrots instead of the large carrots. Omit pineapple, tomato purée, sugar and vinegar. Add 2 finely chopped jalapeño peppers with the onions. Reduce water to 120 ml; add 120 ml salsa; cook as directed.

Prepare Vegetables

- When buying carrots, look for a bright orange colour and firm texture. The carrots should feel heavy for their size.

- There shouldn't be any soft or brown spots on the carrots, or scars or tough areas.

- If you're buying new season carrots with leaves attached, the leaves should not be wilted.

- Carrot leaves are edible; wash them, chop and stir into the dish at the end, or use in salads.

Add Tomato Purée

- The tomato purée adds a rich flavour, some pretty colour and lots of goodness to this already nutritious dish.

- If you choose to use baby carrots, just rinse them well and drain them, then add to the slow cooker.

- To make this recipe simpler, use a bottled sweet and sour sauce instead of the tomato purée and other ingredients.

VEGETABLE SIDES

BEETROOT
Beetroot takes on a new twist in the slow cooker

Many people look askance at beetroot. But it is a delicious vegetable, with a rich, earthy and sweet taste. Preparing it can seem challenging, but it's easy.

There are three kinds of beet: sugar beet, which is used to make granulated sugar, fodder beet, which is used as animal food, and the beautiful red beetroot we eat. The general rule is that the smaller the beetroot, the sweeter it will be. Large beetroots take longer to cook, and always need to be peeled before use. Baby beetroots are tender, with a thinner skin, so they are just scrubbed before using.

You can make a beetroot dish or just cook the roots in the slow cooker for use in salads and other recipes.

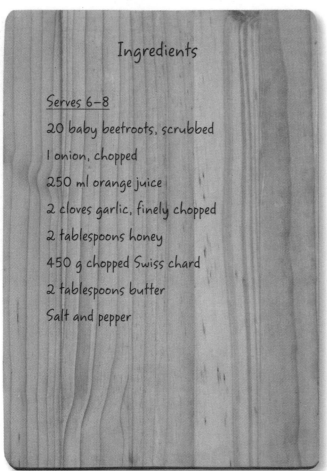

Ingredients

Serves 6–8

20 baby beetroots, scrubbed

1 onion, chopped

250 ml orange juice

2 cloves garlic, finely chopped

2 tablespoons honey

450 g chopped Swiss chard

2 tablespoons butter

Salt and pepper

Beetroot with Swiss Chard

- Scrub the baby beetroot and cut off any rough spots with knife; no need to peel.

- Combine in 3- or 3.5-litre slow cooker with onion, orange juice, garlic, honey, salt and pepper.

- Cover and cook on low for 6–7 hours or until beetroot

is almost tender. Add chard and butter.

- Cover and cook on low for 1–2 hours longer or until beetroot and chard are tender. Serve.

There are many varieties of beetroot. If all you've ever seen are the deep red globes, look for cylindrical varieties, pink globe beetroot with bullseye rings of pink and white; white beets, which are very mild; and golden beets, which are a beautiful gold colour and are mildly sweet.

Harvard Beetroot
This classic sweet and sour recipe is very simple. Peel 5 large beetroots and cut into 1-cm slices. Place in 3.5-litre slow cooker. In bowl, combine 75 g sugar, 1 tablespoon plain flour, 1 tablespoon cornflour, 75 ml vinegar, 50 ml water, salt and pepper; pour over beetroot. Cover; cook on low 8–9 hours.

Scrub Beetroot

- Scrub beetroot using a vegetable brush. Cut off and reserve the greens, if attached.

- If the beetroot comes with green tops, you can wash and chop them and add along with the chard.

- Look at the beetroot carefully; if there are any soft spots or bruises, cut them out. Baby beetroot shouldn't need peeling.

- You could leave out the onion and garlic if you like; just add more beetroot.

Swiss Chard

- Swiss chard is sometimes known as the 'bottomless beet' because it looks so much like beetroot greens.

- Chard, like many dark sturdy greens, tastes better after frost has hit the garden. It's often one of the last harvested vegetables.

- To prepare, immerse the greens in a sink full of cool water to remove all the grit.

- Shake off excess water and coarsely chop the chard. You can prepare it ahead of time.

VEGETABLE SIDES

CLASSIC STUFFING

For festive meals, make stuffing in your slow cooker

Well, technically this bread and vegetable mixture is not stuffing as it's cooked separately in the oven or slow cooker rather than inside a turkey or other bird.

Whatever you call it, this is a delicious and easy way to prepare this popular side dish. And since there's never enough stuffing, double your recipe and cook part in the bird and part in the slow cooker.

If you have a favourite stuffing recipe, convert it to the slow cooker. Just reduce the liquid by half, make sure any meat you add is fully cooked first, and fill the slow cooker one-half to three-quarters full. Cook for at least 6 hours on low.

Classic Bread Stuffing

Ingredients

Serves 8–10

6 slices oatmeal bread

6 slices whole-wheat bread

2 onions, chopped

2 cloves garlic, finely chopped

225 g mushrooms, sliced

115 g butter

3 sticks celery, chopped

2 eggs, beaten

250 ml chicken or vegetable stock

1 teaspoon dried thyme

1 teaspoon paprika

1/2 teaspoon dried sage

15 g chopped parsley

Salt and pepper

- Lightly toast the bread – not to brown it, but so it is slightly dry. Cut into cubes.

- Cook onion, garlic and mushrooms in butter in medium pan until tender.

- Combine onion mixture in 3.5-litre slow cooker with bread and celery. Mix eggs, chicken stock and all seasonings in bowl; pour into slow cooker.

- Stir gently so that bread absorbs flavourings evenly. Cover and cook on low for 6–8 hours, stirring once during cooking, until stuffing is hot and blended.

Not only is it easier to cook your stuffing in the slow cooker, but it is safer too. When stuffing made with eggs or meat is cooked inside a bird, it's difficult to make sure that the stuffing cooks thoroughly all the way through, and it can slow the cooking of the bird.

Sage Stuffing
Prepare as directed, but increase garlic to 4 cloves. Use chestnut mushrooms in place of button mushrooms. Omit thyme and paprika and use 1 teaspoon dried sage and 2 tablespoons chopped fresh sage. Cook as directed.

Prepare Ingredients

- The slow cooker is almost as moist as the inside of a turkey. No evaporation takes place.

- So don't make the stuffing too wet. The vegetables will release liquid into the bread mixture.

- The bread is toasted to remove moisture so it will absorb the flavours in the recipe.

- Beat the egg and stock mixture well so it will evenly coat the bread and the vegetables. Use your favourite herbs and vegetables.

Toss Ingredients

- Toss the bread mixture as you add the egg mixture. Toss gently but thoroughly so all the food is coated.

- There shouldn't be any standing liquid in the bottom of the slow cooker; the stuffing should absorb it all.

- For lightly toasted edges, first cook on high for 1 hour, then reduce heat to low and cook 5–6 hours.

- If you like, add 350 g cooked and drained pork sausagemeat to the mixture with the bread.

VEGETABLE SIDES

ROOT VEGETABLES

These vegetables become tender and sweet in the slow cooker

Root vegetables and the slow cooker were made for each other. All root vegetables cook well using low heat, a moist environment, and long cooking time.

These vegetables contain lots of natural sugars. The roots are storage systems for the plant, and they store the plant's energy as sugar. As the vegetables cook, the sugars become more prominent, concentrate and develop.

Vary the choice of vegetables, using sweet potatoes, turnips, swedes, carrots and other types of potatoes. They can all be cooked in the same way. You can also use hard winter squash such as butternut and acorn.

You can also season the vegetables with herbs, hot peppers, salsa or cheeses. Serve with roasted or grilled meats, casseroles or as a vegetarian main dish.

Ingredients

Serves 6–8

1 onion, chopped

3 cloves garlic, finely chopped

3 carrots, cut into chunks

1 parsnip, peeled and cubed

1 turnip, peeled and cubed

2 sweet potatoes, peeled and cubed

3 potatoes, peeled and cubed

120 ml water

50 ml honey

2 tablespoons brown sugar

2 tablespoons butter

1 tablespoon cornflour

Salt and pepper

Glazed Root Vegetables

- Combine onion, garlic, carrots, parsnip, turnip, sweet potatoes and potatoes in 3.5- or 4.5-litre slow cooker.

- Add water, season with salt and pepper and stir. Cover and cook on low for 7–9 hours, or until vegetables are tender.

- In bowl, combine honey, brown sugar, butter and cornflour and mix well. Pour into slow cooker.

- Cover and cook on high for 45–60 minutes or until vegetables are glazed and tender.

Moroccan Tagine
Make recipe as directed, but add 1 teaspoon turmeric, 1 teaspoon cinnamon, ¼ teaspoon cayenne pepper and 1 teaspoon cumin. Add 150 g sultanas and 115 g currants. Omit honey and brown sugar. Sprinkle finished dish with chopped parsley and coriander.

Apple Root Vegetables
Make recipe as directed, but use 250 ml apple juice instead of 120 ml water. Add 120 ml apple sauce with the apple juice. Omit brown sugar; add 1 teaspoon dried thyme and 1 teaspoon dried marjoram.

Prepare Vegetables

Pour Glaze Over

- When you choose root vegetables, look for firm produce with no soft or wet spots.

- The vegetables should feel heavy and solid. They will look 'rough', especially the swede and parsnip: that's not a problem.

- Peel them until you get to the moist interior. Discard the peel or use it in your compost heap.

- Cut all the vegetables to the same size so they cook evenly. Fill the slow cooker ¾ full.

- You can flavour the glaze any way you like. Use the basic ingredients: honey, butter and cornflour.

- Then add heat with jalapeño or habañero chillies, or with chilli powder or ground chillies.

- Double the glaze for a richer stew, or flavour it with cinnamon, allspice, nutmeg and cardamom.

- You can make the glaze ahead of time; cover it and store in the refrigerator. Stir before adding to the food.

VEGETABLE SIDES

UPDATED STUFFING
Use unusual ingredients for a new twist on stuffing

One of the fun things about stuffing is that it's such an adaptable recipe. You can use just about any ingredient, as long as you include some kind of bread, some vegetables or fruit, and liquid to moisten.

There are many delicious and different recipes for stuffing in cookbooks and online. Try using unusual breads, like challah, cornbread, muffins or flatbread.

Use meats and seafood such as sausage, bacon, oysters, prawns or offal. Make sure the meats are fully cooked before adding to the stuffing.

The fruit and vegetable combinations you can use are limitless. Fresh fruits, dried fruits, dried mushrooms and all vegetables are fair game. Dried and fresh herbs provide additional flavour.

Ingredients

Serves 8–10

2 onions, chopped

2 tablespoons butter

2 Granny Smith apples, peeled and chopped

1 batch cornbread, cubed (see opposite)

50 g dried cranberries

50 g fresh cranberries, cut in half

75 g sultanas

75 g butter

1 cup chicken stock

1 teaspoon dried thyme

Salt and pepper

Onion and Cranberry Stuffing

- Cook onions in 2 tablespoons butter until tender, about 6 minutes. Remove to large bowl. Add apples and toss.

- Add cornbread, dried and fresh cranberries and sultanas; toss gently.

- Melt butter in small pan. Stir in stock and thyme, season with salt and pepper and drizzle over stuffing; toss lightly.

- Place in 3.5- or 4.5-litre slow cooker. Cover and cook on low for 6–8 hours, stirring once during cooking time, until stuffing is hot.

Cornbread

Combine 115 g cornmeal, 115 g flour, ½ teaspoon salt, ½ teaspoon baking soda, 50 g sugar. Cut in 75 g butter. Stir in 2 eggs, 50 ml double cream and 150 ml buttermilk; spread in greased 22-cm tin. Bake at 190°C for 35–40 minutes until skewer inserted in centre comes out clean. Cool.

Pumpkin Stuffing

Crumble 8 pumpkin muffins. Add the onion and apple mixture; add 2 crushed garlic cloves. Omit fresh and dried cranberries; add 100 g dried cherries and 120 ml apple sauce. Make butter mixture as directed; cook as directed.

Precook Vegetables

- Because there is so much food in the slow cooker, and the mixture is fairly dense, the vegetables won't cook through.

- They have to be sautéed, baked, or microwaved before being added to the bread mixture.

- This is an opportunity to add more flavour, too; let the onions caramelize, or add peppers or chillies.

- Fruits such as apples and pears will soften in the slow cooker without precooking.

Mix Ingredients

- The gentle, low heat cooks the stuffing without drying it out, and blends the flavours.

- At the end of cooking time, taste the stuffing. If it needs more moisture, add more butter or chicken stock.

- If it is wet or mushy, turn the heat to high and cook for 30–40 minutes with the lid off.

- If you're making this for a festive meal, you can keep the stuffing warm on low for 1–2 hours after it's done.

VEGETABLE SIDES

BAKED BEANS
Classic baked beans are easily made in the slow cooker

Beans are native to the Americas, and this is among the most traditional of American recipes. It is very inexpensive, easy to make, and has to cook for a long time. The slow cooker is the perfect way to make it.

In New England, the home of baked beans, they are served with brown bread. Not only is this traditional, it also makes a meal with complete protein. Beans eaten with grains provide all the amino acids your body needs. And the combination tastes wonderful.

You can make your beans vegetarian, with no meat, or start by cooking bacon or salt pork until crisp; add the meat to the beans at the end of cooking time.

Serve slow-cooked baked beans as a side dish or a vegetarian main dish.

Ingredients

Serves 6–8

450 g dried haricot beans

2 onions, chopped

4 cloves garlic, finely chopped

3 tablespoons butter

1.5 litres water

75 g brown sugar

50 ml maple syrup

2 tablespoons molasses

2 tablespoons Dijon mustard

75 g chopped smoked back bacon, if desired

250 ml tomato ketchup

120 ml chilli sauce

3 tablespoons tomato purée

Salt and pepper

Rich Baked Beans

- Pick over the beans to remove extraneous material, rinse and drain. Place in large saucepan; cover with water and soak overnight.

- Next day, cook onion and garlic in butter for 4–5 minutes. Add to 3.5-litre slow cooker with beans and water.

- Cover; cook on low for 8–9 hours until beans are almost tender. Drain, reserving liquid.

- Stir in remaining ingredients, including enough liquid to make everything moist, cover and cook on high for 1–2 hours; stir well and serve.

Brown Soda Bread
Mix 225 g whole-wheat flour, 50 g flour, 50 g cornmeal, 50 g brown sugar, 1 teaspoon bicarbonate of soda and ¼ teaspoon salt. Add 1 egg, 250 g molasses, 250 ml buttermilk and 120 ml water; mix. Stir in 150 g raisins. Bake in 2 greased 12.5 x 7.5-cm loaf tins at 180°C for 40–45 minutes.

Bacon Baked Beans
Make recipe as directed, but when ready to cook, fry 225 g smoked streaky bacon until crisp. Drain, crumble and refrigerate. Drain fat from pan, but don't wipe out. Add butter to pan; cook onions and garlic 4–5 minutes. Omit back bacon. Cook as directed; stir in bacon with tomato ketchup.

Soak Beans

- Most beans you buy nowadays are fairly clean. They used to be full of dirt, twigs and leaves.

- Modern harvesting and cleaning methods have reduced that material. Still, it's a good idea to pick over the beans.

- Remove any beans that feel very light or are broken, shrivelled or wrinkled.

- As a shortcut, you can boil the beans 2 minutes, then leave to stand 2 hours instead of soaking overnight.

Stir in Acidic Ingredients

- Salt and acidic ingredients will prevent the beans from becoming tender.

- These ingredients should be added at the end of cooking time, when the beans are almost soft.

- If you live in an area that has hard water, add a pinch

of bicarbonate of soda to the soaking water; this will compensate for the low pH of the water.

- And if you have very hard water, use bottled water to cook the beans. Or add another pinch of bicarbonate of soda.

BEANS & GRAINS

169

QUINOA PILAF
This ancient seed is nutty and delicious when slow cooked

When you say 'pilaf', most people think of rice. But a pilaf can be made from any grain. Quinoa, that ancient seed that has recently come back into popularity, makes an excellent pilaf cooked in the slow cooker.

Quinoa is known as a super grain, even though it's a seed. It provides complete protein: it contains every amino acid your body needs for good health. It's also gluten-free, so is a great choice for those who can't eat wheat. Quinoa has a nutty, mild flavour with a tender inside and slightly crunchy exterior. It pairs well with just about any vegetable. Use your favourite combination, or make a classic pilaf with just the quinoa, onions and garlic.

Ingredients

Serves 6

350 g quinoa, rinsed

1 onion, chopped

2 cloves garlic, finely chopped

2 tablespoons butter

500 ml vegetable stock

500 ml water

1 teaspoon dried marjoram

1 (425-g) can chickpeas, drained

15 g chopped flat-leaf parsley

2 tablespoons chopped coriander

Salt and pepper

Quinoa Pilaf

- Rinse quinoa very well to remove bitter coating. Place in 3.5-litre slow cooker.

- Cook onion and garlic in butter until tender; add to slow cooker along with stock, water, marjoram and chickpeas; season with salt and pepper.

- Cover and cook on low for 2–3 hours or until quinoa is tender.

- Stir in parsley and coriander; cover and cook on low for 20–30 minutes. Stir again and serve.

Spicy Quinoa Pilaf

Make recipe as directed, but add 1 finely chopped jalapeño and 1 chopped poblano chilli with the onions and garlic. Omit marjoram, chickpeas and parsley. Add 1 chopped red pepper and 250 ml salsa to the slow cooker. And increase coriander to 15 g.

Vegetable Quinoa Pilaf

Make recipe as directed, but cook 225 g mushrooms, sliced, 1 chopped green pepper and 175 g chopped courgettes with onions. Omit chickpeas. Add 1 teaspoon dried thyme with the marjoram. Stir in 40 g Parmesan cheese before serving.

Add Quinoa

- Make sure that the quinoa is thoroughly rinsed before using to remove its bitter coating. Rinse until the water runs clean and doesn't foam.

- For a slightly different texture and flavour, toast the quinoa before adding it to the slow cooker.

- Dry the quinoa in kitchen towels, then add to 1 tablespoon olive oil in a frying pan. Toast for 2–3 minutes over medium heat.

- Then proceed as directed with the recipe. This makes quinoa slightly crunchier.

Stir Quinoa

- Stir the mixture thoroughly, both before cooking and before serving.

- You want to evenly mix the ingredients. They all cook at the same time, so layering isn't necessary.

- Add other vegetables, like carrots, or potatoes. But

since the cooking time is short, make sure they are almost cooked before adding.

- Dice these ingredients and sauté or microwave until almost tender, then add to the slow cooker.

171

BEAN CASSOULET

A vegetable cassoulet is a great side dish or vegetarian main dish

Cassoulet is a complex recipe based on beans, with onions, garlic and usually several types of meat. But this version of the recipe is also delicious, and it's very healthy too; it's made without any meat at all.

Cassoulet is originally from southwest France, and is named after a deep, round pot called a *cassole*, in which the dish is cooked. The recipes can get very complicated, using duck or goose *confit*, sausages, pork and sometimes mutton. The dish has humble origins, having been made by peasants for hundreds of years.

And the dish traditionally uses only haricot beans, although many versions using mixed beans appear in cookbooks.

Serve your cassoulet with a spinach salad and some crisp toasted garlic bread.

Ingredients

Serves 6–8

350 g dried lima beans

350 g dried black beans

2 onions, chopped

4 cloves garlic, finely chopped

2 sticks celery, chopped

450 g baby carrots, cut in half crosswise

750 ml vegetable stock

750 ml water

1 bay leaf

1 teaspoon dried thyme

1 teaspoon dried basil

1 (400-g) can chopped tomatoes

2 tablespoons cornflour

3 tablespoons tomato purée

Salt

Vegetarian Bean Cassoulet

- Pick over beans and rinse; drain and cover with cold water. Soak overnight.

- Next day, drain; place in 3.5-litre slow cooker with onions, garlic, celery, carrots, stock, water, bay leaf, thyme and basil.

- Cover and cook on low for 8–9 hours or until beans are almost tender.

- In small bowl, mix tomatoes, cornflour and tomato purée; season with salt. Stir into slow cooker; cover and cook on high for 45–55 minutes until cassoulet is bubbling. Remove bay leaf, stir and serve.

172

Lima Bean Cassoulet

Make recipe as directed, but use all lima beans. Brown 450 g Toulouse sausage; drain and add to slow cooker along with beans. Omit baby carrots and thyme; add 1 teaspoon oregano. Cook 50 g fresh breadcrumbs in 2 tablespoons butter until crisp; scatter over cassoulet.

Classic Cassoulet

Make recipe as directed, but reduce beans to 175 g each. Add 450 g Toulouse sausage, browned and sliced, and 450 g cubed chicken thigh meat to the slow cooker. Add 120 ml dry red wine with the tomatoes. Cook as directed. Cook 50 g fresh breadcrumbs in 2 tablespoons butter until crisp; scatter over cassoulet.

Pick Over Beans

- Sort the beans well, discarding any that are shrivelled or broken.

- You can boil the beans for 2 minutes, then leave to stand for 2 hours instead of soaking overnight.

- Since most cassoulet is baked in the oven for a long period of time, it develops a crunchy crust.

- This can be approximated in the slow cooker by browning coarse breadcrumbs in butter, then adding just before serving.

Combine Tomato Mixture

- As with all dried bean dishes, add tomatoes and other acidic ingredients such as lemon juice at the end of cooking.

- Acid reacts with proteins in the beans' coating, slowing down the absorption of water.

- The beans will be firm, not soft and tender, even after hours of cooking, if there is too much acid.

- After you add the tomato mixture, the beans can be cooked for 2–3 hours more to develop the flavours; they will not get mushy.

BEANS & GRAINS

BARLEY WHEAT BERRY CASSEROLE
Whole grains such as wheat berries are perfect for the slow cooker

Wheat berries are actually the whole kernel of the grain. Just the hull, or tough outer coating, has been removed, so the berries are very high in fibre and B vitamins.

The wheat grains, with their nutty taste and slightly crunchy texture, are the perfect foil for barley. Barley is also nutty tasting, but it becomes almost creamy when it is cooked for a long time.

These grains mix well with just about any ingredient – from meat to vegetables to fruits to herbs to cheese. Using the same proportions of grains to liquid, you can create many new, delicious and healthy recipes.

Serve this as a side dish for grilled or barbecued meats, or as a main dish with a green salad and some crusty bread or cornbread.

Fruity Barley Wheat Berry Casserole

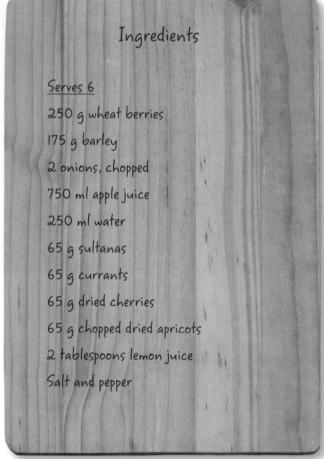

Ingredients

Serves 6

250 g wheat berries

175 g barley

2 onions, chopped

750 ml apple juice

250 ml water

65 g sultanas

65 g currants

65 g dried cherries

65 g chopped dried apricots

2 tablespoons lemon juice

Salt and pepper

- Rinse wheat berries and barley and place in 3.5-litre slow cooker.

- Add all remaining ingredients in order listed, except lemon juice.

- Cover and cook on low for 8–9 hours, or on high for

4–5 hours, until wheat berries and barley are tender and dried fruits are plump.

- Stir in lemon juice; cover and cook on low for 20 minutes. Stir gently and serve.

Wheat Berry Breakfast

Rinse 250 g wheat berries and place in 3-litre slow cooker. Add 250 ml water, 500 ml apple juice, and 250 ml orange juice. Stir in 50 g sugar, 1 teaspoon vanilla extract, 65 g currants and 65 g dried cherries. Cover and cook on low 7–8 hours.

Spicy Wheat Berry Casserole

Prepare recipe as directed, but increase wheat berries to 350 g. Omit barley, apple juice, sultanas, currants, cherries, apricots and lemon juice. Use 1 litre vegetable stock. Add 1 chopped onion, 3 crushed garlic cloves, 2 chopped jalapeño peppers, 1 tablespoon chilli powder and 25 g chopped sun-dried tomatoes in oil.

Combine Ingredients

Add Lemon Juice

- The wheat berries, because they are a whole grain and minimally processed, should be rinsed before using.

- You're just rinsing away the dust left over from processing, plus any dirt or sand.

- You can use any combination of dried fruits; just keep the proportions of wheat and barley to fruit the same.

- If you're cooking on high, stir the mixture once during cooking time so that nothing sticks.

- Stir in the lemon juice at the end to add a pop of flavour. You could also add orange or lime juice.

- As with beans, whole grains cook better when not in a high-acid environment, so the citrus juice is added at the end of cooking time.

- Barley is a high-fibre food. More importantly, it has soluble fibre, which removes cholesterol from your body.

- You should eat whole grains such as barley or wheat berries six times a week.

175

BEANS & GRAINS

ASIAN RICE AND LENTILS

Rice and lentils provide complete protein in a delicious dish

Rice and the slow cooker isn't exactly the ideal combination. It's very easy for white rice to overcook and become mushy.

Brown rice, because it has only the hull removed and still contains the bran and germ, absorbs liquid more slowly, so it does cook well in the slow cooker.

Featuring rice combined with lentils, this dish provides complete protein to the vegetarian. And the flavours and textures are wonderful. Flavour this combination any way you like. Asian flavourings are a natural, but you can also use the flavours of Greece, Mexico, France, Spain or Morocco.

Serve as a side dish with roast chicken, or as a vegetarian main dish with a nice salad.

Ingredients

Serves 6

450 g brown lentils

2 tablespoons butter

1 onion, chopped

2 cloves garlic, finely chopped

1 tablespoon grated fresh ginger

200 g long-grain brown rice

2 tablespoons soy sauce

1 litre vegetable stock

500 ml water

1 tablespoon rice vinegar

Curried Rice and Lentils

- Rinse lentils and place in 3.5-litre slow cooker.

- Melt butter in frying pan and cook onion and garlic for 5 minutes.

- Add ginger and rice; cook and stir for 3–4 minutes longer. Place in slow cooker.

- Add soy sauce, vegetable stock and water. Cover and cook on low for 7–9 hours, until lentils and rice are tender.

- Stir in rice vinegar, fluff mixture with fork, and serve immediately.

Lentils, also known as daal, are a type of pulse. They are legumes, or the fruit of a plant in the family Fabaceae. Other legumes include peas, beans and peanuts. Lentils cook fairly quickly, so don't need the presoaking dried beans do. They are nutty and delicious, and cook well in the slow cooker.

Tex-Mex Rice and Lentils
Make recipe as directed, but add 2 finely chopped jalapeño peppers with the onions and garlic. Omit ginger, soy sauce and rice vinegar. Add 250 ml salsa with the vegetable stock and water. Stir in 115 g grated Pepper Jack or Cheddar cheese at the end of cooking time.

Cook Rice in Frying Pan

Fluff Mixture with Fork

- One way to make rice successfully in the slow cooker is to toast it in a dry pan or in butter or olive oil.

- This firms up the rice coating, which helps delay the absorption of liquid.

- This step also adds a nice nutty taste to the dish, and helps the rice absorb other flavours in the recipe.

- Look for soy sauce with less salt for a milder flavour. Choose regular soy sauce for more flavour.

- Most rice mixtures benefit from fluffing with a fork just before serving.

- This helps distribute the starch so the grains of rice don't stick together. It also introduces air into the mixture.

- You could add lots of vegetables to this dish. If you add mushrooms, cook them with the onions and garlic until tender.

- Or add peppers, sliced green or yellow courgettes or tomatoes. Chop all vegetables to about the same size before adding.

BARLEY MUSHROOM CASSEROLE

This classic combination can be flavoured in so many ways

There's something about the combination of barley with mushrooms that's very satisfying. The nutty barley, which is still slightly chewy even after hours of cooking, blends well with the earthy, sweet tenderness of mushrooms.

This dish can be served as a vegetarian main dish, perhaps with a salad and some bread, or as a side dish with roast chicken or a piece of beef cooked on the barbecue.

Take some time to browse through your supermarket's produce aisle to look at what's new. Ingredients that were difficult to find even five years ago, such as shiitake or morel mushrooms, are now available almost everywhere. Use your favourite mushrooms and herbs in this easy dish.

Ingredients

Serves 6

175 g barley

2 tablespoons butter

225 g chestnut mushrooms, sliced

225 g shiitake mushrooms, sliced

1 onion, chopped

3 cloves garlic, finely chopped

500 ml vegetable stock

1 teaspoon dried thyme

Pinch of white pepper

15 g chopped parsley

Barley Mushroom Casserole

- Place barley in 3.5-litre slow cooker.

- Melt butter in large frying pan. Add mushrooms; cook and stir 4–5 minutes. Remove to slow cooker.

- Add onion and garlic to pan; cook and stir 4 minutes. Add to slow cooker.

- Add stock, thyme and pepper. Cover and cook on low for 4–6 hours, until barley is tender.

- Fluff with fork, top with chopped parsley, and serve.

Barley Risotto
Cook 1 chopped onion and 3 garlic cloves in 2 tablespoons butter. Add to 3.5-litre slow cooker with 175 g each pearl barley and grated carrots and 75 g chopped mushrooms. Add 750 ml vegetable stock. Cook on high 2–3 hours, stirring twice, until thick. Stir in 40 g Parmesan cheese.

Barley Vegetable Casserole
Make recipe as directed, but add 1 chopped green pepper, 1 chopped red pepper, and 175 g chopped courgettes. Omit shiitake mushrooms. Add 175 g diced carrots. Cook recipe as directed, but stir in 40 g grated pecorino cheese before serving.

Prepare Mushrooms

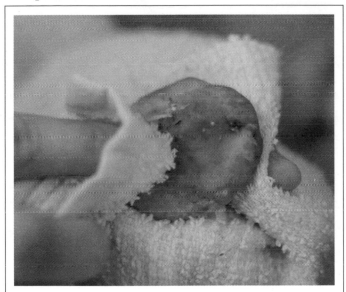

Combine Ingredients

- To prepare mushrooms, wipe with a damp cloth. Don't immerse them in water or they will get tough.

- The mushrooms may also absorb water during washing, which will make the dish too runny.

- Don't worry about the dirt on mushrooms; it's sterilized dirt. Just brush it off or gently wipe.

- Fresh mushrooms have a lot of water, which they release during cooking, so they must be browned before adding to slow cooker recipes.

- You could use any type of stock. For a heartier dish, use beef stock.

- Other herbs that would be delicious in this recipe include basil, rosemary, sage or marjoram. Those herbs complement the earthy flavour of the mushrooms and the mildness of the barley.

- For a heartier dish, stir in 50–100 g grated cheese just before serving. Leave to stand 5 minutes and serve.

BEANS & GRAINS

RISOTTO

The classic Italian dish is made with ease in the slow cooker

Risotto seems like a simple dish, and it's easy to make, but it takes patience and you have to follow some rules to make a true risotto in the usual way.

The rice you use is important. Look for Arborio rice, which is a short-grain rice from Italy. This rice is high in the starch amylopectin, which is a branched molecule that makes the liquid creamy when it's released from the grain.

The rice is usually stirred constantly when making risotto in a pan over heat. This disturbs the outer coating of the rice, letting the grains release more starch. This is where the slow cooker shines: the longer cooking time eliminates the need for constant stirring.

At the end, leave the risotto to stand with the heat off for 5 minutes to thicken a little and finish cooking. Then enjoy!

Ingredients

Serves 6

I onion, finely chopped

2 cloves garlic, finely chopped

2 tablespoons olive oil

350 g Arborio rice

1.2 litres chicken stock

120 ml dry white wine

2 tablespoons butter

40 g grated Parmesan cheese

Salt and pepper

Classic Risotto

- Cook onion and garlic in olive oil until tender. Add rice; cook and stir for 4 minutes. Place in 3- or 3.5-litre slow cooker.

- Add stock and wine and season with salt and pepper. Cover and cook on high for 2–3 hours, until rice is tender, stirring once.

- Add the butter and cheese. Turn off slow cooker and leave to stand for 5 minutes.

- Uncover, stir risotto. If it is runny, leave it to stand uncovered for 10 minutes, then stir again and serve.

· · · · · · · · · RECIPE VARIATIONS · · · · · · · · ·

Vegetable Risotto
Make recipe as directed, but add 2 thinly sliced carrots and 1 red pepper to olive oil; cook with onions. Use 1 litre vegetable stock in place of the chicken stock. Add 1 teaspoon dried thyme with the rice. Cook as directed; add 50 g baby spinach leaves with butter.

Spicy Risotto
Make recipe as directed, but add 2 finely chopped jalapeño peppers with the onions and garlic. Add 1 tablespoon chilli powder, 1 finely chopped chipotle chilli, and 1 tablespoon chilli sauce with the stock. Increase Parmesan cheese to 75 g.

Toss Rice with Olive Oil

- The rice needs to be cooked with the olive oil to slow down the cooking process slightly.

- This step also enhances the flavour of the rice, adds a nutty touch to the dish, and helps incorporate the onion and garlic flavours.

- During the long cooking time (regular risotto takes about 30 minutes to cook) the rice releases lots of starch.

- This naturally thickens the risotto. Stirring the rice once during cooking time helps this process along.

Add Butter and Cheese

- Butter and cheese stirred in at the end is a classic finish for risotto.

- It adds creaminess and more flavour to the dish. Don't substitute margarine; the butter flavour is essential.

- Parmesan cheese is the classic finish to risotto. You could also use pecorino or Asiago cheese for a bit more flavour.

- At this point you could also stir in fresh herbs. A tablespoon of fresh thyme is traditional.

RICE PILAF

Rice pilaf is the perfect side dish for many meat dishes

Rice pilaf can be as simple as cooked rice mixed with some cheese, or it can be complicated, with lots of vegetables, a white sauce and herbs.

This classic dish is easy to dress up for a special occasion. And with a little help, it cooks beautifully in the slow cooker. Use brown rice, season the mixture well, and add your favourite vegetables and fruits for perfect results.

Rice is one of those staple foods that blend well with the flavours and ingredients from every cuisine. And it's used in most of the world's cuisines. It's an inexpensive grain that can be healthy when you choose brown, red or wild varieties. Enjoy these easy recipes.

Ingredients

Serves 6

2 links chorizo sausage, chopped

1 tablespoon olive oil

2 tablespoons butter

1 onion, chopped

3 cloves garlic, finely chopped

400 g long-grain brown rice

120 ml tomato juice

1 red pepper, chopped

3 sticks celery, chopped

4 plum tomatoes, chopped

850 ml chicken or vegetable stock

1 bay leaf

1 teaspoon dried thyme

1/2 teaspoon dried oregano

1/4 teaspoon pepper

Creole Rice Pilaf

- Cook chorizo in frying pan until done. Remove and drain. Pour off fat from pan, but do not wipe out.

- Add olive oil and butter to pan. Cook onion and garlic for 4 minutes. Add rice; cook for 3 minutes.

- Add tomato juice and bring to a simmer, stirring to deglaze pan. Place in 3.5-litre slow cooker along with all remaining ingredients.

- Cover and cook on low for 5–7 hours or until rice is tender, stirring once during cooking time. Remove bay leaf and serve.

• • • RECIPE VARIATIONS • • •

Creamy Rice Pilaf
Prepare recipe as directed, but add 250 ml white sauce to the slow cooker. Omit chorizo, tomato juice, plum tomatoes, oregano and bay leaf. Add 1 teaspoon dried basil. Stir in 115 g grated Emmental cheese at the end of the cooking time.

Fruited Rice Pilaf
Make recipe as directed, but use apple juice in place of the chicken or vegetable stock. Omit chorizo, tomato juice, pepper, tomatoes, bay leaf and oregano. Add 115 g currants, 75 g raisins, 75 g cherries and 75 g cranberries. Add 1/2 teaspoon salt with the pepper; cook as directed.

Cook Vegetables

- Onion and garlic almost always need to be fully cooked until tender before adding to rice mixtures.

- The low heat required for cooking rice just won't cook these foods through and they'll be too harsh tasting.

- Softer vegetables like peppers, mushrooms, courgettes and celery will cook well without sautéing.

- In fact, in rice pilaf mixtures these vegetables will still retain a bit of crunch, lending nice texture to the dish.

Stir Pilaf

- It's important that all the food in a pilaf cooks evenly and at the same time.

- You do need to stir the pilaf just once in the slow cooker. Do it quickly, so you lose as little heat as possible.

- Stirring also makes sure that there aren't any clumps of undercooked or overcooked rice in the pilaf.

- When the pilaf is done, you can keep it warm for 1–2 hours until the rest of dinner is ready.

183

MIXED RICE PILAF
Different types of rice make a flavourful and interesting pilaf

Mixing rice together in a pilaf creates an interesting dish with lots of flavour, colour and texture. If you really look at the different varieties of rice, you'll be amazed at the quantity and range available.

There are more than 40,000 varieties of rice cultivated in the world. These include pecan rice, red rice, jasmine rice, black rice, glutinous rice and baby basmati rice. All of them have distinctive textures, colours and flavours, and many different types are widely available.

When you make a mixed rice pilaf, choose different varieties of rice that will cook in about the same time. If you want to use two kinds of rice with different cooking times, just parboil the longer-cooking variety, then combine everything in the slow cooker.

Ingredients

Serves 6

1 tablespoon olive oil

2 tablespoons butter

1 onion, chopped

2 cloves garlic, finely chopped

225 g chestnut mushrooms, sliced

1 teaspoon dried thyme

150 g wild rice

175 g long-grain brown rice

900 ml vegetable stock

250 ml white sauce

40 g grated pecorino cheese

15 g chopped parsley

Salt and pepper

Mixed Rice Pilaf

- In large pan, melt olive oil and butter; cook onion, garlic and mushrooms until tender, about 6–7 minutes.

- Add thyme and both types of rice; season with salt and pepper. Cook and stir for 4 minutes. Pour into 3.5-litre slow cooker.

- Add stock; stir, then cover and cook on low for 5–6 hours until rice is almost tender. Stir in white sauce.

- Cover and cook on low for 1–2 hours longer until rice is tender. Stir in cheese and parsley and serve.

WILD RICE

• • • • RECIPE VARIATION • • • •

Tex-Mex Rice Pilaf
Make recipe as directed, but add 1 finely chopped habañero chilli to the onion mixture. Add 3 chopped garlic cloves and use brown basmati rice in place of the long-grain brown rice. Omit white sauce; use 250 ml salsa. Stir in 115 g shredded Pepper Jack or Cheddar cheese at end of cooking.

ZOOM

Pilaf, also known as pilau or pulao, is defined as a recipe in which rice or wheat is browned in oil first, then cooked in broth or stock. This dish is served often in Middle Eastern, Latin American and Caribbean cuisines. It was invented in the Persian Empire hundreds of years ago.

Sauté Vegetables

Stir in White Sauce

- Make sure that you stir almost constantly when cooking the rice. You don't want it to burn; just toast.

- Try different types of onions and mushrooms in this dish. Spring onions make a nice change of pace, as do sweet red onions.

- There are lots of varieties of fresh and dried mushrooms on the market, such as shiitake and morel.

- Soak dried mushrooms in hot water, then cut off the stems, chop and add to the pilaf for intense flavour.

- The white sauce adds a creamy texture to this dish as it envelops the rice and vegetables.

- You can substitute a bottled creamy pasta sauce if you wish.

- The cheese adds great flavour and even more creaminess to the pilaf. Grate it just before adding to the slow cooker so it doesn't dry out.

WILD RICE CASSEROLE

Wild rice becomes tender and nutty cooked in the slow cooker

Wild rice is not really rice at all, but the seed of a water grass, *Zizania aquatica*, that is native to North America. Traditionally, the rice was harvested by Native Americans as they glided through reedy lakes in their canoes.

One species, northern wild rice, is the state grain of Minnesota, where you can still find it harvested in the traditional way. Much of the USA's wild rice is now grown on

farms, but nothing compares to the flavour and texture of wild rice harvested by hand. Once harvested, it must be cured by parching in a fire or high heat.

The texture of wild rice is quite chewy. It can be cooked to either of two end points: chewy but tender, or popped. Popped rice has literally exploded, and is very tender.

Enjoy these easy recipes for wild rice.

Ingredients

Serves 6–8

2 tablespoons butter

2 shallots, finely chopped

300 g wild rice

1 teaspoon salt

1 teaspoon dried thyme

500 ml pineapple juice

250 ml apple juice

250 ml pear juice

65 g sultanas

65 g dried cherries

65 g dried cranberries

115 g chopped dried apricots

50 g slivered almonds

Fruity Wild Rice Casserole

- In small frying pan, melt butter; cook shallots until tender, about 4 minutes.

- Combine all ingredients except almonds in 3.5-litre slow cooker. Stir, cover, and cook on low for 6–8 hours until rice is tender.

- Toast the almonds in a small pan over low heat until they are fragrant and light brown.

- Stir almonds into pilaf and serve immediately.

• • • • • • • • • • • • • • • • RECIPE VARIATIONS • • • • • • • • • • • • • • • •

Vegetable Wild Rice Casserole
Make recipe as directed, but cook 1 chopped onion and 3 cloves garlic in butter. Use 1 litre vegetable stock in place of the fruit juices. Omit shallots, sultanas, cherries, cranberries, apricots and almonds. Add 1 chopped red pepper and 225 g sliced mushrooms.

North Woods Wild Rice Casserole
Make recipe as directed, but add 150 g button mushrooms and 50 g dried, reconstituted morel mushrooms, chopped, to the shallot mixture. Add 2 finely chopped garlic cloves. Use vegetable stock in place of the fruit juices; omit all dried fruit. Omit almonds; add 115 g grated Havarti cheese.

Stir Ingredients

Toast Almonds

- Make sure that the wild rice is completely covered with liquid in the slow cooker. You may need to add more.

- It's important to stir the ingredients in the slow cooker once during the cooking time.

- If you cook the casserole for 8–10 hours, the wild rice may pop. It will curl up and become very tender.

- The dish can be kept hot on the keep-warm setting for 1–2 hours after it's finished cooking.

- To toast almonds or any nuts, place them in a single layer in a dry pan.

- Cook over low heat, stirring or tossing the nuts frequently, until they are browned. The nuts will smell fragrant as the oils in the nuts are developed.

- You can also microwave the nuts for 4–5 minutes on high per 100 g.

- Always cool toasted nuts before chopping them, or they can become greasy or mushy.

VEGETABLE RICE PILAF

This delicious recipe could be a vegetarian main dish

The more vegetables the better! Rice and vegetables are a natural combination, and the slow cooker is the ideal appliance in which to cook them. This pilaf can be served as a vegetarian main dish. The combination of rice and lots of vegetables provides complete protein in a delicious package.

Other ingredients add to the texture and flavour of these dishes. Chopped nuts should be stirred in just before serving so they retain their crunch. Fresh herbs add a pop of flavour when added right at the end. And cheese adds an incomparable flavour and creaminess to any pilaf recipe.

Use your favourite ingredients and flavour combinations to create your own special rice pilaf recipe.

Ingredients

Serves 6
2 tablespoons olive oil
1 onion, chopped
3 cloves garlic, finely chopped
1 red pepper, chopped
1 green pepper, chopped
2 teaspoons chilli powder
1 teaspoon paprika
2 cups long-grain brown rice
1 (400-g) can chopped tomatoes
15 g sun-dried tomatoes, chopped
50 g chopped kalamata olives
750 ml vegetable stock
50 g slivered almonds
2 tablespoons butter
75 g grated Manchego cheese
Salt and pepper

Spanish Vegetable Rice Pilaf

- In large frying pan, heat olive oil over medium heat. Add onion and garlic; cook and stir for 4 minutes.

- Place in 3.5-litre slow cooker with all remaining ingredients except almonds, butter and cheese.

- Stir well, then cover and cook on low for 6–8 hours or until rice is tender.

- Cook almonds in butter until light brown. Stir cheese into pilaf, sprinkle with almonds; cover and leave to stand for 5 minutes before serving.

• • • • • RECIPE VARIATION • • • •

Greek Vegetable Rice Pilaf
Make recipe as directed, but add 1 teaspoon dried oregano and 2 tablespoons lemon juice to slow cooker. Omit chilli powder, paprika and almonds. Add 50 g sliced green olives with the kalamata olives, and stir in 75 g feta cheese just before serving.

Sauté Vegetables

- Cook onions and garlic until tender so they become soft and sweet in the pilaf.

- The sun-dried tomatoes to use in this recipe are dried, not packed in oil. They absorb some of the stock as the pilaf cooks.

- The texture of the sun-dried tomatoes will be tender but slightly chewy when the recipe is done.

- The almonds are cooked in butter to add even more flavour. Nuts toasted in butter are rich-tasting and crisp.

Mix Ingredients

- Stir the ingredients in the slow cooker well, both before cooking and after, just before serving.

- It's a good idea to grease the inside of the slow cooker insert before adding ingredients.

- This makes washing up easier, and also prevents the pilaf from sticking to the sides and burning.

- Serve this pilaf as a main dish with a spinach salad, along with breadsticks for crunch.

CHICKEN RISOTTO

Add chicken, and risotto becomes an easy main dish

Risotto is an excellent and elegant side dish, and is made with ease in the slow cooker. Adding meat to this dish turns it into a hearty main dish.

Chicken is the perfect addition to risotto. Its mild taste, velvety texture and low cost turn risotto into an ideal dish to cook when entertaining.

You can use chicken breasts or thighs in this recipe. Cook the breasts whole on top of the risotto; cube the chicken thighs, because they take longer to cook.

Make sure that your chicken stock is nice and rich. If you aren't using homemade stock, chilled fresh stock is a good substitute that adds long-cooked flavour to the recipe.

Serve this risotto with roasted carrots and a salad.

Ingredients

Serves 6

2 tablespoons butter

1 tablespoon olive oil

2 onions, chopped

2 cloves garlic, finely chopped

350 g Arborio rice

1 litre chicken stock

$1/2$ teaspoon saffron or turmeric

1 teaspoon dried oregano

4 boneless, skinless chicken breasts

40 g grated Parmesan cheese

50 g crumbled feta cheese

2 tablespoons lemon juice

Salt and pepper

Greek Chicken Risotto

- In large saucepan, melt butter and olive oil over medium heat. Cook onions and garlic for 5 minutes.

- Place in 3.5-litre slow cooker and add rice, chicken stock, saffron and oregano; season with salt and pepper and mix well.

- Top with chicken breasts. Cover and cook on high for $2^{1}/_{2}$–3 hours until rice is tender and chicken is cooked.

- Remove chicken and cut into cubes. Stir into risotto with cheeses and lemon juice. Cover and cook on high for 10–20 minutes.

190

RECIPE VARIATIONS

Tex-Mex Chicken Risotto
Make recipe as directed, but add 1 (115-g) jar chopped green chillies, drained. Omit saffron and feta cheese. Add 1 tablespoon chilli powder to onion mixture along with 1 chopped green pepper. Stir in 115 g grated Pepper Jack or Cheddar cheese with the Parmesan cheese.

Creamy Chicken Risotto
Make recipe as directed, but add 120 ml double cream with the cubed chicken at the end of cooking time. Omit saffron, oregano, feta and lemon juice; use 1 teaspoon dried thyme. Stir in 115 g grated Gouda cheese and 2 tablespoons butter at end of cooking time.

Cook Onions

Cube Chicken

- For more flavour, you can caramelize the onion and garlic mixture before assembling the risotto.

- Just let it keep cooking in the butter and olive oil mixture. Cook on medium-low heat for 15–25 minutes.

- The onion mixture will start to turn brown. This means that the sugar in the onions is beginning to caramelize.

- The caramelized onions add lots of rich flavour to the risotto. The onions will almost dissolve during the long cooking time.

- While you're cubing the chicken, keep the lid on the risotto so it stays hot.

- If you're using chicken thighs, you can shred them, or just stir them into the rice mixture.

- Immediately stir the chicken back into the

risotto along with the cheeses and lemon juice, so it stays hot.

- This final cooking time allows the starch released by the rice to thicken up a bit so the risotto has the perfect texture.

SALT-ROASTED POTATOES

Salt flavours the potatoes and shields them from heat so they cook to perfection

Potatoes are one of the perfect foods to cook in the slow cooker. And there are lots of ways to do this.

One of the more unusual methods is to cook the potatoes completely buried in coarse salt. This shields the potatoes from the direct heat and the results are spectacular. The flesh becomes buttery and the skin very tender.

This recipe is a great idea for a large party. The potatoes will stay hot in the salt mixture even when the slow cooker is turned off. And you can reuse the salt up to 10 times; just chip it away, leave it to cool, and store.

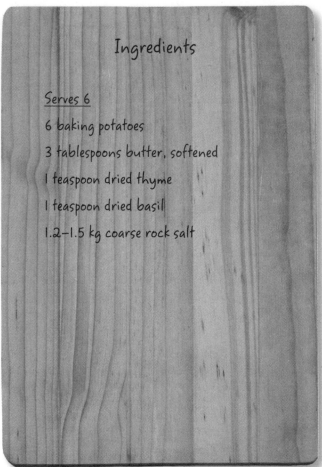

Ingredients

Serves 6

6 baking potatoes

3 tablespoons butter, softened

1 teaspoon dried thyme

1 teaspoon dried basil

1.2–1.5 kg coarse rock salt

Salt-Roasted Potatoes

- Scrub potatoes well, then dry thoroughly.

- Prick the potatoes several times each with a fork. Rub all over with butter, then sprinkle with mixture of thyme and basil; rub in well.

- Pour 500 g salt over the bottom of a 3.5- or 4.5-litre slow cooker; add some of the potatoes.

- Pour more salt in and add remaining potatoes, layering them evenly. Cover with salt. Cover and cook on high for 2–3 hours until potatoes are tender.

· · · · · RECIPE VARIATION · · · · ·

Bacon Roasted Potatoes
Make recipe as directed, but substitute 3 tablespoons bacon fat for the butter. Omit thyme and basil leaves; add a pinch of pepper and 1 teaspoon dried marjoram to the potatoes before layering in the slow cooker.

Layer Salt and Potatoes

- Snuggle the potatoes into the salt. You can add as many potatoes as you can fit into the slow cooker.

- But still keep the ½ to ¾ fill ratio in mind. Make sure the potatoes are completely covered with salt.

- You can use gourmet varieties of salt. Sea salt and grey salt, while more expensive, have more flavour than regular salt.

- You can bake any variety of potato using this method.

Remove Cooked Potatoes

- The potatoes will stay hot in their salt casing, with the slow cooker turned off, until you're ready to serve them.

- These potatoes will be slightly higher in sodium content than regular baked potatoes, but not overly high.

- Break through the crust carefully with a knife and remove potatoes with a large spoon or tongs, keeping them intact.

- Brush off excess salt and serve them with butter, sour cream and chives for an excellent side dish.

SWEET POTATO CASSEROLE
This classic recipe is ideal for the slow cooker

Sweet potatoes are another fabulous food to cook in the slow cooker. They make a great side dish when cooked with lots of sweet and savoury ingredients.

Sweet potatoes are sometimes confused with yams, but they are a completely different species. Yams are natives of Africa and Asia, while sweet potatoes are the tubers of a vine native to tropical South America.

Sweet potatoes are among the most nutritious vegetables on the planet: far more than the ordinary potato. They are rich in complex carbohydrates and fibre, and packed with vitamin A, as evidenced by their deep orange colour. And they're delicious!

Whether your dish is sweet or savoury, sweet potatoes are the perfect side dish.

Ingredients

Serves 6–8

100 g butter

2 onions, chopped

1 tablespoon curry powder

4 sweet potatoes, peeled and cubed

2 tablespoons flour

1 teaspoon salt

250 ml apple juice

120 ml orange juice

65 ml brown sugar

Pinch of grated nutmeg

½ teaspoon cinnamon

2 teaspoons vanilla extract

65 g sultanas

50 g dried cranberries

50 g chopped pecans

115 g granola

Curried Sweet Potato Casserole

- Melt 25 g of the butter in large pan and cook onions until brown, 8 minutes; add curry powder.

- Combine onion mixture and sweet potatoes in 3.5-litre slow cooker. Melt 50 g butter in same pan; cook flour and salt until bubbling.

- Add apple and orange juice; bring to simmering point. Add brown sugar, nutmeg, cinnamon, vanilla, sultanas and cranberries; pour into slow cooker.

- Melt remaining butter and mix in pecans and granola; sprinkle over top. Cover; cook on low 6–8 hours.

Spicy Sweet Potato Casserole

Make recipe as directed, but add 2 finely chopped garlic cloves to onions. Omit cider, orange juice, brown sugar, cinnamon, nutmeg, fruits, nuts and granola. Add 1 chopped red pepper, 1 tablespoon chilli powder, 1 teaspoon cumin, and 115-g jar chopped green chillies. Sprinkle with 50 g crushed tortilla chips just before serving.

Simple Sweet Potato Casserole

Make recipe as directed, but increase sweet potatoes to 6. Omit everything after orange juice. Add 150 g raisins, 115 g brown sugar, 1 teaspoon cinnamon and $1/4$ teaspoon nutmeg. Cook as directed; drizzle with 50 ml maple syrup.

Cook Onions and Curry Powder

Prepare Sweet Potatoes

- Curry powder should always be cooked before eating. The complex of spices has much better flavour when heated.

- Curry powder isn't a spice; it's a combination of up to 20 spices. You can make your own, or experiment with ready-made blends.

- Turmeric or saffron in the curry powder adds a nice yellow colour to the dish.

- Use your favourite dried fruits in this recipe. Try mixed dried fruits, dried cherries, currants or chopped apricots.

- Sweet potatoes look rather rough in their raw state. You need to remove the skin before cooking.

- Use a swivel-bladed vegetable peeler or a sharp paring knife to remove the skin.

- Cut off the ends and remove any eyes or soft spots, then cube the sweet potatoes.

- Choose a granola that's nice and crunchy so it retains some texture after cooking.

NEW POTATOES
Waxy potatoes are delicious cooked with lots of cheese

Waxy new potatoes are usually recommended for use in potato salad. But when cooked in a creamy, cheesy sauce, they become true comfort food.

There are several types of waxy potatoes on the market. Large, waxy red potatoes are ideal for potato salad because they keep their shape when cooked. Tiny new potatoes are also perfect cooked in the slow cooker. They stay whole during the long cooking, but become creamy on the inside and tender outside.

You can add lots of vegetables to these potatoes. Peppers, mushrooms and celery are all good additions. But, like beans, potatoes aren't a good match with tomatoes; the acidity of the tomatoes will keep the potatoes firm, even with hours of slow cooking.

Ingredients

Serves 6

1.3 kg small waxy potatoes

1 onion, chopped

5 cloves garlic, finely chopped

2 tablespoons butter, melted

500 ml white sauce

1 teaspoon dried thyme

75 g cream cheese, cubed

115 g grated Emmental cheese

Salt and pepper

Cheesy Potatoes

- Scrub potatoes. If any are larger than 2.5 cm across, cut them in halves or quarters so all the pieces are about the same size.

- Add to 3.5-litre slow cooker with onion, garlic, butter, white sauce, thyme, salt and pepper; mix.

- Cover and cook on low for 6–8 hours until potatoes are tender. Add cream cheese and partially mash potatoes, leaving some whole.

- Stir in Emmental cheese. Cover and cook on low for 1 hour longer, then stir and serve.

Bacon and Potatoes

Make recipe as directed, but fry 450 g smoked streaky bacon; drain and crumble. Pour off excess fat from pan; add onion and garlic; cook until tender. Omit white sauce and cream cheese. Add bacon to slow cooker with 75 ml vegetable stock. Don't mash potatoes.

Simple Italian Potatoes

Make recipe as directed, using whole baby potatoes. Omit white sauce, cream cheese and Emmental cheese. Add 1 teaspoon dried oregano and 1 teaspoon dried basil to potatoes. Stir in 40 g grated Parmesan cheese at end.

Prepare Potatoes

- New or baby potatoes are delicate, so handle them gently. Rinse them and dry before proceeding.

- They may need just a little scrubbing with a soft vegetable brush under running water.

- Cut off any brown or tough pieces of skin, and any eyes. Then just add to the slow cooker.

- The potatoes should all be around the same size. If some are larger, cut to make the same size.

Mash Potatoes

- To mash potatoes, you can use a potato masher or a mixer.

- Don't use an immersion blender. Like a regular blender or food processor, it will over-process the potatoes and they will become gluey.

- You can mash the potatoes smooth, or leave some whole for a rustic texture. The peels add colour, nutrition and texture.

- Throw in a bunch of fresh herbs at the end for a pop of flavour and colour.

BAKED POTATOES

Potatoes become creamy and silky when cooked in the slow cooker

Technically, these potatoes aren't baked. Baking is a dry-heat cooking method, and the slow cooker is a wet-heat cooking method. Still, the slow cooker turns out potatoes with creamy, velvety flesh and a fabulous flavour, which is the point.

You can just pile potatoes into the slow cooker and cook them as they are. But adding some extra flavouring ingredients is easy and makes the potatoes much more special.

Cut the potatoes in half, slice them thickly or cut into chunks. Then toss with butter or olive oil, vegetables, and herbs, and roast to perfection in your slow cooker. With just a few minutes of work you'll have a side dish worthy of a perfectly grilled steak or piece of salmon.

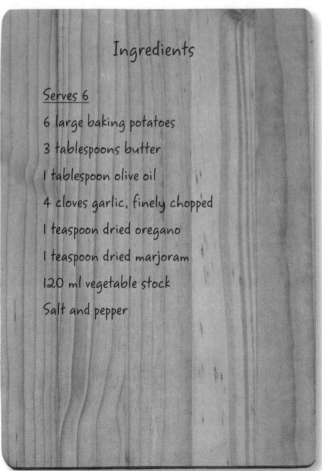

Ingredients

Serves 6

6 large baking potatoes

3 tablespoons butter

1 tablespoon olive oil

4 cloves garlic, finely chopped

1 teaspoon dried oregano

1 teaspoon dried marjoram

120 ml vegetable stock

Salt and pepper

Baked Potatoes

- Scrub potatoes and dry. Cut each in half lengthwise. In small pan, melt butter with olive oil over medium heat.

- Add garlic; cook and stir until fragrant. Remove from heat and add oregano and marjoram; season with salt and pepper.

- Layer potatoes in 3.5- or 4.5-litre slow cooker, drizzling each layer with butter mixture. Pour vegetable stock over.

- Cover and cook on low for 5–7 hours or until potatoes are tender. Carefully remove from slow cooker and serve.

Hasselback Potatoes

Scrub each potato, then place in a large spoon. Slice the potato crosswise, cutting down to the spoon, into thin slices. The bottom of the potato should be uncut. Make herb mixture as directed; drizzle over potatoes. Layer and cook in slow cooker as directed; omit vegetable stock.

Roasted Cubed Potatoes

Make recipe as directed, but cut the potatoes into 4-cm chunks, leaving a bit of peel on each potato. Or peel the potatoes and cut into chunks. Reduce vegetable stock to 50 ml. Before serving, sprinkle 25 g pecorino cheese over potatoes; toss to coat and serve.

Cut Potatoes

Layer in Slow Cooker

- When you cut potatoes in half, sometimes you'll find a brown or black spot in the very centre.

- This is just an indication of low calcium while the potatoes grew. While unsightly, this spot isn't dangerous.

- You can just cut out the spot and throw it away, or use other potatoes. Save the discarded potato for another use.

- The potatoes you buy should be firm and heavy for their size, with no wet or soft spots.

- Try to layer the potatoes evenly in the slow cooker. As they cook, you can rearrange them halfway through cooking time.

- The potatoes may be very tender and fall apart when done, no matter how carefully you lift them from the slow cooker.

- That's OK – just break them up with a spoon and serve them as smashed potatoes.

- If they do break apart, take advantage of the situation and throw in some grated cheese.

MASHED POTATOES

Make mashed potatoes and keep them warm in the slow cooker

Creamy, smooth, fluffy mashed potatoes are one of the most comforting foods of all. And they're easy to make in the slow cooker. Best of all, you can keep the mashed potatoes perfectly hot and moist in the slow cooker while you're finishing the rest of the meal.

For the best mashed potatoes, make sure that the potatoes are thoroughly cooked. They must be completely tender,

with no firm areas. Then, add the butter or other fat when you first start mashing. This helps coat some of the starch in fat so the potatoes don't become gluey. Finally, add warm milk, cream or stock to the potatoes to keep them warm.

Ingredients

Serves 8–10

1.8 kg potatoes, peeled and cubed

2 onions, chopped

6 cloves garlic, finely chopped

250 ml vegetable stock

115 g butter

120 ml sour cream

120 ml single cream

1 teaspoon dried thyme

1 teaspoon dried chives

Salt and pepper

Creamy Mashed Potatoes

- In 4.5- or 5.5-litre slow cooker, combine potatoes, onion and garlic. Pour vegetable stock into slow cooker.

- Cover and cook on low for 6–7 hours until potatoes are very tender. Drain liquid.

- Add butter; mash potatoes coarsely. Add remaining ingredients and mash potatoes thoroughly.

- Cover and cook on low for 2–3 hours, or keep-warm for 3–4 hours. Stir before serving.

Smashed Potatoes

Make recipe as directed, but don't peel the potatoes before cooking. Scrub the skins well before cutting into cubes. Reduce the garlic to 2 cloves. When mashing the potatoes, don't mash completely; leave some chunks of potato visible.

Cheesy Mashed Potatoes

Make potatoes as directed. Ten minutes before serving, stir in 200 g grated Cheddar cheese and 50 g grated Parmesan cheese.

Cook Potatoes

- The potatoes should all be cut to the same size so they cook evenly and in the same time.

- If you like, you can omit the onions and garlic completely for plain mashed potatoes.

- For a milder onion and garlic flavour, sauté the onion and garlic in half the butter before mixing with the potatoes.

- You can also caramelize the onion and garlic before adding to the slow cooker: sauté for 20–25 minutes.

Mash Potatoes

- Mash potatoes using a potato masher or a large fork. Don't use an immersion blender.

- You can keep these potatoes hot in the slow cooker, on low or keep-warm setting, for 2–3 hours before serving.

- This is a huge advantage when you're entertaining a crowd for dinner.

- If you want potatoes to serve more people, fill another slow cooker with a second batch rather than just increasing the amount.

SCALLOPED POTATOES

This classic side dish is so easy to make in the slow cooker

To scallop a vegetable means to slice it thinly and cook it in a white sauce, with or without cheese.

Potatoes are the vegetable most often scalloped. The dish is similar to a gratin, in which the ingredients are baked in a shallow dish, often with a cheese or breadcrumb topping, so that a browned crust forms. Scalloped potatoes can be made *au gratin* by topping them with buttered crumbs or cheese.

In the slow cooker the potatoes have to be cooked in a white sauce, which stabilizes and adds structure to the dish. Making a white sauce isn't difficult; it just requires patience and a wire whisk.

Enjoy these easy scalloped potatoes; serve them with meatloaf and a green salad for a comfort food meal.

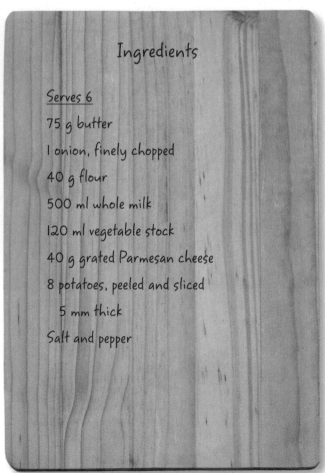

Ingredients

Serves 6

75 g butter

1 onion, finely chopped

40 g flour

500 ml whole milk

120 ml vegetable stock

40 g grated Parmesan cheese

8 potatoes, peeled and sliced
   5 mm thick

Salt and pepper

Scalloped Potatoes

- In large saucepan, melt butter over medium heat. Add onion; cook and stir until very tender, about 7 minutes.

- Stir in flour; cook 3 minutes. Add milk and stock.

- Cook and stir the sauce, using a wire whisk, for

8–9 minutes until sauce thickens slightly; season with salt and pepper. Remove from heat and stir in Parmesan cheese.

- Layer potatoes with sauce in 4-quart slow cooker. Cover and cook on low for 6–8 hours or until potatoes are tender.

Tex-Mex Scalloped Potatoes
Make potatoes as directed, but cook 2 finely chopped jalapeño peppers and 3 finely chopped garlic cloves with the onion. Add 1 tablespoon chilli powder and 1 teaspoon cumin with the flour and salt.

Scalloped Potatoes au Gratin
Make recipe as directed, but add 3 finely chopped garlic cloves with the onion. Cook for 7 hours, then sauté 75 g fresh breadcrumbs in 50 g butter until crisp. Sprinkle over the potatoes; cook, uncovered, for 20 minutes longer on high; serve.

Make White Sauce

Layer Potatoes in Slow Cooker

- The flour has to cook in the butter for a few minutes to help open up the starch granules.

- The starch will absorb some of the liquid and form a branched structure that thickens the sauce.

- It's important to stir the white sauce constantly as it cooks, so it thickens evenly and no lumps form.

- You can make the white sauce ahead of time; refrigerate it, covered, then reheat just before layering with the potatoes.

- Make sure that there is some white sauce on all of the potatoes. There shouldn't be any potatoes without sauce.

- If you'd like to include other tender vegetables in this dish, like peppers, layer them with the potatoes.

- Mushrooms should be cooked with the onions until they turn brown, or they'll add too much liquid.

- Think about adding other ingredients to these potatoes. Some crisply cooked bacon would be delicious, as would different types of cheese.

STEWED FRUIT

This old-fashioned recipe is updated by using the slow cooker

Dried fruit is a good choice for the slow cooker. The fruit plumps in the moist heat as it absorbs the cooking liquid.

Dried fruit is good for you, too. It is high in iron, fibre and antioxidants, and low in fat. These fruits have a greater nutrient density than their fresh counterparts.

Dried fruits include dried figs, prunes, cherries, apricots, dates, raisins, currants and cranberries. You can find them in the baking supplies aisle of your supermarket, and they are ideal for making fruit dishes when soft fruits are out of season. Keep a selection in your store cupboard for inspirational winter meals.

You can serve this stewed fruit as it is, or pour it over ice cream, sponge cake or even your breakfast porridge. Enjoy this healthy treat flavoured many ways.

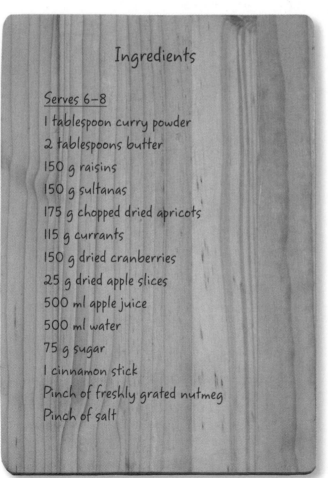

Ingredients

Serves 6–8

1 tablespoon curry powder

2 tablespoons butter

150 g raisins

150 g sultanas

175 g chopped dried apricots

115 g currants

150 g dried cranberries

25 g dried apple slices

500 ml apple juice

500 ml water

75 g sugar

1 cinnamon stick

Pinch of freshly grated nutmeg

Pinch of salt

Curried Stewed Mixed Fruit

- In small saucepan, cook curry powder in butter for 2 minutes; set aside.

- Combine all remaining ingredients in 3- or 4-litre slow cooker. Add curry mixture; stir well.

- Cover and cook on low for 7–9 hours or until fruit is softened and liquid has slightly thickened.

- Remove cinnamon stick and discard. Serve fruit hot or cold over pancakes or waffles.

Vanilla Stewed Fruit
Prepare recipe as directed, but omit butter and curry powder and add 1 vanilla pod. Cut open the pod and scrape out the seeds. Add seeds to the liquid, and add the pod to the fruit. Remove cinnamon stick and vanilla pod before serving.

Citrus Stewed Fruit
Make recipe as directed, but substitute 225 g chopped prunes for the dried apples, and use dried cherries in place of the currants. Reduce water to 250 ml; add 250 ml orange juice, 1 teaspoon grated orange zest and 2 tablespoons lemon juice.

Cook Curry Powder

Prepare Fruit

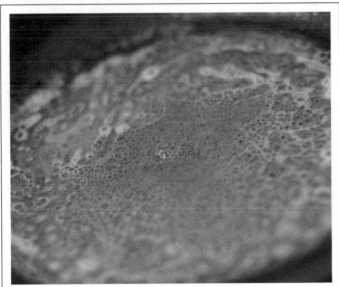

- Cook curry powder in butter before adding to the fruits to bring out its flavour.

- Curry powder Is a complex blend of many spices. Heating releases some aromatic oils, which intensifies the flavour.

- Cook the curry powder in butter over low heat just for a few minutes; don't let it burn.

- In place of curry powder, you could add 1 teaspoon cinnamon and ¼ teaspoon cardamom; omit the cinnamon stick.

- All the fruit can be cut to the same size, or you can leave the fruits whole for a different look.

- Since the fruits cook for such a long time, even fruits like whole apricots or prunes will plump up and absorb liquid.

- Use any combination of dried fruits that you'd like; just keep the proportion of fruit to liquid the same.

- This recipe can be served warm or cold. If serving cold, stir before use to mix the fruits and the liquid.

BREAD PUDDING
Slow cooking is the ideal way to make bread pudding

Bread pudding is the ultimate in comfort food. It's made from stale or toasted bread, layered with a sweetened custard of eggs, milk, and anything from dried fruits to chocolate.

For a pudding that has a nice crust, place a knife between the lid and the slow cooker insert during the last 30–40 minutes of cooking time. This allows some of the moisture to evaporate and creates a crust on the pudding.

The amount of bread you add to the pudding can vary depending on how dry it is. The mixture should be well moistened, but not overly wet. If there are dry areas, add a bit more milk or cream. Don't try to make bread pudding with fresh bread, as it won't absorb the custard.

Serve your bread pudding hot with brandy butter or ice cream melting over it.

Ingredients

Serves 8–10

12 slices cinnamon swirl bread or firm white bread

150 g raisins or dried cherries, if desired

500 ml milk

250 ml single cream

2 tablespoons brandy, if desired

6 eggs, beaten

225 g brown sugar

2 teaspoons vanilla extract

1/2 teaspoon cinnamon

75 g butter, melted

1 tablespoon plain flour

Pinch of salt

Bread Pudding

- Leave bread out overnight, uncovered, to dry. Then cut into cubes.

- Place in 4.5- or 5.5-litre slow cooker with raisins. In large bowl, combine milk, cream, brandy, eggs, brown sugar, vanilla, cinnamon, butter, flour and salt; mix well.

- Pour into slow cooker. Push bread cubes down into slow cooker until bread absorbs most of the liquid.

- Cover and cook on high for 2–2 1/2 hours or until pudding is puffed and set. Serve with brandy butter.

Brandy Butter

In bowl combine 75 g softened butter with 75 g icing sugar and 1 teaspoon vanilla extract; beat until smooth. Stir in 1 tablespoon brandy. Cover and keep refrigerated until serving time. Spoon over warm dessert and allow to melt.

Caramel Cherry Bread Pudding

Make recipe as directed, but use dried cherries. Increase brown sugar to 350 g and increase cinnamon to 2 teaspoons. Drizzle top with 50 ml honey before cooking. Serve with brandy butter made with brown sugar instead of icing sugar.

Prepare Bread

Add Custard and Cook

- The bread should be dry to the touch, so the final pudding is firm and not mushy.

- The pudding will expand as it cooks, so fill the slow cooker only ²/₃ full.

- You can use other types of bread, or a combination of breads. French bread, challah, egg bread or fruit breads all work.

- Use other dried fruits too, if you like. Dried cranberries or chopped dried apricots would be nice.

- It's best to cook bread pudding on high because of the delicate nature of the custard.

- The custard should cook fairly quickly as it is absorbed by the bread.

- The pudding is done when the edges look brown and start to pull away from the sides of the slow cooker.

- If the pudding is done but you're not ready to eat, turn it to keep-warm and place some paper towels under the lid to catch condensation.

POACHED FRUIT
Hard fruits like apples and pears poach nicely in the slow cooker

Poached fruit is another classic dessert that is made for the slow cooker. Choose firm fruits, preferably stone fruits like peaches or plums, or autumn fruits like apples or pears.

Whether you peel your fruits for poaching or leave them unpeeled is a matter of personal choice. If you choose to leave the peel on, you'll need to remove a thin strip of the peel at the top of the fruit so the skin doesn't split in the heat.

Fruit can be poached in fruit juices, wine or a light syrup of sugar and water. The poaching process turns hard fruits juicy and tender, and adds a wonderful flavor.

Serve with ice cream or cream for the perfect finish.

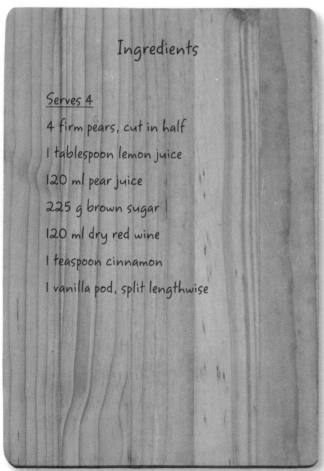

Ingredients

Serves 4

4 firm pears, cut in half

1 tablespoon lemon juice

120 ml pear juice

225 g brown sugar

120 ml dry red wine

1 teaspoon cinnamon

1 vanilla pod, split lengthwise

Cinnamon Poached Pears

- Gently remove core from each pear; leave stem attached. Sprinkle with lemon juice.

- In saucepan, combine remaining ingredients and bring to a simmer.

- Place pears, cut side up, in 3.5-litre slow cooker. Slowly pour sauce over to coat well.

- Cover and cook on low for 2¹/₂–3¹/₂ hours, or until pears are tender when pierced with fork. Remove vanilla pod; serve pears with sauce.

Poached Apples

Make recipe as directed, but use 6 firm apples, peeled, cored and cut into quarters. Substitute 120 ml apple juice for the pear juice. Omit dry red wine; use 120 ml water instead. Serve with ice cream or sponge cake.

Poached Peaches

Use firm peaches with no soft spots. Cut peaches in half; remove stones. Leave skin on. Place in slow cooker. In bowl, mix 120 ml dry white wine, 120 ml water, 75 g sugar, and 2 teaspoons vanilla extract. Pour over peaches. Cover; cook on low 2–3 hours.

Core Pears

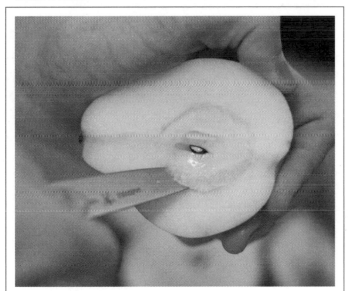

Make Sauce

- Choose firm fruit for this type of recipe. It's a good use for slightly unripe fruit.

- Coring any fruit can be a little bit tricky. You can use an apple corer or a sharp knife. Work gently.

- Since the fruit isn't stuffed, core whole fruit from the bottom so the stem stays attached; that makes the fruit look pretty.

- To prevent enzymatic browning, sprinkle the cut sides of the fruit with lemon juice as you work.

- When making the sauce, be sure to simmer until the mixture combines and is smooth.

- Poached fruit can be served warm or cold. If serving cold, refrigerate in the poaching liquid.

- Spoon the liquid over the fruit from time to time until it is very cold to coat it with a glaze.

- Serve the fruit upright in a dessert dish and pour some of the poaching liquid over and around the fruit.

RICE PUDDING

Creamy rice pudding is a classic comfort food

Rice pudding is comforting and delicious, and very easy to make in the slow cooker. This is one time when white rice is a good choice. It will cook until the grains almost dissolve, making a thick and creamy pudding.

If you like your rice pudding very thick, you can use medium- or short-grain rice. Stir in any type of dried fruit, or add pieces of chocolate.

This recipe is very tolerant. If it's too thick, stir in some more milk; if it's too thin, cook on high for 20–30 minutes with the lid off to thicken it.

Serve hot or cold, with some softly whipped sweetened cream or a drizzle of caramel or chocolate sauce.

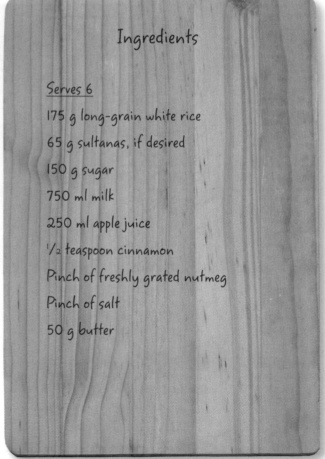

Ingredients

Serves 6

175 g long-grain white rice

65 g sultanas, if desired

150 g sugar

750 ml milk

250 ml apple juice

½ teaspoon cinnamon

Pinch of freshly grated nutmeg

Pinch of salt

50 g butter

Rice Pudding

- Combine all ingredients in 3.5-litre slow cooker and stir well to combine.

- Cover and cook on high for 2½–3 hours or until rice is tender, stirring once during cooking time.

- Turn off slow cooker and leave to stand 15 minutes.

Add more milk if too thick; cook uncovered on high 20–30 minutes if too thin.

- You can serve this warm, or remove from slow cooker and chill 3–4 hours before serving. If chilled, stir pudding before serving.

Curried Rice Pudding

Make recipe as directed, using 150 g brown sugar in place of the white sugar. Cut milk to 500 ml; increase apple juice to 500 ml. Add 1 tablespoon curry powder with the cinnamon and nutmeg. Use raisins instead of sultanas.

Arborio Rice Pudding

Make recipe as directed, but substitute 175 g Arborio rice for the long-grain white rice. Omit apple juice; increase milk to 1.2 litres. Cover and cook on low for 5–7 hours until thick. Stir in 2 teaspoons vanilla extract and serve.

Mix Ingredients

- Some recipes tell you to rinse the rice before cooking, but that isn't necessary.

- Rinsing washes away surface starch, and in rice pudding, we want as much starch as we can get.

- Grease the slow cooker insert to stop sticking.

- You could also use a slow cooker cooking bag for the easiest washing up. Just serve the pudding and throw the bag away.

Stir Pudding

- As the rice cooks, it will expand while absorbing liquid. For an evenly cooked dish, stir once during cooking time.

- Make sure that you scrape the bottom and the sides of the slow cooker when you stir, so nothing sticks and burns.

- Serve the rice pudding with a simple sauce made by puréeing 275 g thawed frozen raspberries.

- Or use a purchased ice cream topping. Toasted nuts or granola are also a nice finish.

CLASSIC DESSERTS

FRUIT CRISP

Granola is the secret ingredient to a candy-like topping

Fruit crisps are made from fruits topped with a crumble of flour, sugar, butter, oatmeal and nuts. They are similar to fruit crumbles but with extra crunch. When baked in the oven, the topping becomes crisp. In the slow cooker, the topping becomes thick, chewy and sweet.

Use the same varieties of eating apples for fruit crisps that you'd use for poaching. They will keep their shape and

become tender and juicy when cooked in the slow cooker.

Granola helps to add a bit of crunch to the topping. You can use homemade or purchased granola; look for types with large and very crunchy clusters of oats and sugar.

These crisps are best served hot or warm, straight out of the slow cooker. Top with brandy butter, ice cream or softly whipped cream.

Ingredients

Serves 6–8

4 crisp eating apples

3 firm pears

2 tablespoons lemon juice

50 g plain flour

175 g brown sugar

175 g granola

115 g rolled oats

1 teaspoon cinnamon

115 g butter, melted

50 g crushed butterscotch toffee

Toffee Fruit Crisp

- Peel and core fruits and cut into 2.5 cm chunks. Toss with lemon juice and place in 3.5-litre slow cooker.

- In large bowl, combine flour, brown sugar, granola, oats and cinnamon and mix well. Stir in butter until crumbly.

- Add toffee bits and sprinkle evenly over fruit in slow cooker to coat.

- Cover and cook on low for 4–6 hours or until fruit is tender and topping is bubbling and hot.

Apple Fruit Crisp

Make recipe as directed, but use 8 apples, peeled and sliced, and omit pears. Sprinkle apples with 115 g brown sugar before topping. Omit toffee; add 75 g chopped walnuts to topping mixture. Cook on low for 5–6 hours until apples are tender. Serve with vanilla ice cream.

Pear Fruit Crisp

Make recipe as directed, but use 7 pears, peeled and sliced; omit apples. Sprinkle pears with 100 g white sugar before adding topping. Add ¼ teaspoon nutmeg to topping mixture; omit toffee. Add 75 g chopped pecans to topping.

Prepare Fruits

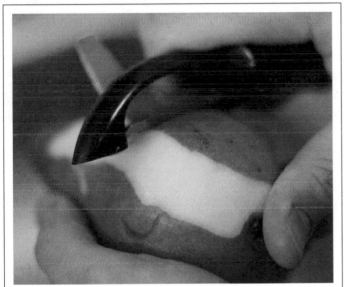

- Peel and toss the fruits with lemon juice so they don't turn brown before you add the topping.

- You can sprinkle the fruits with 50–75 g sugar, either brown or white, for a sweeter dessert.

- Or drizzle the fruit with a caramel ice-cream topping or honey, then add the granola topping.

- Or add dried fruits, like raisins, currants, dried cherries or dried cranberries, for more flavour and colour.

Mix Toppings

- Mix the flour, brown sugar, oatmeal and granola well together before adding the melted butter.

- Mix in the butter using your fingers until the mixture is crumbly. When you hold some in your hand and push it together, it should hold the shape.

- If you like a lot of topping, you can increase the topping proportion.

- Still, make sure that the slow cooker is filled ⅔ to ¾ full for best results.

CLASSIC DESSERTS

213

STUFFED FRUIT

Hard fruits, like apples and pears, pair beautifully with a sweet stuffing

Stuffed fruit is an excellent dessert for the slow cooker. Use the same fruits that you'd use for poaching or in fruit crisps, because they hold their shape in the low, slow heat.

You can stuff the fruit with anything from nuts to sugar mixtures to dried or candied fruits. And there are several ways to stuff the fruit.

You can core the whole fruit from the top or the bottom and fill the cavity, or cut the fruit in half, cut out the core, then fill and place the halves back together.

Or you can cut the fruit in half, remove the core, and fill; then layer, rounded side down, in the slow cooker.

Enjoy with ice cream.

Ingredients

Serves 6

6 large Granny Smith
   or Braeburn apples

2 tablespoons lemon juice

50 g chopped walnuts

65 g raisins

75 g brown sugar

2 tablespoons brandy or apple juice

1 teaspoon ground cinnamon

Pinch of freshly grated nutmeg

350 ml cloudy apple juice

120 ml honey

Stuffed Apples

- Carefully remove core from each apple starting at the top. Leave the bottom 6 mm intact.

- Peel a small strip from the top of each apple. Sprinkle with lemon juice.

- Mix walnuts, raisins, brown sugar, brandy or juice, cinnamon and nutmeg; overfill apples with mixture.

- Place apples in single layer in 3.5-litre slow cooker. Mix apple juice and honey; pour over and around apples. Cover and cook on low for 4–5 hours, until apples are tender.

214

RECIPE VARIATION

Stuffed Pears

Core 6 pears, leaving the bottom skin intact, and remove 1 cm of the peel from the top of the apples. Fill with a mixture of 65 g dried cranberries, 115 g brown sugar, 1 teaspoon cinnamon, and 50 g pecans. Place in slow cooker; add 250 ml cranberry juice. Cover; cook on low 5–6 hours.

RED●LIGHT

To check an older slow cooker for safety, fill it with water and leave it to cook, covered, on low for 8 hours. The water temperature should be 85°C or higher. If the temperature is any lower, discard the slow cooker.

Prepare Filling

- You can use any warm spices in this filling. Warm spices include cinnamon, nutmeg, allspice, cloves and cardamom.

- Try different nut and fruit combinations in your stuffed fruit. In fact, you could stuff each apple with something different.

- You could use chopped cashews with dried cranberries, or chopped pecans with white chocolate and dried cherries.

- Use your imagination; you could also mix apples and pears and vary the stuffing to create a fruit buffet.

Fill Apples

- Overfill the apples. This means fill them higher than the core; just heap the filling on top.

- The filling will sink into the apples as it cooks, so you want to add more than you think you'll need.

- If there's any leftover filling, just sprinkle it on top of the apples in the slow cooker.

- Serve these apples hot or warm from the slow cooker, with brandy butter, vanilla ice cream or whipped cream.

CHOCOLATE CAKE

The slow cooker bakes a velvety cake for a sumptuous pudding

Ah, chocolate. The ultimate dessert, chocolate is irresistible in every kind of pudding and cake. It can be used very successfully in the slow cooker, but with a few caveats.

Chocolate burns at around 80–85°C, so even with the slow cooker set on low you do run the risk of chocolate burning. Prevent this by keeping an eye on it, stirring when the recipe directs, and checking the dish at the earliest cooking time.

When chocolate is enveloped in a cake mixture, the burning point goes up, so it's safer in the slow cooker on the low setting. And when you use a baking tin, the metal shields the cake mixture from the slow cooker's heat.

Always use the best chocolate you can afford when cooking, as it makes all the difference to the result, and enjoy these comforting and indulgent recipes.

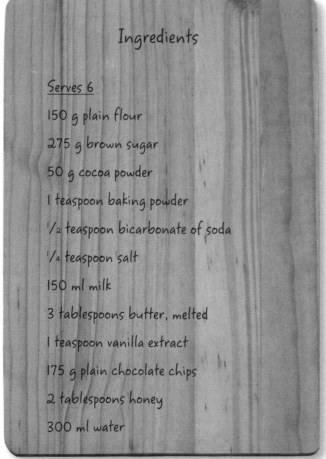

Ingredients

Serves 6

150 g plain flour

275 g brown sugar

50 g cocoa powder

1 teaspoon baking powder

1/2 teaspoon bicarbonate of soda

1/4 teaspoon salt

150 ml milk

3 tablespoons butter, melted

1 teaspoon vanilla extract

175 g plain chocolate chips

2 tablespoons honey

300 ml water

Chocolate Fudge Pudding Cake

- Butter a 2-litre cake tin. In a bowl, mix flour, 175 g of the brown sugar, 25 g of the cocoa, baking powder, bicarbonate of soda and salt.

- Add milk, butter and vanilla; mix until combined. Pour into cake tin; top with chocolate chips.

- In saucepan, combine remaining cocoa and brown sugar, honey and water; bring to the boil.

- Pour over cake mixture in tin. Place on rack in 4.5-litre slow cooker. Cover and cook on high 3–4 hours or until edges are set.

White and Dark Chocolate Pudding Cake
Make recipe as directed, but increase cocoa in cake to 40 g. Reduce plain chocolate chips to 75 g; add 75 g white chocolate chips. Proceed as directed. After cake has baked for 3 hours, sprinkle top with 75 g white chocolate chips.

Chocolate Caramel Pudding Cake
Make cake as directed, but increase cocoa in cake to 40 g. Unwrap 10 caramels and cut into quarters. Push caramels partway into cake mixture in tin. Instead of honey in topping, use 3 tablespoons caramel ice-cream topping.

Whisk Cake Mixture

Place Tin in Slow Cooker

- Stir the cake mixture with a wire whisk to ensure there are no lumps. Make the mixture just before you bake the cake.

- Both baking powder and bicarbonate of soda are used. Baking powder is made from bicarbonate of soda and cream of tartar.

- Both are necessary to the cake. The bicarbonate of soda raises the pH of the batter so it rises evenly.

- Baking powder has an expiration date on its box: follow it to the letter. Bicarbonate of soda does not deteriorate.

- Be sure to grease the tin with unsalted butter. Salted butter can cause the cake to stick to the tin.

- The cake tin has to be placed on a rack in the slow cooker so the heat circulates around it as it cooks.

- Because this cake has a moist pudding layer, you don't need to add a layer of paper towels under the lid.

- Serve the cake with some vanilla or chocolate ice cream for a wonderful treat.

CHOCOLATE DESSERTS

CHOCOLATE FONDUE

Make and serve a rich and creamy fondue in the slow cooker

The fondue originated in Switzerland, and is a communal dish heated by a small burner, filled either with oil for cooking meat or with a sauce, usually cheese, into which all the diners dip food. Dessert fondues can be caramel, honey or other sweet sauces, but chocolate is the most popular.

The slow cooker is ideal for fondue making because you can cook and serve the fondue in one pot. Fondue pots, with

their central burners, can burn the chocolate while you're eating it. The slow cooker's low heat, or keep-warm feature, prevents this and keeps the chocolate at the ideal temperature for dipping.

Use your imagination when thinking of dippers for this dessert. Cake squares and fruit are obvious choices; crisp biscuits, marshmallows and profiteroles are delicious, too.

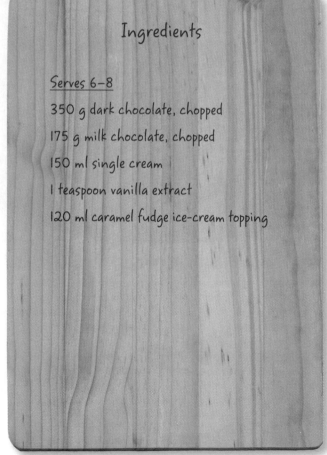

Ingredients

Serves 6–8

350 g dark chocolate, chopped

175 g milk chocolate, chopped

150 ml single cream

1 teaspoon vanilla extract

120 ml caramel fudge ice-cream topping

Chocolate Caramel Fondue

- In 2-litre slow cooker, combine chocolates with cream. Cover and cook on low for 2–3 hours, stirring twice during cooking time.

- Stir; if chocolate is melted, proceed with recipe. If chocolate is not melted, cook for another 30–40 minutes on low.

- Add vanilla and fudge topping; stir well. Cover and cook on low for 20–30 minutes longer.

- Serve from the slow cooker insert with biscuits, angel food cake squares, sponge cake squares and fruit for dipping.

White Chocolate Fondue
Make recipe as directed, but use 500 g white chocolate, chopped. Mix in 2-litre bowl; place in 3.5-litre slow cooker. Omit single cream and caramel fudge ice-cream topping; add 350 ml evaporated milk. Cook on low 1–2 hours until melted; stir in 2 tablespoons amaretto, if desired.

Black and White Fondue
Make the Chocolate Caramel Fondue, but omit the caramel fudge topping. An hour later, make the White Chocolate Fondue. Pour both at the same time into a 3.5-litre slow cooker; stir lightly to marble and serve immediately.

Chop Chocolate

Stir Chocolate

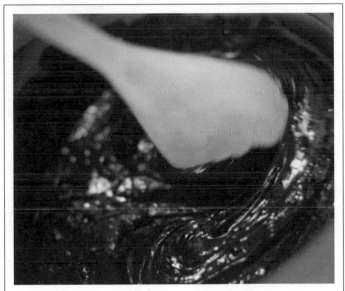

- To chop a bar of chocolate, place it on a chopping board and chop using a chef's knife.

- Just cut across the chocolate with a knife, occasionally bringing the pile together, until the pieces measure about 1 cm.

- The cream not only adds richness and smoothness to the fondue, it helps shield the chocolate from the heat.

- For an even richer fondue, use double instead of single cream. You can also vary the chocolate proportions; use more or less milk chocolate.

- Stir the chocolate using a heatproof silicone spatula or wooden spoon. Be sure to scrape the sides and bottom of the slow cooker.

- If you have a newer slow cooker and are afraid of burning, cook the fondue mixture in a bowl inside the slow cooker.

- The vanilla extract is added at the end of cooking because it has volatile oils that release with heat.

- You want to keep those oils within the fondue mixture, so don't heat it for long after adding the vanilla.

CHOCOLATE DESSERTS

CHOCOLATE CHEESECAKE
Cheesecake cooks to perfection in the moist slow cooker environment

Cheesecake can be quite temperamental. Often, cheesecake baked in the oven has a crack running right down the centre.

There are two culprits in this disaster. First, a cheesecake isn't meant to be airy. Don't beat the mixture very long; just enough to incorporate the sugar, eggs and chocolate. If the cheesecake rises as it bakes, it may crack upon cooking. Second, the oven's dry heat cooking method can cause the mixture to dry out too quickly and lead to cracking, which is why cheesecakes are often baked in a water bath to provide a steamier atmosphere. The moist environment of the slow cooker helps prevent cracking.

The cheesecake has to be chilled before serving. Remove from the slow cooker and place in the refrigerator for 4–5 hours, then enjoy.

Ingredients

Serves 8–10
50 g digestive biscuit crumbs
50 g finely chopped pecans
50 g butter, melted
450 g cream cheese, softened
115 g brown sugar
2 eggs
75 ml double cream
175 g good quality plain chocolate, chopped
1 teaspoon vanilla extract

Topping

120 ml double cream
115 g brown sugar
2 tablespoons butter
75 g salted pecans

Chocolate Praline Cheesecake

- Mix biscuit crumbs, pecans and butter. Press into greased 17-cm springform cake tin.

- Beat cream cheese until smooth. Add brown sugar, then eggs.

- Melt cream with chocolate and vanilla; stir into cheese.

- Pour into tin. Cover with foil; place in 5.5-litre slow cooker. Pour 250 ml water around tin. Cook on high 3–4 hours until edges are set.

- To make topping, cook cream, brown sugar and butter together until smooth. Pour over cake. Top with salted pecans; chill.

Salted Pecans

Sweet and salty is the latest craze in desserts. To salt nuts, melt 2 tablespoons butter in medium pan. Add 175 g whole pecans or almonds; cook and stir until nuts are fragrant. Remove to paper towel; spread nuts out. Sprinkle with ½ teaspoon coarse salt and leave to cool.

Double Chocolate Cheesecake

Make recipe as directed, but use chocolate biscuit crumbs in place of the digestive biscuit crumbs. Stir 175 g dark chocolate chips into cheesecake mixture. Omit brown sugar topping; melt 175 g chocolate chips with 3 tablespoons cream; pour over top and chill.

Beat Chocolate into Cheesecake

- Beat the cream cheese with an electric mixer just until smooth, then beat in the sugar and eggs until smooth.

- Make sure that the chocolate is completely melted, but not very hot when added to the mixture.

- You can melt the chocolate ahead of time, then let it cool to lukewarm. Then stir into the cheese mixture.

Cover Tin Tightly

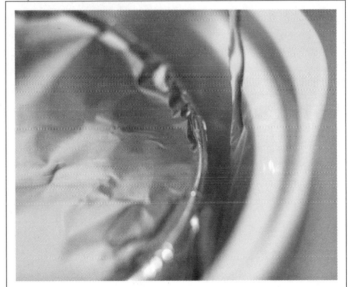

- Wrap the springform tin completely, from top to bottom, in a single large sheet of heavy-duty foil so no water leaks into the cheesecake as it cooks.

- Pour the water carefully around the foil-covered pan. Don't let any get on the cheesecake.

- Don't start cooking the topping until the cheesecake is done; it will harden quickly.

- Stir the topping while it cooks. It will seem as if it is not coming together, then all of a sudden the sauce will blend.

CHOCOLATE DESSERTS

CHOCOLATE BREAD PUDDING
Chocolate is a wonderful addition to bread pudding

Chocolate is the perfect addition to turn bread pudding into an elegant dessert. You can use white chocolate, milk chocolate, dark chocolate, or even the newest kinds of chocolate chips: chocolate swirled with caramel or peanut butter.

Bread pudding was originally a very humble dessert, created to use up leftover stale bread. It has evolved into quite a treat, served at the best restaurants in the world.

Chocolate is very important in this recipe, so buy the best you can find. Makers like Godiva, Lindt and Callebaut make the best chocolate, with a high percentage of cocoa butter. That is what makes chocolate smooth and creamy.

Serve this rich pudding with some plain double cream.

Ingredients

Serves 8–10

10 slices firm white bread

175 g white chocolate chips

115 g chopped toasted pecans

175 g dark chocolate chips

5 eggs

350 ml milk

250 ml single cream

225 g brown sugar

40 g cocoa powder

1 tablespoon cornflour

2 teaspoons vanilla extract

Pinch of salt

Pinch of ground cardamom

White and Black Bread Pudding

- Cube bread and layer in slow cooker with white chocolate chips, nuts and dark chocolate chips.

- In medium bowl, combine remaining ingredients and beat until smooth. Pour into slow cooker.

- Cover and cook on high for 4 hours, or until pudding is puffed and set.

- Serve with whipped cream, vanilla ice cream or chocolate sauce.

Chocolate Sauce

Combine 3 tablespoons butter, 2 tablespoons brewed coffee, 50 ml golden syrup, 115 g brown sugar and 40 g cocoa powder in saucepan. Cook and stir until thick. Stir in a pinch of salt and 1 teaspoon vanilla extract; remove from heat. Store in refrigerator; reheat in saucepan to use.

Dark Chocolate Bread Pudding

Make recipe as directed, but add 175 g plain chocolate chips to the bread mixture. Omit the white chocolate chips. Omit the cardamom; increase vanilla extract to 1 1/2 teaspoons. Cook as directed; serve with vanilla ice cream.

Cube Bread

Layer Ingredients

- The bread should be cubed evenly and into fairly small pieces, about 1–2 cm square. Layer evenly with the chocolate chips.

- It's important to toast the pecans before adding to the pudding mixture so they retain some crunch

in the middle of the soft pudding.

- To toast, place nuts in a dry pan. Cook over low heat, shaking the pan occasionally, until fragrant. Let the nuts cool completely before adding to the bread mixture.

- Place a layer of bread in the slow cooker before you add the chocolate chips. The chips should be suspended in the bread.

- You can use any combination of chocolate chips and nuts you like.

- Chopped cashews, pistachios, walnuts, pecans and even mixed nuts are excellent.

- This dessert is meant to be decadent; don't use low-fat ingredients. Just eat small portions and enjoy.

CHOCOLATE DESSERTS

CHOCOLATE CUSTARD
Add chocolate to custard for a decadent twist

This chocolate custard cooked in the slow cooker is like a whipped pudding, but thicker. It will hold its shape when cut or lifted with a spoon.

Like a chocolate version of a crème caramel, the custard is creamy, rich and smooth when properly made. It's important to follow the directions carefully and take your time when assembling the ingredients.

Like all egg desserts, custard can be temperamental. There's a fine line between smooth custard and scrambled eggs. It's best baked at low heat for a long period of time, and that's where the slow cooker comes in. Blend all the ingredients well, and strain the mixture before cooking.

Serve this custard warm or cool, with a drizzle of chocolate sauce or some whipped cream.

Ingredients

Serves 6–8

250 ml milk

250 ml double cream

2 tablespoons cocoa powder

115 g brown sugar

175 g plain chocolate, chopped

3 eggs

1 egg yolk

Pinch of salt

1 teaspoon vanilla extract

Chocolate Custard

- Grease a 1-litre baking dish with unsalted butter. In saucepan, combine milk, cream, cocoa, brown sugar and chocolate.

- Cook and stir over low heat until chocolate melts and mixture is smooth. Remove from heat.

- Add eggs and egg yolk, salt and vanilla and mix well. Strain into baking dish and cover with foil.

- Place on rack in 4.5-litre slow cooker. Pour 250 ml hot water around dish. Cover and cook on high 2–3 hours, until custard is set. Cool 1 hour; chill.

Pots de Crème

Make recipe as directed, but strain the chocolate mixture into a bowl. Grease 6 (175-g) ramekins with unsalted butter. Divide chocolate mixture among ramekins. Place on rack in slow cooker; add water. Cook on high for 1½–2½ hours until just barely set; cool.

Chocolate Ginger Custard

Make recipe as directed, but reduce plain chocolate to 115 g. Add ½ teaspoon ground ginger to mixture; strain. Then stir in 2 tablespoons very finely chopped candied ginger. Pour into baking dish and cook as directed.

Strain Chocolate Mixture

- Beat the mixture until smooth and combined. As with cheesecake, you don't want to add too much air to a custard.

- Egg custard should be perfectly smooth. To accomplish this it has to be strained.

- Straining removes any lumps from chocolate or sugar, and removes the chalaza of each egg – the part that attaches the yolk to the white.

- Use a fine-mesh strainer, not a colander, to strain the custard mixture.

Cook Custard

- Make sure that the baking dish fits in the slow cooker with at least 2.5 cm to spare around all sides.

- The rack ensures that heat circulates evenly around the custard as it cooks.

- The custard is covered with foil; still, when you pour the

- water into the slow cooker, pour it around the pan, not on top of it.

- Custard is best served chilled; chill for 3–5 hours in the refrigerator before serving.

CHOCOLATE DESSERTS

HANDMADE CHOCOLATES

Melt chocolate in the slow cooker for some delicious and easy treats

Homemade chocolates are quite a delicacy, and will impress everyone. Yet they're quite easy to make, especially in the slow cooker.

This isn't a recipe that you can walk away from. Don't make the recipe, turn on the slow cooker, and leave the house. Because of chocolate's low burning point, it has to be stirred often, even when it's melted in the slow cooker.

There are several types of chocolate, defined by the amount of cocoa solids they contain. Cocoa powder and unsweetened baking chocolate have the highest content, 100 per cent. Dark or bittersweet chocolate ranges from 35 to 90 per cent cocoa solids, and milk chocolate has a minimum of 25 per cent. White chocolate is made with cocoa butter, but contains no cocoa solids.

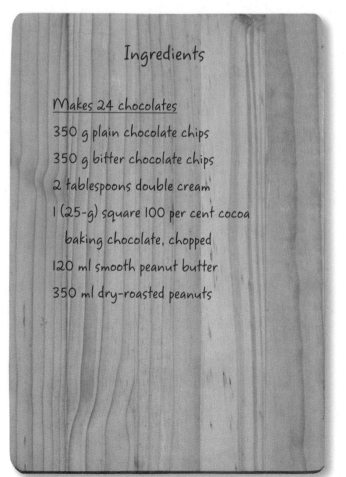

Ingredients

Makes 24 chocolates

350 g plain chocolate chips

350 g bitter chocolate chips

2 tablespoons double cream

1 (25-g) square 100 per cent cocoa
   baking chocolate, chopped

120 ml smooth peanut butter

350 ml dry-roasted peanuts

Chocolate Peanut Roundels

- In 3.5-litre slow cooker, combine chocolate chips, cream and baking chocolate.

- Cover and cook on high for 1 hour and stir. Reduce heat to low. Cover and cook for 1–2 hours longer until mixture is smooth, stirring once.

- Stir well, then add peanut butter. Stir until peanut butter melts and mixture is smooth.

- Add peanuts and stir to coat. Turn off slow cooker; drop mixture by the tablespoonful on to baking parchment; leave to set.

GREEN ● LIGHT

Chocolate, in moderation, is good for you. It contains antioxidants, compounds that help protect you from free radicals. Dark chocolate is one of the best sources of flavanol antioxidants because it has a high percentage of cacao, the nib or centre of the cocoa bean.

• • • • RECIPE VARIATION • • • •

Chocolate Truffles
Melt 350 g dark chocolate chips, 350 g milk chocolate chips and 350 ml double cream in slow cooker. Stir together, then add vanilla extract. Pour into bowl and refrigerate until firm. Beat with electric mixer until fluffy; form into balls and roll in cocoa powder.

Prepare Ingredients

Form Candies

- You can use chocolate bars instead of chocolate chips if you prefer. Chocolate chips may be slightly sweeter.

- If using chocolate bars, chop by cutting with a chef's knife on a chopping board. Cut into pieces roughly 1–2 cm in diameter.

- You can use any combination of dark, milk or bitter chocolate in this recipe.

- Just keep the proportion of chocolate to cream and peanut butter the same, so the chocolates will set.

- Nonstick baking parchment is useful for holding the chocolates as they cool.

- To speed up setting, you can refrigerate the chocolates until firm to the touch.

- Don't store the chocolates in the refrigerator. If chocolate is exposed to

- temperature contrasts, it will 'bloom', or form a greyish coating.

- Make several different kinds of chocolate with different chocolates and nuts; make your own chocolate box for Valentine's Day.

CHOCOLATE DESSERTS

GLOSSARY

Learn the language first

Al dente: Italian phrase meaning 'to the tooth', which describes desired texture of cooked pasta.

Baking powder: A leavening agent used in baking and sweet making.

Beat: To manipulate food with a spoon, mixer or whisk to amalgamate ingredients and incorporate air.

Blanch: To briefly cook food, primarily vegetables or fruits, to remove skin or fix colour.

Braise: Cooking method in which meats or vegetables are browned, then simmered slowly in liquid until tender.

Brown: To cook food so that the surface caramelizes, adding colour and flavour before cooking in the slow cooker.

Caramelize: To cook until the sugars and proteins in a food combine to form complex compounds, browning the food and creating appetizing flavours.

Chop: To cut food into small pieces, using a chef's knife or a food processor.

Coat: To cover food in another ingredient to provide a protective flavoured or textured surface, such as coating chicken breasts with breadcrumbs.

Curry Powder: A blend of warm spices used in Indian cooking to flavour meat and vegetable dishes.

Deglaze: To add liquid to a pan that has been used to sauté meat, fish or vegetables, to release caramelized residue stuck to the pan, which flavours the sauce.

Dice: To cut food into small, even cubes, usually about 6 mm square.

Dry rub: Spices and herbs rubbed into meats or vegetables to marinate and add flavour.

Flake: To encourage cooked fish to break into small pieces; also to cut food into thin slivers.

Fold: To combine two soft or liquid mixtures together, using a gentle over-and-under action with a large spoon, to avoid beating out previously incorporated air.

Grate: To remove small pieces or shreds of food such as cheese, chocolate or citrus fruit zest, using a grater or microplane.

Grill: To cook food quickly close to the heat source, as under an overhead grill or on a griddle or barbecue.

Marinate: To steep meat, fish or vegetables in a mixture of an acid and oil, to tenderize and add flavour and succulence.

Melt: To turn a solid into a liquid, by the addition of heat.

Pan-fry: To cook quickly in a shallow pan, in a small amount of fat over relatively high heat.

Pare: To remove the skin of fruits or vegetables, usually using a swivel-bladed peeler.

Roux: A mixture of butter and flour, cooked together and used to thicken a white sauce.

Shred: To use a coarse grater to create small strips of food, or to pull meat such as chicken apart into small pieces.

Simmer: A state of liquid cooking over very gentle heat, where the liquid stays just below boiling point.

Slow cooker: A thermostatically controlled appliance that cooks food by surrounding it with low, steady heat.

Steam: To cook food by immersing it in steam. Food is set in a perforated container over boiling liquid.

Stir: To mix with a spoon or whisk until foods are combined.

Toss: To combine food using two spoons or a spoon and a fork until mixed.

Whisk: Both a tool, which is made of loops of steel, and a method, which combines food until smooth while incorporating air in the mixture.

White sauce: A sauce made by cooking flour in fat, then adding liquid and cooking until smooth. Used to stabilize sauces in the slow cooker.

Zest: The coloured part of the skin of citrus fruit, used to add flavour to food.

MANUFACTURERS AND WEBSITES
Find equipment through these resources to stock your kitchen

Manufacturers

Breville
www.breville.com.au

- Range of slow cookers including 6.5-litre size.

Crock-Pot
www.crock-pot.com

- The original manufacturer of slow cookers in USA and Canada. Website includes recipes and useful hints and tips.

Cuisinart
www.cuisinart.co.uk

- Good-looking slow-cookers with stainless steel housing, automatic timers and 'keep-warm' features.

Morphy Richards
www.morphyrichards.co.uk

- Cooking range includes steamers, breadmakers, rice cookers and slow cookers.

Russell Hobbs
www.russellhobbs.co.uk

- Range includes a 5.5-litre oval model with a divided insert, enabling two different dishes to be cooked simultaneously. Recipes are available to download.

Tefal
www.homeandcook.co.uk

- Range includes a 4-in-1 rice cooker that can also be used for steaming and slow cooking.

Cookware Online
www.cookwareonline.co.uk

• Wide range of cooking appliances including slow cookers.

John Lewis
www.johnlewis.com

• Range of good quality slow cookers includes Crock-Pot and Cuisinart.

Kitchen Manuals Online
www.kitchen.manualsonline.com

• Website offers contact information for dozens of slow cooker manufacturers, and downloadable manuals for specific models.

Online suppliers and resources

About.com
www.cookingequipment.about.com

• Reviews of cooking equipment include tips on what to look for when buying a slow cooker, and how to use it.

Amazon
www.amazon.co.uk

• Comprehensive selection of European and American slow cookers of every size and shape on this large site.

Argos
www.argos.co.uk

• Numerous slow cookers.

INDEX